Kent State/May 4

KENT STATE/MAY 4

ECHOES THROUGH A DECADE

Edited by Scott L. Bills

THE KENT STATE UNIVERSITY PRESS
Kent, Ohio, and London, England

© 1982, 1988 by The Kent State University Press, Kent, Ohio 44242
All rights reserved
Library of Congress Catalog Card Number 87–31685
ISBN 0–87338–278–1
ISBN 0–87338–360–5 pbk.
Manufactured in the United States of America

Articles which previously appeared in whole or in part in the journal
Left Review are used with permission.
Photo on p. 17 courtesy of John A. Darnell, Jr., © 1970.

Third printing and second paperback issue, 1990

Library of Congress Cataloging-in-Publication Data

Kent State/May 4 : echoes through a decade / edited by Scott L. Bills.
    p.   cm.
  Bibliography: p.
  Includes index.
  ISBN 0–87338–360–5 (pbk. : alk. paper) ∞
  1. Kent State University—Riot, May 4, 1970. 2. Kent State
University—Students—Attitudes. I. Bills, Scott L.
LD4191.072K45   1988
378.771'37—dc19   87–31685
                                                    CIP

British Library Cataloging-in-Publication data are available.

for
J. L.
1940–1980

Contents

Illustrations

Preface to the Paperback Edition

"**A**T KENT STATE UNIVERSITY TODAY FOUR PERSONS WERE KILLED AND OTHERS INJURED IN A CONFRONTATION BETWEEN OHIO NATIONAL GUARD TROOPS AND A MOB OF UNIDENTIFIED PERSONS," telegraphed Ohio Governor James Rhodes to J. Edgar Hoover, director of the Federal Bureau of Investigation. "TELL ME FATHER DID THEY AIM?" asked a telegram from singer Mary Travers. A firestorm of protest and indignation flared across the landscape of American higher education. There was fear and anxious anticipation. Army and National Guard units were on hand in Washington at week's end as "a great crowd of youths" gathered for an antiwar demonstration on Saturday, May 9. "A moatlike ring of 59 city buses, parked bumper to bumper along Executive Avenue, separated the protesters from the White House and President Nixon . . . ," reported the *New York Times*. Max Frankel wrote on Sunday, May 10: "America was a nation in anguish last week, her population divided, her campuses closed, her capital confused, her President perplexed. The lines of conflict ran zigzag across the land." The domestic upheaval in response to expansion of the U.S. war in Southeast Asia and the deaths at Kent State, observed Frankel, "sent tremors of fear through the White House that revolt and repression might be nearer than anyone had dared to imagine." One Kent State student was quoted as saying, "What's the use? . . . I feel, what can we do? What kind of democracy is this?"[1]

Zigzag lines of conflict was the persistent theme of May 4—re-

---

[1] Rhodes to Hoover, May 5, 1970, in *FBI Files on the Fire Bomb and Shooting at Kent State* (Wilmington, Del.: Scholarly Resources, Inc., 1985, microfilm), reel 2, sec. 1; Travers to Hoover, May 5, 1970, ibid.; John Herbers, "Big Capital Rally Asks U.S. Pullout in Southeast Asia," *New York Times,* May 10, 1970, p. 1; Max Frankel, "Nixon: He Faces a Divided, Anguished Nation," *New York Times,* May 10, 1970, sec. 4. See also the editorial titled "Change of Heart . . . ," *New York Times*, May 9, 1970, p. 24.

lated controversies during the ensuing years, as discussed in this book: sparring and countersparring in the courts, through the hearts and minds of several generations, over and around the grassy hillside in the center of the Kent State campus. What has changed? Whereas the terms of reference in the May 4 debate formerly and typically expressed anger and exuded polemic, the sentiments most frequently voiced since 1985 have been those of reconciliation and healing. It is not an inconsequential change. In the midst of familiar props from the past years of contention, there has emerged a shared desire for an commitment to a permanent memorial, near where the shots were fired, to the death and disruption of May 1970.

This paperback reprinting of *Kent State/May 4: Echoes Through a Decade* retains the same title, though we are now nearly two decades distant from the spring of 1970. The book is unchanged except for an addendum to the annotated bibliography and this preface, which serves as an update to the introduction, "The Past in the Present," primarily with regard to the discussion of, planning for, and selection of a new memorial. Referents to May 4 already dot the campus, as indicated in the introduction: sculptures, a granite marker, the activities of the Center for Peaceful Change, a resource room in the library, a major archival collection, and a brief statement in University catalogs. But this assemblage represents years of increments sponsored by numerous individuals and organizations, spawned by differing issues and viewpoints, rather than a single, uniform impulse toward reflection and remembrance. Hence, with plans for a permanent memorial, there is a consensus at least on the issue of historical significance; and there is a new dimension to the life of the past in the present—one which is in part the product of a new willingness to embrace ambiguity and pain in the course of marking epochal events and movements.

A New May 4 Memorial

In December 1983, prompted by a proposal from the May 4th Task Force and acting with the encouragement of University President Michael Schwartz, the Kent State Board of Trustees took the first step toward an officially sanctioned physical memorial to the May 4 shootings. The Trustees authorized the establishment of a special committee, to be appointed by Schwartz, charged "with assessing the historical significance of the events which took place on this campus on May 4, 1970, including the killing of four students, and, in light of this assessment, with determining what sort of permanent memorial, if any, should be established."[2] Meeting for the first time in latter March 1984, the ten members of the May 4th Memorial Committee represented students, faculty, administrators, and alumni of the University as well as community interests. The committee's report and recommendations were made available in December 1984.

In a brief survey of the significance of the May 4 shootings, the committee concluded that after fifteen years the Kent State shootings remained "a visible milestone in a war that belongs to another generation." As such, the events of May 1970 had a measurable impact on national politics as well as a profound influence on the course of Kent State University. In pointing to a positive as well as a negative legacy for the institution, the report stated: "The annual memorial activities, the work of dedicated students and faculty, suggest the meaning May 4th will have for the future at the University. It is that a place of learning cannot escape the outside world, but can mobilize its resources to work toward a better, more equitable, and above all, a more peaceful society." Surveying the existing memorials on campus, the committee noted that they "do not choose sides. All society was the victim on May 4th—students, Guardsmen, townspeople, and faculty. The four dead paid the ultimate price." The committee concluded that the Kent State shootings were of such significance that a permanent memorial was appropriate and necessary, that May 4 "sensitized America to regimented lines of communications and authority. May 4th changed forever how future demonstrations—peaceful and otherwise—must be perceived, analyzed, understood, and settled non-violently." Yet, the committee noted that even so many years after the shootings, there was still no single accepted explanation for why the shootings had occurred; further, it was apparent "that the many constituencies at Kent State University and in the community in early May of 1970 had multiple and often conflicting purposes for their activities." That is, many different viewpoints had been represented by the people who gath-

[2] Press release, December 9, 1983, KSU Communications Services.

ered on the Commons and observed events from off campus in the spring of 1970.

> Therefore, the Committee believes that in order to memorialize these events effectively, a site which reflects the diverse constituencies and meanings would be most appropriate. This reflective site should present the visitor with the opportunity to *inquire* into the many reasons and purposes of the events that led to the killing and wounding of students on May 4, 1970 and to encourage a *learning* process to broaden the perspective of these events. The site should encourage visitors to ask what differences were confronting this community and this nation at that time and to *reflect* on how those differences may have been resolved peacefully.

The committee then made three specific recommendations: (1) the University should commission a physical memorial designed as a "reflective site," one which included "a physical expression regarding the deaths of the four students" and provided a facility for the distribution of certain informational materials; (2) the memorial should be constructed "on the wooded site Northeast of Taylor Hall on top of the small hill facing the tennis courts"; and (3) the University should initiate research grants to encourage scholarly investigation of May 1970 events, Vietnam-era themes, and strategies for peaceful change.[3]

Thus, the committee's report offered an analysis which asserted the historical importance of the May 4 shootings and favored University action to secure a permanent memorial; the purpose of such a memorial would be to commemorate potent, tragic events rather than to hallow individuals or particular principles. Also, the memorial would encourage personal reflection rather than political activism. On January 23, 1985, the Trustees accepted the recommenda-

---

[3] "Report of the Kent State University's May 4th Memorial Committee," December 1984, pp. 4, 5–6, 9, 10–11, KSU Communications Services; italics in original. The informational materials would include a brochure; the text of the conclusions of the President's Commission on Campus Unrest, released in October 1970; a statement listing May 4 memorials located elsewhere on the campus; and a partial text of the committee's report. The committee members were Lawrence S. Kaplan, Jerry M. Lewis, Richard A. Bredemeier, associate dean for student life; Cheryl Croskey; Nancy Hansford, mayor of Kent; James T. Kilgallen; James P. Myers; Elizabeth G. Ricksecker, of the May 4th Task Force; and Nancy Whitehead.

tions of the May 4th Memorial Committee and directed President Schwartz to initiate an effective design competition. The chairman of the Board of Trustees emphasized that the report "is not one that engages in the unproductive and divisive practice of seeking to praise or blame."[4]

In the past, such vague references to the tragic character of the May 4 shootings had elicited disapproval from those student groups eager for an official acknowledgment of wrongdoing and a memorial which would exclusively commemorate and possibly consecrate those who were killed in 1970. In the past, assessing blame had been central to recreating and maintaining a sense of outrage at May 1970 events. Nonetheless, the process of depoliticizing May 4 events had steadily acquired greater legitimacy—as a result, most simply, of the inevitable waning of emotions over time. Also important was the 1979 out-of-court settlement of the May 4–related civil suits brought against the state of Ohio, a settlement which featured as much of an apology as state officials would ever concede. The "relevance" of "Kent State" had come, in the mid-1980s, to mean something quite different from the spirited May 4 commemorations of the mid-1970s, when the retelling of protest and death was intended to spur distrust of established institutions and political activism on behalf of a left-liberal agenda. By 1985, the "relevance" of the Kent State shootings seemed to be that a person should use the provocative images of May 1970 to look across time, to experience the dissonance bred by sudden riflefire, and then to find his or her own meaning in the deaths of four students—and that it need not be a meaning which encompassed anger. Sadness, perhaps, and a renewed commitment to worthwhile personal goals was most appropriate.

"What Have We Learned?" asked an editorial in the *Daily Kent Stater* in May 1985. The answer was offered in the context of superseding the emotive power of May 4: "We have learned that the tragedy of May 4, 1970, could have been avoided if both sides would have acted calmly and with reason. Both sides made mistakes. Continuing to put the blame on one side of the other serves little purpose. Let us put behind the anger." We have learned, advised the editorial, that innocent and unnecessary deaths are a deep loss, that such

[4] Press release, January 23, 1985, KSU Communications Services.

losses must not occur again, that the constitutional rights of free speech and free assembly must be protected, and that "violent protest is intolerable and not the way to change our society for the better. . . . Only through peaceful and rational means can we make the world a better place." A year earlier, the student newspaper had endorsed the reconciliatory virtue of a permanent memorial, asserting that it "would finally put the tragedy of May 4 behind the University and put to rest the conflict over how the tragedy should be remembered." Reflecting the theme of personal loss, an April 1985 statement from the May 4th Task Force pointed out: "As in the past, it is our intention primarily to pay tribute to the memories of our four fallen students."[5]

The annual commemoration of May 4, 1985, marking the fifteenth anniversary of the shootings, featured a reunion of eight of the wounded students from May 1970. For the first time since 1976, Elaine Holstein returned to the campus where her son, Jeffrey Miller, had been shot by National Guardsmen. As had been true for some years, the sponsoring organization was the May 4th Task Force, and its slogan for the fifteenth anniversary was a simple one: "KSU Remembers Allison, Sandy, Jeff, and Bill." About one thousand people gathered on the Kent State Commons to listen to the keynote speaker, Sen. Howard Metzenbaum, and to remember four young people from a violent spring.

However, the fifteenth anniversary represented more than a recapitulation of past injustices or a restatement of the continued symbolic importance of May 1970 to the current generation of students. The 1985 commemoration expressed a mood noticeably different from even several years earlier, when May 4 speakers still felt a need to exhort their listeners to preserve the memory of Kent State's fallen heroes in the face of insensitivity, cowardice, and forgetfulness on the part of the University and the political establishment. For in 1985, it was long-time May 4 activist, Alan Canfora, wounded in 1970, who said, "We're healing the wounds of the past and now this university can address a brighter future. Hopefully, we've seen the end of the May 4 controversy."[6] Other former stu-

[5]*Daily Kent Stater* (hereafter cited as *DKS*), May 3, 1985, p. 6; *DKS,* May 4, 1984, p. 4; *DKS,* April 17, 1985, p. 4.

[6] *Kent-Ravenna Record-Courier,* May 6, 1985, p. 1.

dents, such as Dean Kahler, Joseph Lewis, and Robert Stamps—all wounded in 1970—had praise as well for the University. The planned memorial would satisfy, apparently the diverse constituencies to which it was intended to speak.

The May 4 Memorial Competition

The formula for the memorial design competition was first announced in September 1985, and a booklet detailing the rationale and rules for the contest was available in early October. Funding of the competition was eased by an eighty-five-thousand-dollar matching grant to the University from the National Endowment of the Arts. Registration would take place through November 30, 1985, and the "design phase" of the competition would begin on December 2 and conclude March 1, 1986. According to the registration booklet, the purpose of the May 4 memorial was to "bring a reexamination of this event and its meaning to the University and the nation in the flow of our history, and for our permanent collective conscience."

> It is the hope of the University to create a memorial in relation to the site of the May 4th tragedy through which a person, tracing the path of the events of May 4, will gain a deep sense of the events of that day and thus arrive at a broader realm of feeling and understanding. The University hopes that a visitor's thoughts will be turned to the loss of the lives of four young students, the wounding of nine others, and the emotional and moral injury to so many more. It is the hope of the University that a visitor's reflections will be elevated towards a probing comprehension of a trying moment in our nation's history; that all who experience this place with its memorial will be reminded of the essential tenets which unite us, pondering their delicate yet precious nature.

The memorial must be neither "accusatory" nor "laudatory," nor should the memorial itself become a source of dissension. "It should acknowledge the four young students whose lives were lost, the others who were injured, and contribute to the healing of a receding but still deep and collective wound in the University's and the nation's history."

Paul D. Spreiregen was designated as the professional adviser for the design competition: as such, he would be responsible for organizing and managing the entire effort. Having performed a similar role for the competition which produced the Vietnam Veterans Memorial in Washington, D.C.—and having weathered the controversy which it generated—Spreiregen's participation in the Kent State competition added to the credibility of the project. A seven-person jury was also named, consisting of artists, architects, landscape architects, and environmental author Grady Clay, who served as chairman of the group. Of some import later, section 1.1 of the competition rules stipulated that entrants must be U.S. citizens at the time of their registration. Cash prizes of twenty thousand, ten thousand, and five thousand dollars would be awarded to the top three designs, and up to ten honorable mentions, at five hundred dollars each, could be awarded at the discretion of the jury.[7]

The *Design Program,* made available to competition entrants after the completion of registration, contained more precise guidelines for the memorial plus an elaborate description of the actions of students and guardsmen on May 4, 1970, accompanied by maps. While the University, it was noted, did not have any preconceived notions as to the form of the memorial, "we do have a hope as to what it may accomplish." As before, the University stressed its desire for a nonjudgmental memorial design: one "that hovers about yet transcends the events of May 4" and one which was not a political expression. "The purpose of the Memorial is to emphasize inquiry, learning, and reflection and to elevate the thoughts of visitors to a larger realm of awareness. It is the University's hope that those who experience it will gain a strengthened sense of our highest values as Americans." Design requirements stipulated, among other things, that the wooded character of the site must be preserved, such that the memorial "should be an artistic 'incident' alongside a pedestrian pathway." Also, the memorial should be easily accessible year-round, made from durable and noncorrosive materials compatible

[7] *Kent State May 4 Memorial, National Open Design Competition,* competition description booklet, October 1985, p. 2, Kent State University Archives; the booklet also contained a brief description of the events of April 30−May 4, 1970, with photographs, and a summary of May 4−related litigation and the gym controversy of 1977. In addition to Clay, the jury members were William A. Behnke, Robert M. Hanna, Richard H. Hunt, Gyrgy Kepes, William N. Morgan, and William C. Muchow.

with the climate of northeastern Ohio, conceived at a cost of no
more than five hundred thousand dollars, and suitable for use by
small-scale gatherings. It should include "a physical expression" of
the four students killed and provide for a "distribution device" for
informational brochures. Entrants could submit a short written
statement with their illustrations.[8]

The jury finished its work on April 3, 1986, and the announcement of the winning design, submitted by Michael Fahey and Ian
Taberner, was made at a press conference of April 4. As it turned
out, Taberner was chiefly responsible for the final design, and his
statement emphasized the manner in which the memorial would encourage reflection and transcendence. His design featured a walk-
way and five rooms cut into the hillside along the northeast edge of
the Commons: four small circular rooms and "a square open air
room for assembly meetings." A key theme, as Taberner later explained, was "subtraction": the absence of the four students killed,
the loss of their lives and talents.[9]

Paul Spreiregen, a strong advocate of design competitions, has
observed nevertheless that they "are not magic tools of political or
professional reform."[10] But the competition had provided a unique
opportunity for Kent State's president, Michael Schwartz, to identify himself and the institution with a new perspective on May 4
affairs: cognizant of the historical importance, sensitive to the human loss, willing to support a permanent memorial to such tragic
events. In May 1985, Schwartz had characterized the Kent State
shootings as the "single most important domestic event of the Vietnam era." Earlier, in his interview for this book, he had acknowledged: "People were killed here, people who hadn't really done anything. They were killed by the authorities of their own government."
To Schwartz, the vitality of May 4 issues through subsequent years
had as much to do with the University's handling of its May 4 legacy

[8] *Design Program, Kent State May 4 Memorial: National Open Design Competition,* December 1985, p. 16, Kent State University Archives; additionally, the
booklet contained sections providing information on the University and the city of
Kent, the layout of the campus, and a text-and-photograph description of the intended memorial site.

[9] *DKS,* April 8, 1986, pp. 1–2; *DKS,* April 15, 1986, p. 13.

[10] Paul D. Spreiregen, *Design Competitions* (New York: McGraw-Hill Book
Company, 1979), p. 2.

as it did with the original events themselves. Thus, the final paragraph of the "May 4, 1970" section of the *Design Program* referred to "an untended void in the University's conscience."[11] This was the central issue which could be and would be addressed by a memorial. Kent State would come to terms with its own pivotal moment, and in doing so would at last heal the scars left by years of indifference and uncertainty. At his April 4, 1986, press conference, Schwartz remarked:

> With this announcement today, Kent State University formally acknowledges its own history and its place in recent American history. The loss of four young lives, the wounding of nine other students, the psychological pain and suffering inflicted upon countless others on the campus, in the City of Kent, and even beyond—all of that is remembered here today with the establishment of this commemorative memorial. . . . To reflect and inquire into our own values and ideals as Americans, knowing our past and concerned for our future, has been our purpose. It is a tribute to the University's students of today that they reminded us of the need to remember the past in order to safeguard the future. As president of Kent State University, I am proud of their patience and persistence.[12]

The statement contained an echo of the May 4th Task Force's slogan of a decade earlier: "Remember the Past, Continue the Struggle." But Schwartz was indicating that the struggle was over, and he thus played a leading role in gathering support for an abstract memorial as an appropriate remembrance of May 4, 1970. Consistently, his remarks sought to legitimize the purposeful ambiguity of the project by linking it to a strong affirmation of the historical vitality of 1970 events. "Fortunately," read an editorial in the *Daily Kent Stater,* "construction can't be far away. Optimism is high. With the design officially accepted, the University is certain to work expediently to have the memorial erected."[13]

---

[11] *Akron Beacon Journal,* May 3, 1985, p. A5; *Design Program,* December 1985, p. 11.

[12] "Statement of President Schwartz to the May 4 Memorial Design Press Conference," April 4, 1986, KSU Communications Services.

[13] *DKS,* April 8, 1986, p. 6.

New Controversy, New Memorial

Shortly after the Fahey-Taberner entry had been proclaimed the winner of the design competition, the latter informed Schwartz that he was a Canadian citizen, a violation of the guidelines on eligibility. Section 11.1 of the competition rules had read: "Any Competitor who breaks any of the Competition Rules, or who fails to comply with the requirements of the Competition Program, will be disqualified from the competition, and his, her, or their design submission will not be considered." However, the initial response of the Kent State administration was to disqualify Taberner only, retain the design, present the cash award to Michael Fahey, and assign to him the task of supervising construction. But since he was not the actual designer, Fahey refused to accept either the award or the responsibility for overseeing the project. Now the memorial design stood alone, while the jury had advised "sensitive collaboration between all responsible . . . , assuring that the intention of the original design concept be realized."[14] It was an unhappy situation which was not eased as negotiations directed toward hiring Taberner as an independent consultant collapsed in mutual disagreement.

On July 2, 1986, the Board of Trustees formally disqualified the Fahey-Taberner entry and declared that the memorial-plaza design submitted by Chicago architects Bruno Ast and Thomas Rasmussen, formerly the runner-up, was the new winner of the May 4 Competition. While this decision received the support of Spreiregen, it was disputed locally, most notably by Alan Canfora and other members of the May 4th Task Force. Temporarily, at least, the rapid movement toward selection and construction of a permanent memorial was slowed. Yet, the abstract character of both memorial designs virtually guaranteed that most observers, including May 4 activists, would hesitate to proclaim one proposal more virtuous or more relevant than the other. Thus, both Dean Kahler and Robert Stamps spoke out against identifying with a particular design at the expense of the overall project.[15]

---

[14] "Additional Jury Recommendations," n.d., KSU Communications Services.
[15] See "Canfora backs original May 4 Memorial," *DKS,* May 1, 1987, p. 5; Kahler and Stamps comments, *Akron Beacon Journal,* April 26, 1987, p. 5B.

By the spring of 1987, with the University and Ian Taberner having settled their differences out of court, fundraising began in order to implement the Ast memorial design. "Our recollections and views may differ," read a letter to Kent State graduates. "But perhaps there is one thing upon which we can agree: the events of May 4, 1970 were so unprecedented, so history-making, so traumatic that any of us associated with this University know they have affected our lives."

> May 4, 1970 is not just Kent State's burden. It is a burden carried by an entire society. It was an event without precedent, it was also an event which must never be repeated. We are long past the period of assigning blame. We are now seeking understanding.
>
> We are asking your help. . . . We must heal the past, aspire to a peaceful future and, most importantly, understand what went before as a prelude to what can be. It is time to realize the real purpose of a university, which is to learn from human events. We believe this effort will help in that mission.[16]

Kent State in History

On July 12, 1986, delegates to the Ohio American Legion convention in Cleveland approved a resolution which opposed construction of a May 4 memorial on the Kent State campus. Such a memorial, stated the resolution, would be an insult to all veterans who had honorably served their country. It was a flamboyant counterpoint to the desultory confusion at Kent State in the immediate aftermath of the design competition. The *Cleveland Plain Dealer* termed the American Legion resolution "nasty" and "misguided," and defended the planned memorial: "The proposed monument is designed not to take a side as to who was right or wrong on that day, but rather to provide a permanent setting in which Kent State students and faculty can reflect on what happened."[17] It was the only flurry of organized opposition to appear and posed no threat to the project. But the legionnaires' action provided a useful reminder of the residue of hostility which still enjoyed a bitter half-life in the region.

---

[16] Form letter to KSU graduates, signed by Michael Schwartz and Anthony A. Petrarca, chairman of the Board of Trustees, March 1987; author's copy.

[17] *Cleveland Plain Dealer,* July 12, 1986, p. 12A; *Akron Beacon Journal,* July 13, 1986, pp. A1, A6.

In his state-of-the-university address of October 10, Michael Schwartz pointed to the American Legion resolution as an example of the kind of "blinding prejudice" which it was the mission of higher education to overcome. He repeated the themes of the memorial design competition: "The time was right for healing, for peace and thought, for learning and reflection. The time of playing childish games of praise and blame were over. The time had come to remember and move forward."[18] Here was the new ethos of May 4: the binding up of wounds in the midst of pondering the complexity and ambiguity of history. "The Memorial marks the event of May 4, 1970 and the promise for an enlightened future," wrote Bruno Ast in his design statement: "It suggests containment and escape." Ian Taberner's proposal had been likewise an exercise in depoliticization. Indeed, the memorial design competition had been founded on the assumption that a "political expression" was inappropriate. Certainly it was not practical. In May 1987, a spokesperson for the May 4th Task Force remarked: "There aren't any right answers to this whole thing [concerning the May 4 shootings], but it's something that Kent State students and society should learn from." But learn what? "The meaning of . . . [a] memorial," wrote two Kent State faculty members, "is created both through the social process whereby it is conceived and in the activities it generates after construction."[19] Public memorials to recent and controversial events, by providing a physical setting for reflection and inquiry, may do much more to encourage us to remember the past than we realize. They may do much less. The May 4 Memorial, when it is built, could prove to be a valuable tool in improving our collective memory; it will surely mark a significant achievement for the University.

Acknowledgments

I wish to thank the following people who provided assistance in gathering materials for this new preface and expanded bibliography:

[18] *Akron Beacon Journal,* October 12, 1986, p. E3.

[19] *DKS,* May 1, 1987, p. 12; Stanford W. Gregory, Jr., and Jerry M. Lewis, "Symbols of Collective Memory: The Social Process of Memorializing May 4, 1970 at Kent State University" (revised version of a paper presented at the 12th Annual Conference on Social Theory, Politics, and the Arts, University of California-San Diego, October 1986), p. 7.

Sylvia Eldridge, Jan Griffey, Gary Harwood, Nancy Hawkins, George Hing, Jerry Lewis, Sanford Rosen, and Lesley Wischmann. At the request of Elaine Holstein, I have substituted a different picture of Jeffrey Miller on page 57, one which was taken only a short time before his death; the negative was supplied by Lesley Wischmann. I would also like to thank John Hubbell, director, and Jeanne West, editor, of the Kent State University Press for their interest in reprinting this book.

October 1987

Preface to the First Printing

This is a book about attitudes, about how people interpret events, about myths and zeitgeist. The deaths of four students and the wounding of nine others at Kent State University on May 4, 1970, sparked a highly emotional response from students and faculty of virtually all university communities; from parents; from residents of college or university towns, many of them hostile toward the youth-dominated antiwar/radical movement and its institutional base; from law enforcement officials of various kinds, some of them uncomfortable with the logistics of campus unrest. The essays and interviews contained in this volume reflect the broad spectrum of this response and the many and conflicting interpretations that have arisen regarding what took place in the spring of 1970, who was culpable, and what significance those events have held for us, as individuals and a society, over the intervening years.

Each person represented here speaks with his or her own voice, polemical or nonpolemical, direct or indirect. There is, of course, a special vocabulary that has developed, quite naturally, to describe the Kent State shootings and their aftermath. There are relatively neutral terms, such as "shootings," "deaths," "events," "slain and wounded students," "incident." But partisan views   and this collection contains such views—regularly employ such words as "murders," "massacre," "rioters," "troublemakers," "triggermen," and so forth. The area where the shootings occurred has become "the site," and the ground where the guardsmen stood and fired— Blanket Hill—is often simply "the hill." A shorthand reference to the whole series of events of May 1–4, 1970, culminating in the shootings, is "Kent State," which is used frequently in this collection. In Kent, people use the term "May 4th issues" to describe a range of political considerations, from an analysis of the root causes of the May 1970 events to the controversies generated by the subsequent debate over proper memorialization and commemoration of the shootings.

The oral history format used for some of the voices in this collection provides an effective means for the expression of viewpoints held by people with little or no inclination to write them down. Yet, their opinions are central to an accurate portrayal of the emotional as well as the political response to the May 4 shootings. And some of the comments made are perhaps more provocative and instructive than those interviewed may have realized. The written essays are equally expressive and offer a variety of perspectives, both academic and nonacademic, on Kent State affairs.

Why have I chosen these people and not others? I have sought contributors who could articulate, in written or oral form, the range of viewpoints that has characterized the political debate over the death of four students in 1970. Most contributors have clear past or current ties to the University or the town; those who do not have become students of Kent State because of the violence of May 1970 and the following years of continuing controversy and lengthy litigation. Some people with whom I corresponded chose not to contribute to this collection for various reasons, among them the feeling that they had already said or written what they had to say. For others it is too painful a memory to revisit.

The introductory essay provides background information on the town and the University, an overview of pertinent events at Kent State between 1970 and 1982, and brief references to each essay or interview in the book. It is not meant to be a complete history of the period, and readers interested in further discussion of particular issues should consult the annotated bibliography which appears at the end of this volume. In order that the bibliography be more current for purposes of reproduction and distribution for classroom or library use, I have included, among the entries, the essays which appear in this book.

Acknowledgments

It has been a long time since I was standing in the street in Morgantown, West Virginia, watching state troopers assemble on my campus to disperse (as I remember it) over one thousand students who had gathered to protest the deaths at Kent State. It seems much longer ago than a simple count of the years would indicate. I have often thought since then of what happened in May 1970, in Kent and elsewhere, and my work on this collection reflects an interest that is both personal and historical.

The preparation of this book has drawn on materials which I first collected in 1977, but the real impetus for such an anthology emerged from a special (and last) issue of the journal *Left Review*, published in May 1980 to commemorate the tenth anniversary of the shootings. The issue was designed to pull together the separate threads and differing political and historical perspectives on the continuing impact and symbolism of Kent State, and I was assisted in that project by E. Timothy Smith and Steven Thulin. This volume contains several of the essays which appeared in the *Left Review*, though they have been, for the most part, substantially revised and updated.

However, this collection is different in character and scope from any other book about the shootings and their aftermath. And many people have participated in its genesis. My wife, Kristi Dixon-Bills, was in Kent in May 1970, and she well remembers her car being searched at gunpoint, traveling back roads to get out of town, the chaos and fear that reigned. Her suggestions and comments have been helpful at every turn. Mary Von Lindern typed nearly all of my extensive correspondence for the book in the spring and summer of 1980; and even though many letters were never answered, her work enabled me to reach many more potential contributors than I could have otherwise. Tim Smith took time from his pre- and post-dissertation research to produce the rough transcripts for the interviews with Lyman, Gibson, Herington, Gabriel, Lewis, and Schwartz—a task of many hours. Steven Thulin worked with me in preparing annotations for the bibliography. Without their help, I cannot say when the collection might have been finished. I have often discussed with Steven Thulin, in the past, the concept and role of the "May 4th Movement," and I am certain that some of his ideas have found their way into my introductory essay.

James Geary, former Kent State University archivist, was always helpful and encouraging. His emphasis on the expansion of the Archives' May 4th Collection resulted in the processing of many new and useful materials during his tenure. Archival Assistant Sylvia Eldridge was very helpful in aiding my search for certain photographs and other specific pieces of information in the University Archives; her patience in the face of my numerous requests was exemplary.

I should like to thank those people with whom I corresponded during the preparation of this book, who gave me permission to quote from their letters. The people who were interviewed for the oral history segments spoke, I believe, with openness and candor, and I learned something from each one of them. Ken Calkins, Lynne Jurkovic, Tim Smith, and my wife all read and commented on drafts of my introductory essay; Gary Hess, Marjorie Dobkin, and John Hubbell read the entire manuscript and offered useful suggestions for its improvement. Marjorie Evans and Millie Keyser typed much of the final draft.

Special thanks must go to Henry Whitney, Lawrence Kaplan, Mary Vincent, Harriet Begala, Thomas Matijasic, Mim Jackson, and James Abraham. Arlene Lawson, Thomas Hensley, Jerry Lewis, Maire Dugan, and Lilas Pratt aided my search for particular articles which appear in the bibliography. John Darnell, Jr., Roger Vance, Douglas Moore, Richard Caputo, John Rowe, Bill Bierman, Sandy Kessler, and Tom Jennings supplied or helped me locate photographs which appear here. David Marquard of the Engineering Department, City of Kent, was kind enough to show me a number of aerial photographs which his office had on file; thanks also to John Reed of the Ohio Department of Transportation. Janet Schaeffer of The Reading Center in Hudson, Ohio, allowed me the use of a tape recorder for more weeks than she originally intended.

The interest shown by the Kent State University Press, specifically by its director, Paul Rohmann, and editor, Laura Nagy, in the publication of a book which capsules intense intrauniversity controversies as well as the larger issues raised by the May 4 shootings is, I feel, noteworthy.

May 1982

Introduction

The Past in the Present

by SCOTT L. BILLS

Each of us," said Sen. Frank Church in eulogy of John F. Kennedy, "tends to remember, in a personal fashion, the cataclysmic occasions of a lifetime. Why else is the question so commonly asked, 'Where were you on Pearl Harbor day? or V-day? on the day F.D.R. died?' "[1] The same is true of the events at Kent State University on May 4, 1970, when four students were killed and nine wounded by Ohio National Guard riflefire. Where were you in the spring of 1970, on April 30, when President Richard Nixon announced that U.S. military forces had entered Cambodia? What were you doing on May 4 when you heard that four students were dead at Kent State University?

In northeastern Ohio, as throughout the country, people were doing what they do every day. They were, as reflected in the interviews and essays in this book, having lunch, working, driving their cars, sitting around the house, teaching classes, listening to classes being taught. And some of them were standing in the large, grassy, open area in the center of the Kent State campus—the "Commons," bordered on one side by Blanket Hill—watching National Guard troops attempt to disperse a noontime crowd of antiwar, anti-Guard demonstrators. At 12:25, the guardsmen stood on the crest of the hill and fired into a crowd of students in a parking lot; and for a moment, at least, the world stopped to listen. Then, almost immediately, the questioning about and assessment of the shootings began: to discern who was at fault, what the "truth" was, and what "lessons" could

---

[1] U.S., Congress, House and Senate, Joint Committee on Printing, *Memorial Addresses in the Congress of the United States and Tributes in Eulogy of John Fitzgerald Kennedy*, comp. Joint Committee on Printing, 88th Cong., 2d sess., 1964, p. 73.

and should be learned. More than a decade afterward, the same questions are being asked. Over the years, views have become more clearly articulated, certainly, but different and contradictory interpretations of the shootings have flourished and are still put forward with only slightly diminished spirit and emotion. As with other sudden, violent historical events, the past lives uneasily in the present.

Kent, Ohio

Founded in 1805 as "Franklin Mills," the town of Kent lay in the center of a region of northeastern Ohio known as the Western Reserve, a 120-mile-wide area "reserved" for Connecticut coastal residents moving westward after suffering British depredations during the Revolutionary War. Harlan Hatcher, in his 1949 history of the Reserve, noted that despite the arrival of latter-nineteenth-century, non-English-speaking immigrants, the area "was Connecticut and New England long enough and exclusively enough to establish a distinctive atmosphere and style of living and culture that set it apart from the other regions of Ohio."[2]

The town began to prosper during the Civil War with the coming of a railroad trunk line and attendant facilities. A local entrepreneur, Marvin Kent, was popularly credited with this new success, and the townspeople were "so grateful," wrote one local historian, that the "City of Kent" was officially incorporated in the spring of 1867. The city's fortunes rose and fell over the next forty-five years based on the lifecycles of local industries and developments in the transportation network, including the growth and failure of a canal. What ultimately transformed the town—with, observed Karl Grismer, an "almost magical" effect—was the founding in 1910 of a "normal school" to train teachers, predecessor to the University.[3]

Kent grew slowly, however, as did the normal school, until after World War II. Between 1940 and the mid-1960s, the city's population virtually tripled, the census figures for 1970 showing slightly

    [2] Harlan Hatcher, *The Western Reserve: The Story of New Connecticut in Ohio* (New York: Bobbs-Merrill, 1949), p. 16.
    [3] Karl H. Grismer, *The History of Kent* (Kent, Ohio: The Courier-Tribune, n.d.), pp. 45 and 103 for quoted material. A very brief narrative of local history to the mid-1950s can be found in *Portage Heritage*, ed. James B. Holm (Ravenna, Ohio: Portage County Historical Society, 1957), pp. 323–45.

over 28,000 residents. Yet, there remained the self-image of a non-industrial, semipastoral environment; residents liked the town's nickname, "Tree City," and many local businesses have consistently incorporated those words into their names. A 1959 brochure, published by the Kent Area Chamber of Commerce, proclaimed that the city, "although located in the heart of an industrial area, retains enough of its Western Reserve heritage to lend it charm and character. An ideal community in which to live, the city is resplendent with attractive houses and beautiful trees."[4]

Indeed, its location approximately thirty-five miles south of Cleveland, forty miles northwest of Youngstown, and eleven miles east of Akron, put Kent in the midst of an industrial belt. Yet, it was a town increasingly shaped not by local industries, which remained small, but by the expansion of the educational institution which became Kent State University. A report prepared by the Tri-County Regional Planning Commission in 1968 included a socioeconomic profile which pointed to the growing importance of the service sector of the town's economy. During the period 1955–65, employment in manufacturing enterprises showed a marked decline while the University's economic role only expanded. By 1965, 21 percent of the employed labor force in Kent was working for the University.[5] The median income for Kent families in 1969 was $10,886. The community was quite racially homogeneous: only 3.7 percent of the local population was black. The county-wide population (125,868) showed only a 2.1 percent black representation. Hence, while located in the heavily industrialized, urban part of northeastern Ohio, Kent remained insulated from the problems of its large neighboring cities, except as the University became—as did such institutions throughout the nation—a reflection of the social and political upheaval in society at large and the source of its own special student revolt.

Physically, Kent is bisected north to south by the Cuyahoga River, the railroad lines that run beside it, and State Route 43—Water Street—which runs roughly parallel about a half block away.

---

[4] "This is Kent, Ohio," vertical file F.7.5.1., American History Research Center, Kent State University Archives (hereafter cited as KSUA), Kent, Ohio.

[5] "Western Portage County Planning Area—Report 2," Tri-County Regional Planning Commission, Community Assistance Division (Akron, 1968). Copies of the report can be found in Box 5 of the John A. Begala Papers, KSUA.

The city is split east to west by State Route 59, or Main Street, with the intersection of Main and Water considered the center of town. The business area surrounding the intersection, today and in 1970, consists largely of banks and drugstores, with jewelry and small grocery stores, the post office, the city hall and police station southward. North Water Street, described in some detail in John Begala's essay in this book, consisted primarily of a series of bars and was well known throughout the area for that reason. This is the part of town described in Irwin Unger's history of the American New Left as a "small, honky-tonk district."[6]

West Main Street bridges the Cuyahoga and runs for several miles to what Mary Vincent, in her interview, refers to as the "automobile end of town": a cluster of auto showrooms and used-car lots where, for instance, Lucius Lyman, Jr. owned the Chevrolet dealership. East Main Street, which runs past a downtown hotel and a cinema, comprises the northern border of the Kent State campus, which is about four blocks from the center of town, and leads to Ravenna, the county seat, five miles to the east. James Michener, in his *Kent State: What Happened and Why*, published in 1971, discussed at length the problems created when long trains would pass through downtown Kent and stop all east-west traffic. "All university settings throughout the world have a town-gown problem," he wrote, "but none more aggravated than Kent's, where one Erie & Lackawanna freight train, coming along at the inopportune moment, can infuriate thousands."[7] Whether or not it was a problem of that magnitude, a bypass was opened in the mid-1970s which enabled drivers, harried or not, to pass over freight trains as well as the river and a section of Franklin Street.

Beginning in the spring of 1969, the local newspaper, the *Kent-Ravenna Record-Courier*, began featuring an increasing number of articles dealing with campus unrest, at Kent State and elsewhere. Editorials reflected now-familiar themes, denouncing "young activists," for instance, who demonstrated at Richard Nixon's inaugural in January 1969, for "playing their dangerous games with reckless abandon." Protests, read the editorial, certainly had a legitimate

---

[6] Irwin Unger, *The Movement: A History of the American New Left, 1959-1972* (New York: Dodd, Mead, 1975), p. 185.

[7] James A. Michener, *Kent State: What Happened and Why* (Greenwich, Conn.: Fawcett Crest, 1971), p. 41.

place in American politics: "But are we to be greeted by these activists at every event, every occasion and every governmental function?" Still, there were favorable remarks about the October and November "moratorium" demonstrations in the fall of 1969. Looking toward a restored national unity in the coming decade, the newspaper's editors observed on October 11: "Breathe a sigh of relief, Americans: we've almost made it through the Frantic Sixties; let's hope that the Seventies will be the calm after the storm, a decade when Americans get to know and trust each other again and join together to construct a more wonderful America." And in the first edition of the *Record-Courier* for 1970, the editorial stated: "There's a clean slate ahead in the next decade, a clean slate that contains none of the mistakes of the past 10 years."[8]

Kent State University

The University, founded in 1910, quickly assumed a key role in the local economy and just as certainly experienced institutional crises before 1970. Phillip Shriver, in his book *The Years of Youth*, notes the growing pains and personal rivalries which were felt by the school in the 1920s. He points to a crisis of spring 1933 when "the very existence of the College was threatened." The Finance Committee of the Ohio House of Representatives formulated a proposal to convert one of the state normal schools into a hospital for the mentally ill. Kent was to be visited by an inspection committee on May 4 of that year. Shriver reports that there was "a mobilization of all civic, fraternal, and educational organizations of northeastern Ohio into a single fighting force" to prevent such action being taken at Kent.[9] The proposal was defeated. Two years later, in May 1935, Kent State officially achieved university status. It continued to grow as an institution, so much so that Shriver reported that after May 1960, Kent State was entering its "second half-century, confident and unafraid." He wrote: "The years of youth were over. The years of maturity were now beginning."[10] This theme of maturation was the title for two long-range planning studies completed in 1967–68.

[8] *Kent-Ravenna Record-Courier* (hereafter cited as *Record-Courier*), January 21, 1969, editorial, p. 4; ibid., October 11, 1969, editorial, p. 2; ibid., January 2, 1970, editorial, p. 4.

[9] Phillip R. Shriver, *The Years of Youth: Kent State University, 1910–1960* (Kent, Ohio: Kent State University Press, 1960), p. 129.

[10] Ibid., p. 239.

A report contained within the study, distilling the views of forty newer faculty members, indicated concern over the quality of the expanding undergraduate program, questioning whether "a real university atmosphere yet exists," with mild critiques of certain administrative procedures. But, said the report, there were "high aspirations." It continued:

> Many of us dream of a university with a national and international reputation for academic excellence; of a place with a free and vital atmosphere of questioning and learning; of a place where the explosion and implosion of ideas are the all-consuming activity; and, hopefully, of a place where excellence and the pursuit of excellence are no longer goals, but assumptions felt in the blood.[11]

Such "aspirations" were shared by other institutions and widely recognized as appropriate goals for higher education. As Kent State President George Bowman wrote in April 1956, "The University which fails to try to lead thought and not follow it is missing a most important objective."[12]

In the 1960s, many smaller universities and colleges had experienced significant and often rapid growth and looked forward to continued expansion as well as the orderly stabilization of new academic programs. However, there were other, broader societal forces which undermined and transformed this process. James Huber and Carl Rosen, writing with reference to the events of May 1970, have pointed to the growing alienation of universities from the society of which they were such an integral part and also to the "specialization of the intellectual" which generated increased conformism and departmental insularity within academia. At the same time, the university was achieving, in the words of Clark Kerr, former president of the University of California at Berkeley, a "new centrality" in American political and social life. "Today," he said in 1963, "the large American university is . . . a whole series of communities and activities held together by a common name, a common governing board, and related purposes. This great transformation is re-

---

[11] "On the State of Kent State University—As Seen by Newer Faculty," in *The Years of Maturity: Long Range Planning at Kent State University 1967–1968*, 2 vols. (Kent, Ohio: Kent State University, 1968), 2:324–32. The authors of the faculty report were Ottavio Casale, Stanley Christensen, Richard Goldthwaite, and Thomas Moore.

[12] Bowman to McCormick, April 9, 1956, Box 40, May 4th Collection (hereafter cited as M4C), KSUA.

gretted by some, accepted by many, gloried in, as yet, by few."[13] It was the "multiversity," characterized by deteriorating internal consensus, a splintering of academic holism, and large subsurface growing pains as student enrollment increased dramatically. Kent State University felt this transformation, having, by 1970, an enrollment of 21,000 students on a 900-acre main campus and administering nine regional campus centers.

The major challenge to the surface tranquility in American higher education arose in the form of the student movement, which began in the mid-1960s and was typified by the Students for a Democratic Society (SDS) and similar groups. SDS originated as a youth-oriented organization committed to a strategy of student mobilization to implement its political program. Its founding document, the Port Huron Statement, promulgated in 1962, asserted that the university should be a "community of controversy, within itself and in its effect on communities beyond."[14] For SDS, the multiversity was a depersonalized, authoritarian institution, yet one which presented a great opportunity for building a national network of affiliated dissident student groups who would carry their politics beyond the boundaries of the campus. And the issue which enabled SDS to become truly a national organization—and the spearhead of the radical student movement—was the Vietnam War.

What began as a student-centered antiwar campaign blossomed into a broad-based coalition opposing U.S. involvement in Indochina; by 1970, the antiwar movement was no longer led by radical groups only. SDS had disintegrated in 1969 as a result of internal factionalization, and in its wake had arisen a number of small, competing sectarian groups advocating violent revolution and convinced of the imminent collapse of the American capitalist system. However, while the "New Left" failed to build a lasting organization or political party, its programs and ideology had a major impact on educational institutions. Proposals for the democratization of university decision-making and the elimination of military-related

[13] James Huber and Carl Rosen, "What Should Be, What Could Be: While Educating the Children, Who Will Guard the Guards?" *Left Review* 4 (Spring 1980):9–12; Clark Kerr, *The Uses of the University, With a New Postscript* (New York: Harper Torchbooks, 1973), pp. vi, 1. Kerr's book contains materials he first presented as part of the 1963 Godkin Lectures at Harvard University.

[14] "Port Huron Statement," in *The New Left: A Documentary History*, ed. Massimo Teodori (New York: Bobbs-Merrill, 1969), p. 172.

academic and research programs received strong support from many students and faculty. Nor were student radicals universally condemned by nonleftist observers. Arthur Schlesinger, Jr., for instance, while terming them "fantasists of revolution," nonetheless observed: "Many criticisms launched by the New Left are uncomfortably close to the mark. By forcing the rest of us to take a fresh look at injustices too complacently accepted, the New Leftists have played an undoubted role in stimulating the national conscience."[15]

Kent State University was not excluded from the political upheaval of this period. The Kent chapter of SDS, like the national organization, had worked to implement a radical program integrating points of its anticapitalist critique with its antiwar stance. This included attacks on the administrative structure of the University, charges of complicity between the University and corporate interests, and calls for the termination of ROTC programs on campus. Formed in 1968 and superseding the Kent Committee to End the War in Vietnam, the Kent SDS published its only major paper, a pamphlet titled "Who Rules Kent?" in 1969. It stated: "Our concern . . . is to demonstrate the relation between the ruling class and the university, in this case Kent State University. What we contend is that this relation amounts to domination and control of the university by the ruling class, and the use of the university by the ruling class to serve its own interests."[16]

The pamphlet, after examining the business and professional interests of the members of the Ohio Board of Regents and the Board of Trustees for the University, concluded that the "ruling class" did dominate the institution. In April 1969, the national SDS launched a "Spring Offensive" which resulted, in Kent, in the presentation to the University Trustees of demands for the abolition of ROTC and an end to University participation in war-related research and cooperation with local law enforcement agencies. The organization's actions at a Trustees' meeting led to disciplinary hearings, held on campus at the Music and Speech Building. SDS activists and their supporters attended and attempted to "shut down" the hearings. University police began to seal the building, and although two faculty members, one of them Kenneth Calkins,

[15] Arthur Schlesinger, Jr., "Often Close to the Mark," *Akron Beacon Journal*, May 15, 1970, p. D1.

[16] "Who Rules Kent?" Box 21, M4C, KSUA.

were responsible for assisting the exit of some students, fifty-eight people were arrested. Calkins recounts the experience in his essay, "The Frustrations of a Former Activist," and comments as well on the complex relationship between radical students and sympathetic faculty. "We were well aware of the fact," he writes, "that by teaching our students to think critically we had fostered the cast of mind which encouraged political activism, but we were surprised and perturbed when some of our most able protégés began to turn their developing talents against the institutions which provided us with our status and livelihood—and even against ourselves, their mentors."

After the incident at the Music and Speech Building, the campus SDS charter was revoked by the University administration. As the national SDS organization experienced fatal fragmentation, so too did the Kent group. Former member Ken Hammond recalls: "Even before the Music and Speech bust two tendencies had been growing in SDS. One group . . . was moving towards a position that only action and confrontation organized people and brought them into the movement. . . . On the other hand a group put more emphasis on educational work *followed* by action."[17] Hammond counted himself in the latter group and wrote that contention over the different policies "paralyzed" the local chapter.

Within the University administration, the Music and Speech incident provoked concern over the institution's ability to deal with prolonged and insistent protest. President Robert White asserted that the University would follow a policy of arrests and suspension for those involved in further disruption. "Kent State University undeniably faces a crossroad," he commented, asserting that the survival of the school was at issue. "Universities have never before faced the assaults of the present. They produce tensions and strains, and exact a cost in many ways. Kent State University has become an open and announced target. That seems to be the unfair reward of those institutions which have been the most open." And while President White received much support from within the University, some faculty and students contended that his policy was too inflexible. At a "teach-in" of April 22, 1969, faculty member James Louis stated

---

[17] Ken Hammond, "History Lesson: Kent State, a Participant's Memoir," March 1974, Box 21, M4C, KSUA. Emphasis in original.

that it was not the University's survival that was in question, but
rather "what kind of a university will survive."[18] Nevertheless, the
local SDS failed to create a massive protest over the Music and
Speech affair and subsequent University disciplinary proceedings;
and the organization itself collapsed before the end of the year. By
the spring of 1970, there was no radical, antiwar group active on the
campus. Only the Black United Students organization maintained
an activist front, although it promoted primarily the interest of its
own constituency.

May 1970[19]

Student upheaval in the two years prior to 1970 constituted a series
of spiraling confrontations, engendered by such factors as a growing
emphasis on "violent revolution" within the ranks of the New Left,
increased frustration on the part of antiwar activists at the continuation of the Vietnam conflict, and increased resistance to the demands of radical groups by university and civil authorities. In 1969,
there were two large-scale, nationally organized demonstrations
against the war. In mid-October, there were "moratoriums" on
many campuses and in many towns and cities throughout the
country; in Kent, 4,000 people marched through the downtown area
and 4,500 sat in Memorial Gymnasium on campus to listen to future
Ohio governor John Gilligan, among others, denounce the war effort. In November, there was a demonstration in Washington, D.C.,
that drew as many as 500,000 people. It was the high tide of the antiwar movement. The imminence of the "revolution" was a theme
popularized in songs and writings of the time. Hence, many who
reflect on the events of spring 1970 remember them as part of a process that began earlier, characterized first by growing euphoria, then
followed by shock, disbelief, and sometimes by disillusionment.
     The immediate catalyst for heightened student protest in the
spring of 1970 was the announcement by President Nixon, on April

---

[18] White statement, *Record-Courier*, April 17, 1969, p. 6; Louis statement, ibid., April 23,
1969, p. 33.
     [19] The sources for background material in this section, unless otherwise noted, are Peter
Davies, *The Truth About Kent State: A Challenge to the American Conscience* (New York:
Farrar, Straus, and Giroux, 1973), and U.S., President, Commission on Campus Unrest,
Report, 1970, pp. 233–90.

30, that U.S. troops were engaged in an assault on suspected guerrilla strongholds in Cambodia in order "to go to the heart of the trouble." Nixon had previously promised a "Vietnamization" of the Indochina conflict to permit the gradual reduction of American troop involvement in the region. Therefore, some considered the April 30 announcement a "widening" of the war. But the president also spoke to broader issues, saying that Americans lived "in an age of anarchy, both at home and abroad." He continued: "We see mindless attacks on all the great institutions which have been created by free civilizations in the last 500 years. Even here in the United States, great universities are being systematically destroyed."[20] Speaking to civilian employees at the Pentagon the next day, Nixon was quoted as attacking the "bums" who were "blowing up the campuses." The remark was thereafter often interpreted as a reference to all campus dissidents.

On Friday, May 1, spontaneous demonstrations against the Cambodia "invasion" occurred on campuses throughout the nation, including Kent State, where an ad hoc group of graduate students organized the World Historians Opposed to Racism and Exploitation (WHORE) and called for a noon rally on the Commons. The rally leaflet charged that Nixon had "garnered all governmental power to the executive and committed us to a course of national barbarity" in foreign affairs. The president, it read, had "murdered" the Constitution,[21] and a copy of the document was buried at the rally.

The demonstration was relatively small and not sufficiently threatening to prevent President White from leaving town the same day on a previously scheduled trip, from which he did not return until Sunday afternoon. On the evening of May 1, the first serious disturbance took place. A "demonstration" in the downtown section of Kent began as students and nonstudents emerged from bars along North Water Street and blocked the road. Members of a motorcycle gang were prominent participants. A bonfire was started in the street. The crowd then moved toward the center of town, only two blocks away, and began breaking windows in business establishments. Although some observers have seen a clear political flavor to the crowd's actions, it is often asserted that the warm weather and

[20] New York Times, May 1, 1970, p. 2.
[21] WHORE leaflet, May 1, 1970, Box 3, M4C, KSUA.

"rites of spring" sentiments had the major impact on participants' behavior. Fifteen businesses had windows broken, and damage was later assessed at $10,000, although initial estimates were much higher.

At 12:30 A.M., Kent Mayor Leroy Satrom declared a state of emergency, ordering the closing of all liquor stores and taverns and the discontinuance of liquor sales. He also prohibited the sale of firearms and the sale of gasoline "in any container other than a gasoline tank properly affixed to a motor vehicle." A "dusk to dawn" curfew was established for the town. Later in the day, May 2, Satrom formalized a request for the presence of National Guard units, saying that local law enforcement personnel could "no longer cope with the situation."[22]

Lucius Lyman, Jr. was one local resident who surveyed the downtown damage on Saturday morning. He found it "not nearly as extensive" as it had been depicted to him beforehand. But Lyman was upset at the destruction of property. In his interview for this book, he mentions "how important property is in the mentality of those of us who are in the system. You see, it's life, liberty, *and* property." Nor was window-smashing the only problem. On Saturday evening there was a large rally on campus, followed by the burning of the ROTC building. The military presence represented by ROTC had been a long-standing focus for student antiwar demonstrations. Ruth Gibson recalls the moment in her interview: "I didn't really feel gleeful in particular, but I understood why the building was burning. It was a symbol in everybody's mind of direct oppression: the direct threat of having to go into a war that you didn't believe in, that you didn't want, that you didn't think your country should be involved in." A block from the campus, Lyman and his wife were watching the fire, which they and other townspeople saw as simply another— though more flagrant—act of property destruction. Lyman remarks: "You could look up into the sky [and see the flames] and you'd just have to believe that many people in this town thought their house and their property was going to be next."

The source of the ROTC fire is still disputed. It was initially assumed that the fire was started by student demonstrators or "outside agitators." More recently, however, it has been suggested by

[22] "Proclamation of Civil Emergency," May 2, 1970, Box 21, M4C, KSUA; Satrom to Commander of Troops, Ohio National Guard, May 2, 1970, ibid.

some, such as researchers Peter Davies and Charles Thomas, that the fire was begun by *agents provocateurs*, sent to Kent by a government agency in order to provide an excuse for military intervention in campus affairs.[23] Firemen, arriving on campus to extinguish the blaze, experienced strong resistance as students grabbed and tried to cut the hoses. National Guard units arrived in Kent while the building was in flames, and troops commanded by Maj. Gen. Sylvester Del Corso (adjutant general of the Ohio National Guard) and Brig. Gen. Robert Canterbury (assistant adjutant general) were sent onto the campus and took positions in the town. Since the University was state property, neither commanding officer felt a need to contact the school administration before guardsmen entered the campus. The next issue of the local newspaper contained a dramatic photo of guardsmen's bayonets silhouetted against the burning building.

On Sunday, even with the National Guard on campus, many of those present remember the mood as calm, "even festive," in the words of former University administrator Leigh Herington. Students talked with members of the Guard. A young woman named Allison Krause noticed a flower in the barrel of one soldier's rifle. To a nearby officer she commented, "Flowers are better than bullets." Ohio governor James Rhodes arrived in Kent for a press conference in the morning. Speaking at the downtown fire station, he denounced student radicals, asserting that they were intent on destroying higher education. He outlined new state legislation that would provide harsh penalties for those who "just move from one campus to the other and terrorize a community." In words often quoted in the years that followed, Rhodes said: "They're worse than the Brownshirts and the Communist elements and also the Night Riders and Vigilantes. They're the worst type of people that we harbor in America."[24] Herington, in his interview, contends that Rhodes was deliberately inflammatory in his remarks in order to win votes in an upcoming primary election for the U.S. Senate—which he lost—and that the press conference "had a most volatile effect on the whole situation."

At the same press conference, General Del Corso pledged "full

---

[23] See, for instance, Davies, *Truth About Kent State*, p. 17; and Charles Thomas, "The Kent State Massacre: Blood on Whose Hands?" *Gallery*, April 1979, p. 43. See also Peter Davies's essay in this volume.

[24] Transcript, Rhodes press conference, May 3, 1970, Box 63, M4C, KSUA.

support" to local authorities: "anything that is necessary, like the Ohio law says, use any force that is necessary even to the point of shooting." He said: "We don't want to get into that, but the law says we can if necessary." A statement by "23 concerned faculty," issued that day, repudiated the governor's remarks and urged the removal of troops from the campus. Regarding the ROTC fire, the statement read: "We deplore this violence but feel it must be viewed in the larger context of the daily burning of buildings and people by our government in Viet Nam, Laos, and now Cambodia."[25] The connection between the war in Indochina and the upheaval at Kent State was one that would be made frequently after the events of the following day.

On Sunday evening, students again gathered on the Commons. They were tear-gassed and dispersed. Law enforcement officials had decided that the state of civil emergency meant a complete ban on all rallies or demonstrations, but this was not fully understood by or communicated to all students. And some ignored it. Later that night, a group of students staged a sit-in at the intersection of Lincoln and Main Streets on the northwest corner of the campus. This group was also dispersed by guardsmen. A helicopter searchlight followed students across the campus.

A leaflet had been issued on Sunday by Robert Matson, vice president for student affairs, and Frank Frisina, student body president, which stated: "We plan to resume our normal class schedule on Monday with the exception of classes scheduled for the floor of Memorial Gymnasium. Currently the gym floor is being used to provide barrack facilities for the National Guard troops."[26] What was "normal," town and campus residents began asking, and when would normality return? For some, however, the situation seemed appropriate to the politics of that spring. Ken Hammond recalls of Sunday night: "This was, in my opinion, a true revolutionary moment. People were living very much in the present, and were acting out their feelings of outrage with the war, and with their more or less total alienation from American society."[27]

May 4 was far from normal. Classes were held in the morning, but many students did not attend. Robert White had issued a state-

[25] "Statement by 23 Concerned Faculty," May 3, 1970, Box 16, M4C, KSUA.
[26] "A Special Message to the University Community," May 3, 1970, Box 62, M4C, KSUA.
[27] Hammond, "Participant's Memoir," Box 21, M4C, KSUA.

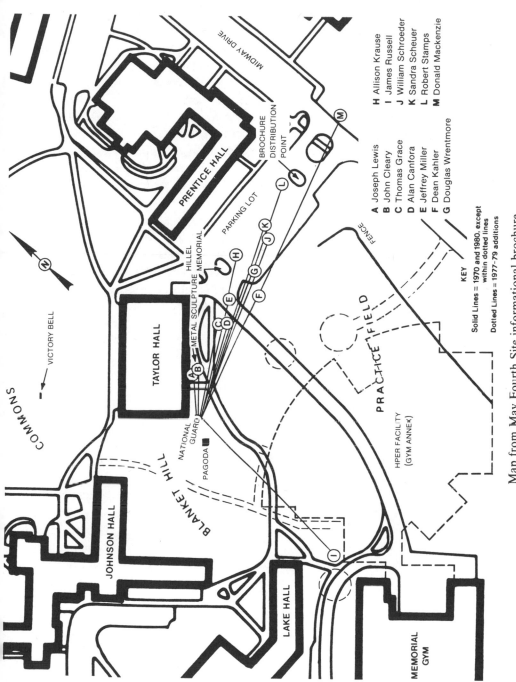

N

COMMONS

VICTORY BELL

JOHNSON HALL

BLANKET HILL

TAYLOR HALL

NATIONAL GUARD

PAGODA

METAL SCULPTURE

HILLEL MEMORIAL

PRENTICE HALL

PARKING LOT

BROCHURE DISTRIBUTION POINT

MIDWAY DRIVE

LAKE HALL

MEMORIAL GYM

HPER FACILITY (GYM ANNEX)

PRACTICE FIELD

FENCE

A Joseph Lewis
B John Cleary
C Thomas Grace
D Alan Canfora
E Jeffrey Miller
F Dean Kahler
G Douglas Wrentmore

H Allison Krause
I James Russell
J William Schroeder
K Sandra Scheuer
L Robert Stamps
M Donald Mackenzie

KEY

Solid Lines = 1970 and 1980, except within dotted lines
Dotted Lines = 1977-79 additions

Map from May Fourth Site informational brochure.

ment after his return to Kent on Sunday saying that the National Guard would remain on campus indefinitely. "Events," he said, "have taken these decisions out of University hands."[28] A rally was scheduled for noon on the University Commons; if it were held, the Guard commanders were intent on dispersing it. When students gathered near the so-called Victory Bell on the east end of the Commons, General Canterbury asked the Kent State police for a bullhorn. When it was delivered, he asked University patrolman Harold Rice to speak to the students, to ask them to leave. Rice was driven in a jeep to the edge of the crowd. "This is an order," he said. "You must leave this area immediately." Few people could hear what he was saying. Rice returned to the line of guardsmen and heard the order for them to advance. He later reported: "At that time I heard the order given for tear gas to be shot. I turned to my partner . . . and told him 'Somebody is going to get killed.' "[29] Rice watched the skirmish line of guardsmen move toward the students.

There were, according to James Michener and Peter Davies, 113 guardsmen moving against a crowd of perhaps 2,000 people. The guardsmen's weapons were "locked and loaded," ready to fire. After a tear-gas barrage, the guardsmen moved to the crest of Blanket Hill at the south end of Taylor Hall, with some of the formation taking positions at the north end of the building. The troops at the top of the hill then walked down the slope and across a football practice field behind Taylor Hall, moving all the way to the fence closing off the field at its east end. While on the practice field, some of the guardsmen knelt and pointed their weapons at students gathered in the Prentice Hall parking lot, adjacent to Taylor Hall. Some observers charge that it was here that a few of the guardsmen "huddled" or "clustered" together as if they were conspiring or receiving a new order.

After approximately ten minutes on the practice field, the Guard contingent began walking in a skirmish line back toward Blanket Hill. Students and guardsmen had thrown tear-gas cannisters back and forth; some rocks had been thrown at guardsmen, but few struck their targets. The guardsmen reached the crest of the hill once again, stood grouped between a cement sculpture known as the

[28] *Record-Courier*, May 4, 1970, p. 16.
[29] Statement by Harold Rice, police report, May 11, 1970, Box 63, M4C, KSUA.

National Guardsmen fire from the top of Blanket Hill into a group of student demonstrators. The "Pagoda" sculpture is in the background.

"Pagoda" and a railing on the south side of Taylor Hall, turned, and fired in the direction of the parking lot. They fired for thirteen seconds and expended, by most accounts, sixty-one rounds of ammunition. It was 12:25 P.M. Four students were killed and nine were wounded. The wounded students were Alan Canfora, John Cleary, Thomas Grace, Dean Kahler, Joseph Lewis, Donald MacKenzie, James Russell, Robert Stamps, and Douglas Wrentmore. Dean Kahler was shot in the lower back, 100 yards from the guardsmen, and was subsequently paralyzed in the lower part of his body. The four students killed were Allison Krause, Jeffrey Miller, Sandra Scheuer, and William Schroeder. Only Krause and Miller had been active participants in the rally. Schroeder was himself an ROTC student. Sandra Scheuer was killed 130 yards from the guardsmen as she was walking to a class.

In Ravenna, Assistant County Prosecutor Charles Kirkwood was waiting in the morgue at Robinson Memorial Hospital as the ambulances arrived from the Kent State campus. Like most people in the Kent area, he had heard the early radio reports that guardsmen had been killed. But the first body brought into the morgue, as he discovered when he lifted the covering sheet, was that of a young girl. It was Allison Krause. "I could see that she had been very beautiful in life," he recalls in his interview. "That's when I assumed that no one had shot guardsmen, that guardsmen had shot the other people."

The Aftermath

The University was closed by court order the day of the shootings and remained closed for the remainder of the spring quarter. National Guard units continued to patrol the campus and town until Friday, May 8. As soon as the firing had stopped, the questions began. Who was to blame? What would happen to the University? What was the "truth" about Kent State?

Student protests had created a strongly negative reaction among townspeople which was evidenced daily in letters to the editor in the *Record-Courier*. Rumors abounded. The first-edition headline of the local newspaper on May 4 had proclaimed that two guardsmen were dead. As Kent resident Mary Vincent indicates in her interview, rumors of impending destruction and arson spread rapidly through the area. It was said that communists dressed in National Guard uniforms had shot the four students in order to create a controversy. It was said that the slain students were so dirty and lice-ridden that the ambulance doors were thrown open on the way to the hospital in Ravenna. "They should have shot more of them"— this was heard often in the town. There was no surge of community support for this university in crisis.

The Kent Area Chamber of Commerce issued a statement on May 7, saying that the events of May 4 had left a "deep scar" on the community and directing attention to the activities of the days preceding the shootings: "The people of Kent were subjected to extensive loss of property, business and personal rights; subjected to profane language, both spoken and written; subjected to threats on the street and in the homes; subjected to the witnessing of abuse to the

RECORD-COURIER

A STRONG VOICE IN A GROWING AREA

RAVENNA and KENT, OHIO, MONDAY, MAY 4, 1970

AM -- 1520 Kc
FM -- 100.1 Mc

140TH YEAR NO. 105

RAVENNA 296-9657

KENT 673-3491

10c A COPY

TONIGHT: Partly cloudy, low 37 to 43.
TOMORROW: Little change. Details on page 6.

2 guardsmen, 1 student dead in KSU violence

Universities must oust hooligans

(AN EDITORIAL)

Ohio will no longer tolerate its state universities being used as sanctuaries by lawbreaking hooligans who destroy, terrorize and burn and then seek protection in the academic community.

That was the major message of Gov. James Rhodes, who visited Kent Sunday morning and termed the rioting in Kent as the worst the state has suffered.

Gov. Rhodes proposed two major pieces of legislation that he will push for in the next assembly — one making it a felony to throw a projectile at a police officer, the other requiring an automatic and permanent suspension for anyone convicted of any crime arising out of campus violence.

In essence, the Governor stated that the days of the "go easy" policy toward campus law breakers is over, and they can expect their violence to be met with every law enforcement tool the state has at its disposal.

Amen to that, for Kent in the past three days has had its fill of these violence-prone toughs who use legitimate causes, such as a drive for peace, as vehicles to allow them to riot and disrupt.

The acts of violence in Kent and on campus during the past two days are so serious as to merit the sternest repression: store windows broken and store owners threatened; a campus building burned, fire hoses cut and firemen and policemen pelted with bricks, stones and bottles.

We are pleased, however, to hear from state authorities that for the most part students aren't that way. The great majority — all but the very few — are on our campuses to get an education and become the leaders of tomorrow.

69 arrested, 10 injured in riots

BULLETIN

Three were killed in a shooting confrontation on the Kent State University campus shortly after noon today. Robinson Memorial Hospital reported three or 14 gunshot victims brought to the hospital were dead. One report said the dead, all unidentified at presstime, included two National Guardsmen and one student. Law enforcement agencies sent an escort to Ravenna Arsenal for more ammunition.

R-C Staff Report

An atmosphere of tense forboding hangs like a pall over Kent and Kent State University today after the campus was shaken Sunday night by another serious student-police confrontation which left 10 injured and 62 arrested.

Ohio National Guard troops still patrolled the campus after thousands of students defied a dusk-to-dawn curfew and confronted police and Guardsmen on the campus and in the streets last night.

Other photos, stories on pages 3, 4, 6, 16, 17

Although demonstrations of any sort have been prohibited by a court order, a rally was scheduled for noon today on the university Commons by dissident students.

Front-page headline of the *Record-Courier*, May 4, 1970. The error was corrected during the pressrun. Used with permission.

American flag."[30] The National Guard had been welcomed by townspeople. Lucius Lyman, Jr. expresses the ambivalent attitude that many experienced, people who were unhappy about the loss of life on the campus but pleased that order had been restored:

> I did feel some sense of . . . relief, and I want to tell you why. I think this is very important for the story. Immediately after the killings, not three or four days later, Kent was as calm as it ever was. The National Guard stayed. There weren't any students on the street; they'd all been sent home, and the University was closed. There was a normalcy in the community, in sharp contrast to what it had been on the days before.

But the hostility toward students and the University continued. Edgar McCormick, associate dean of Arts and Sciences, drafted two letters to local newspapers but never sent them. He wrote: "It is plain from countless letters published . . . that many Kentites consider the University a menace and a liability." It was only slightly with tongue in cheek that he proposed the annexation of Kent State by Brimfield Township to the south.[31]

There were efforts to bridge the gulf between campus and town. It was easier to contemplate such a town-gown dialogue with most of the student body gone and radical leaders in hiding. One of the efforts to ease tensions was initiated by Mary Vincent, who opened her home to students, faculty, and townspeople for "fact-finding." The meetings were structured to avoid political confrontation. People would be reasonable, polite, and the truth would emerge—this was her assumption. Minutes were kept for some of the meetings, but speakers were not identified by name. Instead, meeting minutes read "S" for student, "F" for faculty, and "T" for townsperson. At the gathering of May 18, for instance, a major topic was "channels of communication."[32]

Within the University community, "communication" was also often discussed. After the closing of the campus, a first priority was to offer students a means to complete their coursework for the

[30] "Statement Made by the Executive Committee of the Kent Area Chamber of Commerce," May 7, 1970, mimeograph; courtesy of Mary Vincent.

[31] McCormick to Editor, *Record-Courier*, May 21, 1970, Box 40, M4C, KSUA; McCormick to Editor, *Akron Beacon Journal*, July 9, 1970, ibid. The quote is taken from the second letter draft.

[32] Meeting minutes, May 18, 1970; courtesy of Mary Vincent.

quarter. In every academic department, faculty prepared mimeographed letters to all their students, designating course options and
homework, and sometimes providing a commentary on recent
events. Professors expressed confusion, shock, anger, and uncertainty: directed at the National Guard, student violence, or the
political system in general. Sheila Tabakoff, an instructor of art
history, wrote to her students: "Kent State will never be the same,
nor should it be, and if you do not take, or rather seize, this opportunity to revitalize and reorganize your University, each of you will
be personally responsible for the continuation of an academic environment that is out of touch with life." She expressed the hope that
Kent State would become "a vanguard in modern education." Other
faculty avoided political comments but referred often to the abrupt
end of the school term. John Fridy, in a letter to his math students,
noted: "In closing, I'd like to add one more thought: I miss you. I am
a classroom teacher, and seeing my students regularly is a way of life
to me. So keep in touch, and together we will get our university
operating again."[33]

In responding to the faculty letters, in offering opinions on their
rightful grades—and most students felt they should receive A's for
the term—students frequently provided an interesting commentary
of their own. John Begala, who would be elected to the Ohio House
of Representatives six years later, wrote: "The whole situation, I
believe, didn't come as a response to the President's message on the
30th. I believe that it has been building for some time—the invasion
of Cambodia was the breaking point. The situation comes as a response to having government channels closed to the public. . . ."
He asserted that the University was and should be a center for political action: "Divorcing it from politics puts us all in an 'ivory tower,'
isolated from the events that make, and take our lives." Students returning to their homes found that there was much misinformation
about the shootings and great hostility to young people in general.
One co-ed wrote: "From the news reports that most of the people in
my area had received, you would think that rioters (at *least* the entire
student body) had burned and looted the campus and town area and
all that was left was a pile of smoldering ruins." Another student re-

---

[33] Tabakoff to students, May 13, 1970, Box 59, M4C, KSUA; Fridy to students, May 11,
1970, Box 1, ibid.

counted that when she mentioned attending Kent State, the response was "Oh, a rioter." She remarked: "After reading the newspapers and watching the television, it looks to me as if Kent State is becoming a symbol for a battleground."[34]

The "battle" symbolism was very real for the faculty and students who remained at Kent or lived nearby. The University administration was faced with a shattered institution, and although officials began discussing almost immediately when the school would reopen, there were some fears that it would not. Mail from alumni, for instance, was not encouraging. While many alumni expressed personal support for Robert White, a number of letters attacked "permissiveness" within the institution, urged the expulsion of nonconformist students, and charged that a "trouble-making minority" was responsible for the shootings. "Regrettable as fatalities are," wrote Catherine Kendall, of Dellroy, Ohio, "when students resort to flaunting the laws, damaging and burning public and private property, and endangering the lives of those who are trying to defend the rights of all, it is time that strong action is taken to curb their acts of anarchy." Another woman wrote from nearby Cuyahoga Falls: "I say all of the *students* out on the commons shouting obscenities, throwing rocks and generally harassing the Guard are guilty of murder." But other (fewer) alumni were not so critical, expressing support for the antiwar movement and calling for an investigation of the shootings. Frances Lehman, of Goshen, Indiana, wrote:

> Let me quickly assure you that if students at KSU had taken no stand against the escalation of the war in Southeast Asia by an intransigent president, I would have been sorely disappointed. These young people have given their lives for their country in a purer sense than those on the

[34] Begala to Fishel, May 15, 1970, Box 57, M4C, KSUA; Sutherland to Fishel, May 24, 1970, ibid. (emphasis in original); Koepp to Fishel, May 18, 1970, ibid.

President Robert White
in August of 1970.

battlefield. To give one's life without killing in return is in the finest tradition.[35]

For University faculty members, it was a moment to consider their response to extraordinary circumstances. A faculty resolution of May 5 strongly condemned the actions of the National Guard. "In this moment of grief," it read, "we pledge that in the future we shall not teach in circumstances which are likely to lead to the death and wounding of our students. . . . We can—and do—refuse to teach in a climate that is inimical to the safety of our students and to the principles of academic freedom."[36] The same day, President White held a press conference, releasing the text of a telegram he had sent to the parents of the slain students. The events of May 4, he said, were "terribly unique." He further remarked: ". . . In retrospect it is possible to say that the possibility of death has hovered over us for some time." What had happened at Kent State was "a microcosm of what is occurring over the nation." White was frightened by the political polarization, already clearly evident, concerning the shootings.[37] Nor was this polarization only a local phenomenon. The Kent State shootings attracted national and international attention. The Urban Research Corporation of Chicago has listed 760 campuses which experienced serious disruption in the aftermath of the Cambodia incursion and May 4, and several hundred of them were closed down.

Letters and telegrams from students and nonstudents arrived at Kent State from all parts of the United States and from many areas overseas (largely Great Britain, France, Australia, New Zealand, and South Africa). A few letters were from U.S. servicemen in Vietnam, some condemning antiwar activists and others supporting them. But Gloria Emerson, a journalist in Vietnam in May 1970, who rode with American troops into Cambodia, concluded that the Kent State shootings had little impact on U.S. soldiers. She writes: "So much killing was around us, all of us had seen such unimaginable things, that the information about Kent was information. We

---

[35] Kendall to Nixon (cc: White), May 7, 1970, Box 40, M4C, KSUA; Olex to White, May 8, 1970, ibid. (emphasis in original); Lehman to White, May 5, 1970, ibid.

[36] Faculty resolution, May 5, 1970, Box 1, M4C, KSUA.

[37] Transcript, White press conference, May 5, 1970, Box 2, M4C, KSUA. The telegram to the parents read: "The thoughts of Mrs. White and I are with you in your terrible loss. As parents ourselves, we are filled with horror, knowing full well, of course, that words are inadequate."

heard of the four deaths in Vietnam where there had already been three thousand days of killing, and everybody there seemed to have died in one way or another."[38] Vietnam veteran Robert Gabriel, a National Guard helicopter pilot over the Kent State campus on May 2, 1970, had little sympathy for the dead and wounded on May 4. "If I had been there," he remarks in his interview, "and seen a platoon of armed soldiers, I would've said, 'Well, the fun's over.' Maybe it's my military mind, but if someone has a gun I assume it's loaded. I assume that the individual is trained to use it and that if the situation comes up where he feels he has to use it, he will." Gabriel observes: "I suppose I thought that the shootings were a good thing, because they stopped everything right there. . . . That took the hot air right out of the radical stuff in the nation."

But a former Oberlin College student, living in Germany, wrote that the events in Kent were incomprehensible to him. "How do I explain this to a European," he asked, "when it sounds to him so much like Prague?"[39] His reference was to the occupation of Czechoslovakia by Soviet troops in 1968. The essay by Lawrence Kaplan, "A View from Europe," describes well the student reaction which he encountered while lecturing in Britain and Germany. News of the shootings "catapulted the university into public prominence." Kent State, Kaplan writes, "was the flashpoint of all discontents with American leadership at this moment. . . . In 1970, German universities under sway of a violent radical student movement looked upon Kent State as a red flag to rally others to their cause."

The fear that the shootings would be a "red flag" was a point raised also by Robert White, who felt that the University might become a "Mecca" for political agitators.[40] *Time* magazine reported that Kent State had been converted "into a bloodstained symbol of the rising student rebellion against the Nixon Administration and the war in Southeast Asia."[41] The potency of the events of May 4 was readily apparent, and student anger which grew out of the shootings was only exacerbated by President Nixon's statement of May 5:

[38] Emerson to Bills, October 14, 1980; Emerson is author of *Winners and Losers: Battles, Retreats, Gains, Losses and Ruins from a Long War* (New York: Random House, 1976).

[39] Brown to White, May 6, 1970, Box 3, M4C, KSUA.

[40] White to Millett, May 12, 1970, Box 17, M4C, KSUA. See also White memo to members of the University Commission to Implement a Commitment to Nonviolence, May 21, 1970, Kegley Commission notebooks, vol. 1, KSUA, for a similar statement.

[41] "Kent State: Martyrdom that Shook the Country," *Time*, May 18, 1970, p. 12.

"This should remind us all once again that when dissent turns to violence it invites tragedy."[42] According to memos by FBI Director J. Edgar Hoover, Nixon did feel that the guardsmen had fired in self-defense. Hoover himself thought that "the students invited and got what they deserved."[43]

On May 14, at Jackson State College in Mississippi, two black students were killed by police gunfire. One was Phillip Gibbs, a college junior, and the other was James Green, a high school student. Tim Spofford, who has researched the incident, asserts that the deaths of the black students did not have nearly the same impact as the shooting of white students in Kent, Ohio. "The student peace movement of the 1960s and the Vietnam War are both over," he writes, "yet Americans cannot forget the young white lives lost on Blanket Hill. But the historic campus slayings in Mississippi were part of another great sixties movement—the student civil rights movement—and these we have forgotten."[44] In her essay, "The Kent State Legacy and the 'Business at Hand,' " Miriam Jackson attributes this tendency toward selective memory to "deeply ingrained racism" in American society. But at Kent State, at least, the May 4 and May 14 deaths are always linked, always remembered jointly.

Commissions

Despite the closing of the University, a commencement was held in Kent on June 13, 1970. It was an important ceremony for many graduating seniors, providing a sense of closure to their years at the school. It was also important to faculty and administrators who saw in the commencement a reaffirmation of the institution's vitality. Speaking at the ceremonies, President White remarked: "Reflec-

---

[42] *New York Times,* May 5, 1970, p. 1.

[43] Hoover memorandum, May 11, 1970, in *FBI Files on the Fire Bomb and Shooting at Kent State* (Wilmington, Del.: Scholarly Resources, Inc., 1985, microfilm), reel 4, sec. 17, for quote; see also Hoover memorandum, July 24, 1970, ibid., reel 6, sec. 32, for similar sentiments. Nixon deals only briefly with Kent State events in his memoirs, noting that an "uneasy confrontation" developed on the campus on May 4: "Finally, a large crowd of students began throwing rocks and chunks of concrete at the guardsmen, forcing them up a small hill. At the top the soldiers turned, and someone started shooting." He recalled: "Those few days after Kent State were among the darkest of my presidency." See *RN: The Memoirs of Richard Nixon* (New York: Grosset & Dunlap, 1978), p. 457.

[44] Tim Spofford, "Jackson State," unpublished manuscript; see also idem, "Ten Years Later at Jackson State," *Mother Jones,* June 1980, pp. 11–13, and idem, "Lynch Street: The Story of Mississippi's Kent State—The May 1970 Slayings at Jackson State College" (Ph.D. diss., State University of New York at Albany, 1984).

tions following tragedy force painful thinking. As never before we see the need for some changed actions and attitudes. As a graduating class, you have shared an experience which no other graduating class has had in American history." White mentioned public attitudes which equated "genuinely distressed college students who hold lofty goals and impeccable integrity" with a small group of what he called "committed 'burners' and out-and-out destroyers." He listed new commitments that had emerged from the ordeal of the shootings: (1) greater "personalization" within the University and in contacts with the town; (2) support for "non-violent action"; (3) a "dedication to orderly procedure"; (4) the restatement of the proposition "that constructive change is possible"; and (5) a University effort to promote studies and research in the "peaceful resolution of conflict."[45] During his speech, White was able to announce the creation of a President's Commission on Campus Unrest, established by Richard Nixon, chaired by William Scranton, former governor of Pennsylvania. The major task of the commission would be to investigate the shootings at Kent and Jackson State.

However, this was not the first commission to launch an investigation of the deaths at Kent State. The first agency had been appointed by White on May 8, 1970, chaired by Prof. Harold Mayer, and titled the "Commission on KSU Violence" (CKSUV). The intrauniversity group focused its efforts on two areas: (1) an independent analysis of events leading to the upheaval of May 1–4; and (2) "a broader investigation of the causes of dissatisfaction and unrest which were vulnerable to escalation into the tragic events." The group would then recommend "constructive modifications of policy."[46] In early June, a CKSUV subcommittee began surveying faculty attitudes and ultimately collected a large number of statements and observations. The commission's work, however, was hampered by the task of coordinating its activities with those of smaller campus committees and by the lack of cooperation from local civil and police authorities. Looking back at his chairmanship, Mayer comments: "The operation of the Commission . . . resulted in a sense of complete futility and frustration on the part

---

[45] Commencement speech, June 13, 1970, Box 40, M4C, KSUA.

[46] Harold M. Mayer, "Basic Philosophy of the Report," *Commission on KSU Violence*, 4 vols. (Kent, Ohio: Kent State University, 1972), 1:2.

of myself and most of the other members, and the result was entirely unproductive."[47]

The Commission on KSU Violence was unable, after meeting for ten months, to reach a consensus report. Once it had become clear that the CKSUV was looking at long-range causes of campus violence and intending to make recommendations for substantive changes in University procedures, another group was appointed to deal with the short-term problems of planning for the reopening of the school for fall quarter. This was the Commission to Implement a Commitment to Nonviolence, chaired by faculty member Charles Kegley.[48]

The President's Commission on Campus Unrest, or the "Scranton Commission," as it is often called, had much more success than University agencies in gaining access to all pertinent materials and reaching an internal consensus. The commission held public hear-

[47] Mayer to Bills, August 14, 1980.

[48] For a description and analysis of the operation of the commission, see the following: Charles F. Kegley, "University Commission to Implement a Commitment to Nonviolence," in *Kent State: The Nonviolent Response*, ed. A. Paul Hare (Haverford, Pa.: Center for Nonviolent Conflict Resolution, 1973), n. pag.; and idem, "The Response of Groups to the Events of May 1–4, 1970 at Kent State University" (Ph.D. diss., University of Pittsburgh, 1974).

The Scranton Commission, August 21, 1970. William Scranton, left, arm over chair, listens to Kent State President Robert White's testimony.

ings in Kent on August 19–21, 1970. Its final report, released in October 1970, has become a basic resource for facts and opinions about May 4. The Scranton Commission found that the shootings were a "national" but not a "unique" tragedy: "Only the magnitude of the student disorder and the extent of student deaths and injuries set it apart from similar occurrences on numerous other American campuses during the past five years." The report attacked violent protest and affirmed that those who had taken part in the "havoc on the town of Kent" and the burning of the ROTC building must share responsibility for the deaths of May 4. The main impetus for the noon rally on May 4, said the report, was the presence of National Guard troops on the campus. The Guard's decision to disperse the rally, its subsequent marching tactics, and the use of loaded weapons were all criticized. Then, in a sentence that has become nearly a litany in Kent commemorations and for people who write about the Kent State shootings, the report concluded: "The indiscriminate firing of rifles into a crowd of students and the deaths that followed were unnecessary, unwarranted, and inexcusable."[49]

Although the Scranton Commission had condemned student violence as well as the actions of the National Guard, the release of its report met with a favorable response from students. The report contained, it was widely felt, an "objective" quality not present in local analyses of the spring upheaval. On October 16, 1970, a special state grand jury, convened in nearby Ravenna some weeks earlier to investigate the shootings, issued twenty-five indictments and an accompanying report which was sharply critical of dissidents. Those indicted for criminal offenses were all students or former students, with the exception of one professor, Thomas Lough.

The grand jury's report supported Kent Mayor Satrom's call for the National Guard and further stated: "We find . . . that those members of the National Guard who were present on the hill adjacent to Taylor Hall on May, 1970, fired their weapons in the honest and sincere belief and under circumstances which would have logically caused them to believe that they would suffer serious bodily injury had they not done so." "Verbal abuse" of the guardsmen was said to have "represented a level of obscenity and vulgarity which we have never before witnessed!" The "concerned faculty"

[49] Commission on Campus Unrest, *Report*, pp. 287–90.

who had signed the statement of May 3 were termed "irresponsible." "Major responsibility" for the events of May was assigned to the University administration, which "has fostered an attitude of laxity, over-indulgence, and permissiveness with its students and faculty to the extent that it can no longer regulate the activities of either and is particularly vulnerable to any pressure applied from radical elements within the student body or faculty." The grand jury report criticized a University climate "in which dissent becomes the order of the day" and made reference to faculty who "teach nothing but the negative side of our institutions of government and refuse to acknowledge that any positive good has resulted during the growth of our nation." The report advised that students promoting disorder be expelled.[50]

The grand jury included one caveat in its report: "Let no one assume that we do not consider the University a valued part of our community." But clearly, little affection was expressed for the current state of the institution. The report well represented the division that existed between the campus and the surrounding communities. The contents of the document were leaked before it was made public, and criticism from University constituencies was quick in coming. An October 12 leaflet from the newly organized Kent Liberation Front stated: "These indictments are a direct attack not only on individual people, but on the revolutionary struggle as a whole. The four days of May were an integral part of a Movement against the policies of imperialism and racism which form the principal support for American capitalism."[51] Faculty members were eager to refute the grand jury's charges that the University bore major responsibility for the events of May 4. Prof. Ottavio Casale, for instance, defended the White administration, saying that Kent State was "an extremely democratic institution" and that White and the University had been "victims of a series of chance phenomena." Prof. Martin Nurmi, chairman of the Faculty Senate, remarked: "This university and every other university in the country are in danger of being destroyed." He added: "My personal feeling is that the University has become a scapegoat for actions by the extreme left which attacks it as a tool of the war machine . . . and by the

[50] "Report of the Special Grand Jury," October 15, 1970, Box 16, M4C, KSUA.
[51] Leaflet, Kent Liberation Front, October 12, 1970, Box 21, M4C, KSUA.

right which attacks the University and specifically its professors as the source of all radicalism."[52]

Bill Arthrell, in his essay "The Ones They Missed with Bullets," describes the feelings of student activists in Kent: the anger and shock of spring, the anxiety of fall. Some students wore t-shirts reading "Kent Police State University." Arthrell writes: "It was as if the grand jury wanted to indict the whole campus." He refers also to a decision by Judge Edwin Jones that no one who had appeared before the grand jury could publicly comment on its findings. This "gag rule" was broken by Kent State professor Glenn Frank, in response to a statement attributed to Seabury Ford, special prosecutor attached to the grand jury investigation, or "probe," as it was often called. Ford had said: "They should have shot all the troublemakers."[53]

The "Kent 25" cases were not resolved until late 1971. Only five people were eventually brought to trial in November, resulting in the conviction of one person for interfering with a fireman (on the evening of May 2) and two persons for first degree riot. On December 7, charges were dismissed against the remaining defendants.

Commemoration

Causation and responsibility, of course, are inextricably linked to how we remember events and how we record them. Remembrance is as personal as it is selective. It is political in that we regularly make decisions on what and how to remember in accord with an ideological outlook. This is especially true when events provoke a highly emotional response, as did the Kent State shootings. A letter of May 7, 1970 from an Indiana student raised a critical point: "I only hope that what the Kent State students died for will be realized in the days to come."[54] What did the students die for? Were they martyrs to a noble cause, were they troublemakers and bums, were they victims of a sad, cosmic confrontation? As Kent State English professor Doris Franklin wrote in the fall of 1970, " 'Taking sides,' six months after the events, is still going on all around us, and the 'reality' of

[52] Casale statement, *Akron Beacon Journal*, October 17, 1970, p. A2; Nurmi statement, ibid., October 20, 1970, p. A2.

[53] *Akron Beacon Journal*, October 24, 1970, p. A1.

[54] Kagan to KSU student government, May 7, 1970, Box 3, M4C, KSUA.

May 4 is still being reshaped and reconstructed according to the creative stress of the mind perceiving it."[55]

Taking sides has not abated over the intervening years. The grand jury report of October 1970 epitomized widespread anti-student, anti-intellectual sentiments. The political left, among its various factions, has generally seen the four deaths as an integral part of a long and continuing struggle against militarism, imperialism, and the suppression of dissident rights at home. The families of the slain and wounded students launched a protracted effort to prove government culpability in the May 4 shootings. They sought recognition of their claims that National Guard and state officials had acted wrongfully, violated the constitutional rights of student demonstrators, and then attempted to cover up their mistakes.

Some analysts have used the vocabulary of classic "tragedy" to portray May 1970 events as a culmination of unpleasant but inevitable, depersonalized causal forces. "In my opinion," wrote a Kent State faculty member in June 1970, "the violence on Kent's campus was a rather tragic series of events which unfortunately added up in the wrong way."[56] Leigh Herington saw the shootings as resulting from a "series of mistakes" by all parties, and Martin Nurmi's remarks at a faculty convocation of May 3, 1980, included in this volume, drew heavily on the "great tragedies of literature" as referents.

But another view has also been propounded: that the shootings were the direct result of a government conspiracy. Peter Davies in his essay, "The Burning Question," asserts that the events of May 4 "were a political operation with specific political goals," though the killings were unintended. John Logue, in "An American Tradition," argues against the notion that what happened in Kent was a great aberration and thus examines a history of "official violence" toward dissident movements. He writes: "The names of the dead at Kent State are as accidental as the names of the guardsmen who shot them. That they died is not."

And so the determination of cause and the fixing of responsibility for the shootings has been both unifying and divisive, both abstractive and highly emotional, both scholarly and purposefully polemical. The approaches toward remembering and memorializing

[55] Doris Franklin, foreword to "Minority Report," *Commission on KSU Violence*, 4:1.
[56] Petersham to Ohles and Zink, June 5, 1970, Box 14, M4C, KSUA.

the event have been no different. While the annual commemoration of May 4 has been firmly institutionalized at Kent State over the past twelve years, different and conflicting themes have emerged. On the first anniversary of the shootings, there were already disparate attitudes concerning an "appropriate" memorial ceremony, reflecting opposing analyses of the shootings themselves.

Prof. Jerry M. Lewis, in his interview, describes the candlelight walk and vigil, which began in 1971 and has since become a noted feature of commemorative activities. The walk around campus on the night of May 3 and the lantern-lit all-night vigil in the Prentice Hall parking lot where the four students were shot comprise a remembrance that is highly personal and often spiritual in tone. Lewis points to the usefulness of the vigil as a teaching device, as a historical reenactment, and as a humanitarian ritual. "I suppose what I will find most interesting," he comments, "is some young person attending the vigil who was born after 1970."

The first memorial program, on May 4, 1971, was sponsored by the University administration, featuring Rev. Jesse Jackson as the main speaker. With the approach of the spring ceremony, President White wrote: "Everything for Kent State University is at stake in how well the May 1–4 program is carried off." To the important implicit question—"To whom does May 4 belong?"—White answered: "Emotionally and philosophically the occasion is ours."[57] A summary report by the official May 4th Recognition Committee, chaired by Dennis Carey, a graduate student member of the Kegley Commission, suggested that the observance be limited to the University community. "That is not to say," it read, "that others have not the right, perhaps even the obligation, to recognize the meaningfulness of the moment but rather that this University finds it can best insure the dignity and integrity the occasion surely necessitates through a program focused primarily on the immediate University family."[58] This approach was criticized by a student activist group called the Mayday Coalition, which planned an "alternate" program. A letter to the editor of the school newspaper, written by Alan Canfora, Tom Grace, Robert Stamps, and Dean Kahler—all wounded the year before—charged that the University memorial

[57] Draft statement, April 13, 1971, Box 16, M4C, KSUA.
[58] Summary report, April 1, 1971, Box 16, M4C, KSUA.

committee was "totally unrepresentative of the people and ideas
. . . whom it was designed to commemorate."[59]

The Center for Peaceful Change (CPC), founded in 1971 as a
"living memorial" to the slain students, was seen by many students
and faculty as a significant institutional response to the crisis of May
1970. The essays by Dennis Carey and John Begala discuss the
Center's approval by the Board of Trustees as well as its initial development. Carey, who later became the director of the Center, outlines his concept of the "phoenix reaction" by which the CPC was
established and also addresses the problems encountered in building a stable academic unit under such circumstances, noting that
expectations of the Center were often contradictory.

Subsequent to its founding, the Center for Peaceful Change was
placed in charge of coordinating the May 4 commemorations for
1972–73. However, since some students felt that the CPC was essentially a surrogate for the University administration, the Center's
plans were met both years with proposals for alternate programs,
sponsored by the May 4 United Front. A guest column in the *Daily
Kent Stater*, written by Tobie Fixler, outlined the latter group's
objections to the Center's role in the commemorative process, emphasizing that the "peaceful change" theme was an insult to students, that what happened in May 1970 was "no mistake" but rather
a deliberate action, and that radicals must use the annual occasion
to show a "connection to all struggles of liberation." She wrote:
"What was needed was a peaceful change school for the Ohio
National Guard, not the students who were engaged in a legal assembly."[60]

President White opened the first commemorative program by
saying: "If any one thing unites us, the desire for memorial does just
that. We gather to express that unity."[61] It was true; the desire was
widely shared. But assumptions underlying the method and purpose
of commemoration were not. From the beginning, there was a
struggle over who "owned" May 4 and who should control its potent
symbolism. While some students were pleased to work with the CPC
and the University on May 4 issues, others—more radical—saw
such a connection as an effort to sanitize the imagery of the shoot-

[59] *Daily Kent Stater* (hereafter cited as *DKS*), April 23, 1971, p. 4.
[60] *DKS*, May 2, 1973, p. 5.
[61] Quoted in editorial, *DKS*, May 5, 1971, p. 4.

ings, to "isolate" them in the past and deny a continuing political relevancy.

Hence, a different commemorative tradition was developed in the years after 1970 which expressed, at least implicitly, an anti-capitalist critique of University and society, building on the themes of injustice and government repression. Inspiration was and is drawn from the "martyrs" of 1970, remembering the "revolutionary spirit" of an era of upheaval and using May 4 as a vehicle to discuss the broad range of political issues which formed the focus of New Left activism in the late 1960s. Miriam Jackson's essay suggests a symbolic effort each year "to continue the rally forcibly dispersed in 1970." The "alternate" commemoration of May 4, 1974, which featured Daniel Ellsberg, Jane Fonda, Julian Bond, and Vietnam veteran Ron Kovic as speakers, drew 6,500 people. "The shootings [of 1970]," said Fonda, "happened in the context of repression and terror that was aimed at crushing the antiwar movement." Kovic, crippled by wounds received in Vietnam, placed his wheelchair next to Dean Kahler's. "Our bodies," said Kovic, "were destroyed by the same administration."[62] For most observers, it was a poignant moment and one that was repeated when both men appeared together at the commemorative program of May 4, 1977.

The formation of the May 4th Task Force in October 1975 established over the next few years a kind of left-liberal control over commemorative activities on May 4. The group was initially established by the student government "to coordinate actions concerning the issues stemming from the events at KSU on May 4, 1970."[63] Since its founding, the membership has consisted of veterans of the 1970 demonstration as well as many younger students. The Task Force itself has been an amalgam of various political views, and the balance has shifted from year to year. The two most popular slogans have been "The Truth Demands Justice" and "Remember the Past, Continue the Struggle." Since May 1976, the Task Force has coordinated the annual May 4 program, opening the rally at noon on the Commons with the ringing of the Victory Bell.

There has been, to be sure, opposition to the politicization of the May 4 commemoration, and many of the arguments against it were expressed in a letter by J. Gregory Payne to the *Daily Kent Stater* in

---

62 *DKS*, May 7, 1974, pp. 1, 10.
63 *DKS*, October 7, 1975, p. 1.

Ron Kovic, left, and Dean Kahler, right, at the May 4 commemoration in 1977.

May 1976. He voiced his disapproval of the "radicalization" of the May 4 program, denouncing "the tendency among some to prostitute the incident by using the May 4 memorial as a means of propagating their own causes and revolutionary rhetoric." He further commented:

> The eyes of America turn to Kent each May 4. It is our responsibility to present a program which will enlighten, rather than polarize, which will educate, rather than indoctrinate, and one which will commemorate the death of four fellow students, rather than present a paradoxical haphazard summary of the various political organizations found on today's college campus.[64]

Kent State Litigation[65]

Concurrent with the Task Force and other student activity on May 4 issues was the long courtroom debate over responsibility for the shootings. The concept of disparate families, united by events, acting or seeming to act as a unit is familiar to us. After the seizure of the U.S. embassy in Teheran, Iran, in November 1979, the families of the American hostages were often portrayed as a group, not necessarily single-minded perhaps but nonetheless bound together by circumstances externally imposed. So it was with the "Kent State families," or as they are most often referred to in Kent, simply "the Families"—those parents of the students killed and wounded on May 4, 1970. This small group, pulled together by the violence at Kent State University, launched what Prof. Thomas Hensley has called "one of the longest, costliest, most complex, and most controversial legal struggles in American history."

---

[64] *DKS*, May 5, 1976, p. 4.

[65] The source for background material in this section, unless otherwise noted, is Thomas R. Hensley, "The Kent State Trials," in *Kent State and May 4th: A Social Science Perspective*, ed. Thomas R. Hensley and Jerry M. Lewis (Dubuque, Iowa: Kendall/Hunt, 1978), pp. 41–57.

In August 1971, the U.S. Department of Justice, then headed by Attorney General John Mitchell, announced that there would be no federal grand jury probe of the Kent State shootings. In his essay for this volume, Peter Davies describes his role in the effort to secure such an investigation. For two years, there followed a struggle to get the matter reconsidered by the Justice Department. The Kent State families pressed to have the case reopened, and there was a petition drive on the Kent State campus by students Greg Rambo and Paul Keane. The Reverend John Adams, director of the Department of Law, Justice, and Community Relations of the Board of Church and Society, the United Methodist Church, also played a prominent role in trying to secure a federal grand jury investigation. He served as fund-raiser, counselor, and advocate for the Families throughout the nine years of Kent State-related litigation.

However, these actions had little effect on the Justice Department, even after Mitchell was succeeded by Richard Kleindienst. But "with Kleindienst's resignation," writes Hensley, "the linking of both Mitchell and Kleindienst to the Watergate scandal, and the new appointment of Elliot Richardson to the position of Attorney General in April of 1973, new directions began to emerge in the Justice Department, leading to an announcement on August 3, 1973, that the case would be formally opened."[66] Davies's essay focuses on this event, and he asserts: "What had happened to precipitate this remarkable reversal was the very real threat of a congressional investigation into the Justice Department's handling of the case, an investigation the Nixon administration had to thwart if its Kent State cover-up was not to go the way of the Watergate cover-up." On December 18, 1973, evidence was first presented to the new grand jury, and on March 29, 1974, indictments were handed down against eight guardsmen. The trial itself, which began the following October, ended abruptly on November 9, after ten days of testimony, with the acquittal of the former guardsmen by the federal district judge.

The next step in the process involved lengthy civil suit litigation. In fact, individual suits had been initiated by the Kent State families only a short time after the shootings, but a major court decision was not reached until April 1974, when the families, now the "plaintiffs,"

66 Hensley, in *Kent State and May 4th*, pp. 41–57.

had succeeded in gaining a favorable Supreme Court decision (*Scheuer* v. *Rhodes*) stating that the executive branch of a state government did not enjoy "absolute" immunity for its actions. This allowed the civil suits against Ohio officials and former guardsmen to proceed. Before the beginning of the 1975 trial, all the individual suits were consolidated into one case, *Krause* v. *Rhodes*, which sought $46 million in damages. The trial lasted fifteen weeks; the chief attorney for the plaintiffs was Joseph Kelner of New York. The jury's decision, announced August 27, 1975, found that the plaintiffs had not been denied their civil rights, nor had they been the victims of the "willful or wanton misconduct or of the negligence of some or all of the defendants."

An appeal of this verdict was certain, and attorney Sanford Rosen of San Francisco was chosen to head the new legal team. "Before I accepted the assignment, however, I made it clear that I would be answerable to no one . . . except my clients, the victims," writes Rosen in his essay, "Finishing Unfinished Business." Oral arguments for the appeal were heard in Cincinnati in June 1977, at the same time that a controversy had arisen on the Kent State campus in connection with the disposition of part of the site of the confrontation in May 1970. On September 12, a new trial was ordered, based on the judgment that the first trial judge, Donald Young, had improperly handled a threat made against one of the jurors.

The new trial was scheduled to begin in December 1978. Judge Young withdrew from the case and was replaced by William Thomas, whom the plaintiffs felt was more objective in his conduct of the trial. But Rosen notes: "As we prepared the cases for trial, and even as we tried them, we also prepared to reach a settlement—on terms favorable to the victims." The out-of-court settlement was reached on January 4, 1979. The plaintiffs received $675,000 for injuries received in 1970, and this compensation was accompanied by a statement from the defendants. "In retrospect," read the statement in part, "the tragedy of May 4, 1970 should not have occurred. . . . We deeply regret those events and are profoundly saddened by the deaths of four students and the wounding of nine others which resulted." The settlement, according to the plaintiffs, "accomplished to the greatest extent possible under present law" their main objectives, not the least of which was financial support for Dean Kahler. The settlement monies were distributed as follows: Dean Kahler,

$350,000; Joseph Lewis, $42,500; Thomas Grace, $37,500; Donald MacKenzie, $27,500; John Cleary, $22,500; Alan Canfora, $15,000; Douglas Wrentmore, $15,000; Robert Stamps, $15,000; James Russell, $15,000; the families of the four slain students, $15,000 each. Seventy-five thousand dollars was allocated for attorneys' fees and expenses.

Rosen concludes that acceptance of the settlement by the plaintiffs was a good decision, observing that even a courtroom victory in 1979 could have meant indefinite appeals by the defendants, nor was such a victory at all assured. Rosen asserts that the plaintiffs could not prove that there had been a conspiracy to shoot students on May 4, 1970, and that "no new revelations" would have appeared in the transcript of the new trial. Nonetheless, the settlement has been criticized as an unsatisfactory conclusion to nearly a decade of legal battles over the issue of responsibility for the shootings. In his essay "December Dialogues," Charles Thomas argues that the out-of-court agreement provided a means for the nation at large to evade the central political issues posed by Kent State in 1970. Attorney Joseph Kelner has called the monetary award a "pittance" and contended: "Any experienced trial lawyer would have hung his head in shame upon learning the details [of the settlement]." And yet it is clear that "Kent State" has always resisted closure, as do many complex, violent historical events. Peter Davies has written: "So much effort, dedication, and hope should have produced something more substantial and lasting, but this may well be a short-sighted assessment. In the long run history may well record that the fruits of our labors were much richer than we now realize."[67]

During the years of litigation, there developed a close working relationship between May 4 activists on the Kent State campus and the families of the slain and wounded students. Writing in the spring of 1980, Alan Canfora observed that the settlement was the result not only of "legal finesse" but also of the "longstanding support of the Kent State students and faculty."[68] The interests of the families and student activists had come together in spirit before 1975 or the second trial in 1978, but this unity was most clearly evidenced in

[67] Joseph Kelner, "The Kent State Killings: Among the Victims Was Justice," *Los Angeles Times*, May 4, 1980, p. 3; Joseph Kelner and James Munves, *The Kent State Coverup* (New York: Kayem Books, 1980), p. 268; Davies to Bills, July 16, 1980.

[68] Alan Canfora, "A Decade of Determination," *Left Review* 4 (Spring 1980): 25.

1977 when a major protest was mounted to stop the construction of a gymnasium annex on the Kent State campus.

The Gym Controversy[69]

Plans for a new gymnasium or a gym-annex on the Kent State campus began in the 1960s. Various sites were considered, and an early option was to attach an addition to either of the two gym facilities already on the campus. One of them was Memorial Gymnasium, a building on the south edge of the football practice field behind

[69] The source for background material in this section, unless otherwise noted, is Thomas D. Matijasic and Scott Bills, "The People United: A Tentative Commentary on the Kent State Struggle 1977," *Left Review* 2 (Fall 1977): 10–35.

Aerial view of the central Kent State campus in June 1977, showing the outline of the proposed gymnasium annex. Tent City is partially visible in wooded area, center.

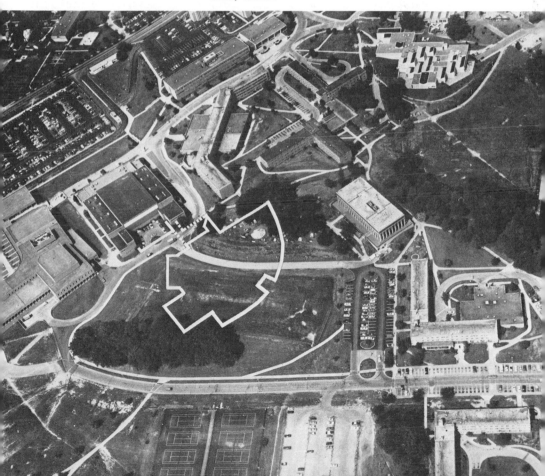

Taylor Hall. By April 1972, the Space Planning Council of what was then called the School of Health, Physical Education, and Recreation (HPER) clearly favored a location "just north of Memorial Gym."[70] In December, this site was formally recommended. For the next two years, however, it was uncertain how large the new facility would be and how it might be attached to the older building.

In June 1975, University Architect Gae Russo approved the site selection. He indicated that this plan would utilize "existing facilities" in order "to avoid the duplication necessitated by a separate facility" and that it would provide for a "unification" of all HPER programs. The vice president for administration, Walter Bruska, in his response to Russo, noted that there should be an effort "to retain as much of the playing field and open vista" as possible to the north of Memorial Gym.[71] There was no indication that the politics of the May 4 controversy had been considered in proposing and approving this location. In mid-November 1975, the *Daily Kent Stater* contained an article concerning the location of the new building which noted that it would be "about twice the size" of the older facility.[72] In July 1976, the *Record-Courier* published a diagram of the proposed structure, showing clearly its contours and the area it would cover. A photograph of the model of the gym-annex appeared in the summer issue of the campus newspaper. The first letter to the editor which opposed construction of the annex appeared in early October. It was written by Nancy Grim, and she emphasized environmental concerns and asserted: "The disruption of this area could be serious for the continuing legal actions [stemming from May 4]. Many people change their minds about the causes and implications of the shootings when they experience the setting."[73]

The Kent State Board of Trustees, meeting on November 11, 1976, voted to proceed with plans for the annex despite objections raised by student representatives who spoke at the meeting. Even so, construction of the new building did not become the principal focus of activity for the May 4th Task Force; instead, the group concentrated on pressing for class cancellation on May 4, 1977, and the

[70] Meeting minutes, Space Planning Council, April 28, 1972, Box 10, Joseph W. Begala Papers, KSUA.

[71] Russo to Bruska, June 13, 1975, interdepartmental correspondence, University News Service Factfile; Bruska to Russo, June 27, 1975, interdepartmental correspondence, ibid.

[72] *DKS*, November 19, 1975, p. 10.

[73] *DKS*, October 5, 1976, p. 4.

dedication of four campus buildings to the slain students. The commemorative program of spring 1977 was held indoors, in Memorial Gymnasium, because of bad weather; and as Thomas Matijasic has observed, "Few [people] had the proposed HPER facility at the forefront of their mind. No major campus organization advocated the relocation of the structure as one of its pressing goals."[74]

The main speakers at the assembly on May 4 were William Kunstler, Dick Gregory, and Ron Kovic. All of them spoke strongly against the location chosen for the gym-annex. Other speakers— Alan Canfora, his sister Roseann "Chic" Canfora, and Dean Kahler —opposed it as well. The annex, it was charged, would be one more element in a series of cover-ups of the "truth" about May 4. It would be a physical alteration of the site of the shootings. "If they build that gymnasium," said Ron Kovic, "they are going to have to bury a thousand students in the cement."[75] After the program, about 1,500 people participated in a march through the downtown area of Kent and back onto the campus. Then, upon hearing that the Trustees were meeting at Rockwell Hall, several hundred students moved to the building to present their views on the gym issue.

After a short meeting with President Glenn Olds, who succeeded White in 1971, and George Janik, chairman of the Board of Trustees, the protestors occupied the first floor of the building. This action led to the formation of the May 4th Coalition. In Rockwell Hall, a steering committee of twenty-eight people was chosen to formulate the group's central concerns, and these were articulated as eight "demands," including: "official" recognition of "the injustice of the Kent State massacre"; no construction "on the site of the shootings"; no change in the status of or dismantling of the Center for Peaceful Change; no classes on May 4; and the dedication and renaming of four campus buildings in honor of the slain students.[76]

The sit-in was ended early in the morning of May 5 by the voluntary exit of the participants. The May 4th Coalition then began preparing arguments to present to the next meeting of the Trustees, on May 12. At this meeting, President Olds asserted that the annex would not violate the May 4 site, nor would it affect the disposition

[74] Matijasic and Bills, "The People United," p. 16.
[75] *DKS*, May 5, 1977, p. 5.
[76] Leaflet, "Meet the 8 Demands," n.d., Box 56, M4C, KSUA.

RALLY 2pm
COMMONS
THURS. MAY 12th

MEET THE 8 DEMANDS

The following demands have been presented to the Board of
Trustees. We do not consider these demands negotiable.
The students of Kent State University are interested in the
truth. The truth demands justice. We uncompromisingly
support the ideals of the slain and wounded students of
May 4, 1970. We uncompromisingly support our faculty.

1) The Kent State University administration must officially
    acknowledge the injustice of the Kent State massacre of
    May 4, 1970.
2) The new p.e. building·(gym) must <u>not</u> be built on the
    site of the shootings of May 4, 1970, and in the future,
    no construction or alteration of the site must be
    permitted.
3) The status of the Center for Peaceful Change shall be
    maintained as it is an all university program.
4) Henceforth May 4 shall be set aside as a day of remembrance
    and education about the Kent State massacre; and the
    regular activities of this University will be cancelled this
    May 4 and every May 4 hereafter.
5) The four buildings which have been named after the four
    slain students shall be officially recognized.
6) Amnesty must be given to all students, faculty and staff
    who commemorated May 4 and,as a result, are threatened
    with punishment of any kind.
7) The administration must reopen negotiations in good faith
    with the United Faculty Professional Association.
8) No punitive actions shall be taken against anyone who
    participated in the sit-in on May 4,1977 in Rockwell Hall.

JOIN US!

May 4th Coalition

Leaflet outlining the initial demands of the May 4th Coalition.

of the civil damages suit. The Board accepted his points and voted 8–1 to grant contracts for the new facility. The same day saw the establishment on Blanket Hill of a protestors' "Tent City" and the beginning of a long campaign by the May 4th Coalition to "move the gym." In her interview, Nancy Grim outlines the major points in the Coalition's opposition to the proposed gym-annex: the link to May 4, 1970; "the aesthetics and environmental issues"; and "the politics of the Vietnam War." On the last point, she comments:

> The argument was that the students of May 4, 1970, were protesting the invasion of Cambodia and United States involvement in Vietnam, and that the shooting of the students was part of the suppression of dissent, part of the U.S. foreign policy in Vietnam which was extended homeward. I think for most people that May 4th was the critical point, in different ways. Some were more sentimental about it than others. Certainly the rhetoric stressed "this is our land" in the sense that it was the peoples' land: this is where our ancestors, so to speak, an earlier generation of students were shot down.

These ideas were emphasized in a Coalition position paper of June 23, which pointed to the "threat to desecrate this sacred ground" as the unifying factor in the antigym effort. "The preservation of this site," stated the paper, "is essential to carry the lessons of 'Kent State' to future generations."[77]

Hence, there were political, historical, and spiritual aspects to the Coalition's activities. Definition of the "site" was central to the issue. The University administration considered the site to be where the students had actually fallen from National Guard riflefire, and clearly the proposed gym-annex did not extend to the Prentice Hall parking lot. Nor by most calculations would the building cover the ground where the wounded students had fallen. The Coalition, however, defined the May 4 site as the entire center area of campus where the events of 1970 had unfolded, where the guardsmen had assembled, marched, and then fired.

Tent City became the focal point of Coalition political activity as well as a social community. The protestors were a mix of older and newer activists, including participants in or observers of the May 4 rally of 1970: Ken Hammond, Bill Arthrell, Dean Kahler, Alan Canfora, Chic Canfora, Miriam Jackson, Tom Grace, and others. This aspect of the protest prompted John Begala to refer to

[77] "Position of the May 4th Coalition," June 23, 1977, Box 58, M4C, KSUA.

it in his essay, "The May 4 Disease," as a "last hurrah" or "an extended old home week" for former student radicals. He dismisses most of the Coalition's objections to the annex and remarks: "In Ohio, with all its urban poverty, 'country justice,' low benefits levels for the poor, low subsidies for education at all levels, *and gross apathy on all these problems*, the great liberal cause was stopping a gym."

The May 4th Coalition directed much energy toward the holding of "national" rallies on the Kent State campus in order to gather wide support; it was certain that the University would act to remove the Tent City encampment. Rallies in June and early July often featured members of the Kent State families as speakers, especially the Krauses, Scheuers, and Canforas. On June 4, Martin Scheuer promised: "If it comes to it this summer and they start to build the gym, I will be there to lie under the bulldozers, even if I am 66 years old."[78] Construction was expected to begin in late June, but Presi-

[78] *Akron Beacon Journal*, June 5, 1977, p. D1.

President Glenn Olds addresses student protestors in June of 1977.

dent Olds did not visit Blanket Hill to deliver a notice to vacate until
July 9. On July 11, the University was granted a court injunction
against Tent City. At an emotion-packed meeting that evening, the
members of the Coalition voted to proceed with plans for a nonviolent mass arrest rather than leave, in the words of Neal Kielar,
"that land that we had held for 62 days."[79]

On the morning of July 12, Portage County sheriff's deputies
established a ring around the area stipulated in the court injunction.
Campus police began making arrests at 8:30 A.M. All policemen in
the immediate area were unarmed. Among the first to be arrested
were Rev. John Adams, Mr. and Mrs. Albert Canfora, and Mr. and
Mrs. Martin Scheuer. A police report which appeared two days later
listed 193 people who had been arrested; it also stated that 63.2 percent of that group had not been students during either the spring
quarter or the first term of summer school.[80] This in part was the
basis for claims, such as that expressed in the interview with Michael
Schwartz, that nonstudents played a "leading role" in the antigym
protest. Other observers have contended that the majority of Tent
City residents were current or former Kent State students, alumni,
or from the northeastern Ohio area.[81] Within the Coalition, there
was little concern with the issue of "outside agitators." As Miriam
Jackson wrote in a letter to the *Record-Courier*: "We have every
right to ask any help we can get from anywhere, on the understanding that those friends pledge themselves, as we have pledged our
selves, to nonviolent action."[82]

Without the organizing base and communal atmosphere of Tent
City, however, the May 4th Coalition began to experience height-
ened internal discord. The strategy of "militant nonviolence" had
effectively carried the group through the mass arrests of July 12, but
future policies were unclear. On July 25, the University was granted
a permanent restraining order against additional encampments. By
the morning of July 27, there was a chain-link fence around the

[79] Interview with Neal Kielar, July 28, 1977; conducted by Thomas Matijasic.

[80] Malone to Herman, July 14, 1977, interdepartmental correspondence. This memorandum, with an attached list of arrestees, was used as a press release; author's copy.

[81] See, for instance, Jerry M. Lewis, "The May 4th Coalition and Tent City: A Norm
Oriented Movement," in *Kent State and May 4th*, p. 156; and Jerry M. Lewis and Betty
Frankle Kirschner, "Public Interpretation of Tent City Arrestees: Kent State, 1977"
(paper presented at the annual meeting of the Southern Sociological Society, New Orleans,
April 1978).

[82] Jackson letter to editor, *Record-Courier*, July 20, 1977, p. 5.

construction site. The next evening, sixty-one people climbed the
fence and established a short-lived mini-Tent City; by 5:00 A.M. on
the morning of the twenty-ninth, the area had been again cleared of
tents and protestors. Construction equipment rolled into the fenced-
in area at the beginning of the workday but only operated for a few
hours. In response to a suit filed by William Kunstler, on behalf of
the Coalition, in the U.S. District Court in Cleveland, Judge Thomas
Lambros issued a temporary restraining order against any site alteration. Under Lambros's auspices, there followed a series of negotiations between University and Coalition representatives. There
was a suggestion that the annex could be "rotated" slightly away
from Blanket Hill; however, it was uncertain whether the plan was
genuinely feasible, and the Coalition issued a statement which said
that a rotated gym-annex would still interfere with the May 4 site.

Judge Lambros suspended negotiations on August 8; he ruled in
favor of the University administration on August 17, although he
extended the prior restraining order until August 24. In this way,
Kunstler was able to file an appeal in Cincinnati; it was denied, however. Coalition attorneys subsequently achieved a brief restraining
order from Supreme Court Justice William Brennan, but this was
removed on September 8. Further legal barriers were removed on
September 12, and construction began at the gym site on September
19. Eighty policemen stood guard around the perimeter of the area,
but there were no demonstrations.

Both the loss of Tent City and the focus on court litigation which
followed imposed strains on the Coalition that were evidenced in
growing factionalism within the group. This was apparent in August
when the "participatory democracy" of the early Coalition had
broken down and many members felt that the group was being
manipulated by a minority element. Additionally, the experience of
the summer's activism had resulted in a high degree of radicalization
within the Coalition regarding tactics and rhetoric, so that students
returning to Kent for the fall quarter found themselves reading leaflets calling for a struggle to smash the capitalist state as well as move
the gym. The political gulf between the spring and fall was too large
to accommodate new members easily or to allow internal reconciliation. Much of the analysis of who "took over" the Coalition has
focused on the Revolutionary Student Brigade (RSB), which was
part of the antigym effort from its inception and whose members

were among the most active in Coalition politics. Other sectarian groups participated as well: the Young Socialist Alliance, the Communist Youth Organization, and the Spartacus Youth League, though the latter did not actually join the Coalition.

The Revolutionary Student Brigade sought to use the "Kent State struggle" as a means to build up its national organization; therefore, RSB chapters at many eastern campuses organized support for "move the gym" rallies in Kent. An article titled "Long Live the Spirit of Kent and Jackson State," which appeared in the organization's newspaper, stated: "Students at Kent have built one of the biggest waves of struggle on a campus in recent years. They've set off a spark that can rekindle the spirit of standing up and fighting back."[83] Plans for an RSB convention in Kent in October were vetoed by the University administration, which prompted a *Record-Courier* headline reading "KSU Takes Stand against Red Meeting" and an editorial titled "Commie Ban Right."

The weakening of the internal bonds of the May 4th Coalition continued through late August and into September. The group continued to exist nominally through the next spring, but Coalition-sponsored rallies in September and October, though large on two occasions, were generally futile and largely fueled by student contingents from outside the Kent area. The length of the protest led to the formation of one student group which began wearing t-shirts proclaiming: "Move the Coalition."

Ken Hammond has commented on the strengths and weaknesses of the May 4th Coalition, terming its activities a "symbolic struggle." In an interview in 1977, he observed:

> It's a contest over images. It's a contest over who controls what we think, who controls our history. It's a fight to gain back our roots, and our own understanding of ourselves and our past. But as a symbolic struggle, it's especially vulnerable, because symbols by their very nature are slippery. And they also by their nature have an element of unreality in them. And to wage a struggle over symbols in the absence of a material struggle, in the absence of a strong grasp of the material reality that you want to be dealing with, I think is perhaps fated to be unsuccessful.[84]

---

[83] Special supplement, *Fight Back!*, October 1977. This issue of the newspaper presented Kent State President Brage Golding with the "Running Dog of the Month" award.

[84] Interview with Ken Hammond, October 3, 1977; conducted by Bills.

Coalition members, nonetheless, have asserted that the antigym effort was an important political struggle, despite the factionalism that it created. Bill Arthrell, for instance, points to the publicity which the protest received, creating "at least for one more time a sense of horror about the whole Kent State situation."[85] Nancy Grim observes: "I think the main success was making May fourth again a major aspect of life at Kent State. The gym struggle brought it back into focus after several years of decreasing interest in the shootings. I think that's important. It's important to Kent State to be aware of its role in history."

Kent's role in history was also the concern of Prof. Lawrence Kaplan in his commencement address of August 27, 1977. His speech, titled "The Kent Heritage," was widely quoted at the time it was given, and is reprinted in this volume. Kaplan stated, in part:

> There is no shelter here. The experience of the Kent universe has been a microcosm of society at large. The turmoil of America in the last decade was and is an integral part of life at Kent. . . . What, then, of Kent State today and tomorrow? Should it be immobilized by the events? Should it be the site of continuing protests against present or future sins of society? . . . May 4 is part of our heritage, as it is part of America's heritage. We should remember the past, not to reopen old wounds or to seek out new villains, but to learn from it and to use it for the building of a greater University.

Administration and May 4

When Robert White retired as University president in 1971, his views on the May 4 shootings were clear: the events were tragic; the institution must learn from the violence, develop new programs, and rededicate itself to its tasks; and commemorations of the four deaths should be restricted to the University "family." White feared that Kent State might become or be seen as a center for radical activity, and he worried that the existence of the school itself could be jeopardized by the recurrence of the polarization and politicization which he had witnessed.

White's successor was Glenn Olds, a Yale graduate and former U.S. representative to the United Nations Economic and Social

---

[85] Interview with Bill Arthrell, November 15, 1980; conducted by Bills.

Council. The essay by D. Ray Heisey, "Sensitivity to an Image," describes the "high expectation" which greeted the new administration. "The latitude which a new president had in dealing with the May 4 image," writes Heisey, "was considerable since he was neither personally nor institutionally involved in the tragic events." Olds, it was widely believed, might be able to heal the divisions in the Kent State community. He did not hesitate to express his personal sentiments—in his poem "Never Again," which appeared in the *Daily Kent Stater* in May 1972, or in his remarks at the dedication of the May 4 Resource Room in the University Library in May 1974. "Some events have a magnitude beyond their moment," he said. "They are full of meaning. They mirror in miniature a whole life, a time, a meaning never to be forgotten." Kent State and the tragedy of May 1970 must be "transformed into new life."[86] But he did not agree with the demands of May 4 activists for class cancellation, renaming campus buildings, and other steps to "officially recognize" or acknowledge University complicity in the events of spring 1970. His resignation, which was announced in November 1976 and took effect the next July, came in the midst of the gym controversy; and the complicated legal battle and the matter of negotiations with the May 4th Coalition were left to Interim President Michael Schwartz.

The controversy was far from over when Brage Golding, former president of Wright State and San Diego State universities, took office in September 1977. The new president was thus plunged immediately into the May 4 debate and forced to concentrate his energies, at least for a brief period, almost exclusively on that single issue. During a preliminary visit to the campus in August, Golding commented that the gym-annex site had been a poor choice. In a special press release of September 13, he reiterated that view but also observed that there was by then "no alternative" to the designated location. Everyone, he said, had been a victim of the shootings—students, guardsmen, townspeople, and the University. The slain students "were victims of a tragedy, a combination of international, national, local and personal forces which exploded in panic and unreason on May 4." The 1978 commemoration, he observed, should be a "quiet anniversary and ceremony for the University com-

---

[86] Glenn Olds, "Remarks on May 4 Dedication"; courtesy of Susan Bleakney.

munity."[87] Several months later, in response to criticism, Golding
wrote a letter to the May 4th Task Force in which he stated: "I have
repeatedly said that we should *not* forget all this but that we must
move ahead. The events of May 1970 must not be forgotten—how
could they be?—but they must not be allowed to so dominate our
lives that our effectiveness as a University is damaged."[88]

Heisey concludes that presidents White, Olds, and Golding were
all sensitive to the issues raised by the shootings and worked within
the constraints of their position to reshape Kent State's image as a
strife-torn institution. Michael Schwartz, provost and vice president
of academic and student affairs at the time of his interview—now
president of the University—refers to a distorted public view of the
University, with "tanks on every corner," a school that "seems to
draw from all over the country . . . a bunch of people who are intent on ripping it apart." Schwartz then observes: "And the facts
were all otherwise: this is a quiet, placid, if anything remarkably
conservative institution, both in terms of its student body and its
faculty." Robert Dyal, however, in his essay for this volume, is
sharply critical of the administrative response to May 4. There was
an opportunity to make positive gains from the experience of the
shootings, he writes, but "a succession of unimaginative administrators, in their headlong rush to return to normalcy . . . missed the
opportunity to transform a minus into a plus." Instead, writes Dyal,
the University's official position on May 4 has been characterized by
indifference, defensiveness, and excessive concern for its public relations image. He is also critical of the official response of the Kent
State faculty—as a group—to the issues raised by the shootings.

However, Golding's comment on the need to "move ahead" is, in
a way, not unlike a point made by Miriam Jackson in her article:
that May 4 must be placed in perspective. She believes that the
"narrow" focus of Kent activists must be broadened: "The task for
those of us associated with the struggle on behalf of the victims of
Kent State ought to be to link the mourning of the vigils and the reaffirmation of the May 4 rallies to much larger issues." The intro-
version of student radicalism at Kent State is a familiar topic of dis-

[87] "President's Statement on Kent State University's New HPER Facility," September 14,
1977, press release; author's copy.
[88] Golding to Task Force, January 19, 1978, Box 56, M4C, KSUA.

President Brage Golding.

cussion among those involved in the annual commemorative programs.

The May 4th Movement

Political activism at Kent State University, from whatever perspective it has been approached, is inundated by the backwash of the events of 1970. The "May 4th Movement," as it has been called, was a decade-long struggle directly energized by the experience and "lessons" of May 4. It has been far from homogeneous, involving reform-oriented as well as self-styled "revolutionary" tendencies; but it has involved many people whose personal politics were shaped by the "injustice" at Kent State and the subsequent pursuit of satisfactory answers to questions raised by the shootings—questions of the legitimacy of dissent, the responsibility of government agencies regarding the use of force, the training and equipment of the National Guard, and the nature and use of power in America.

The May 4th Movement united campus activism with the legal battle of the Kent State families in a way that lent inspiration to both groups. Political activity associated with May 4, highlighted by the yearly commemorations, provided a vivid focal point for the articulation of radical political themes during a transitional period for the American left as a whole. The movement has encompassed political, historical, and spiritual themes of protest, while the emotional reverberations of the shootings and visualization of the event have been the most potent connective force for younger students. It is no coincidence that the cycle of student activism at Kent State peaks each May. Alan Canfora's "Winter Poem in Anticipation of

Spring," which appeared in 1978, spoke to this point. The imagery of spring, the ideas of renewal and rebirth, have reinforced the political echoes of May 1970.

While May 4 organizing committees often provided a working model of leftist unity and coalition strategy, disputes between veteran and newer activists have been endemic in recent years. And differences also typically arise over substantive issues regarding the planning and structure of commemorative activities, the viewpoints to be expressed, and the overall purpose of the annual program. Former student Bill Gordon, for instance, writes: "I never considered myself part of any larger movement, just working for a cause." He identified three reasons for initial May 4-related activities at Kent State: to determine if there had been a conspiracy against students, to see that guardsmen were held accountable for the deaths, "and closely tied to the other two, we wanted to keep Kent State in the public eye."[89]

The theme of not forgetting has been expressed at every commemoration: there was an injustice committed, it was not properly recognized, and the country at large must not let it slip from memory. "The only hope for America is remembering Vietnam," said activist Elizabeth McAlister on May 4, 1975. When Joan Baez appeared on the University Commons on August 20, 1977, to perform at a May 4th Coalition rally, she was presented a dozen roses with a message attached: "Flowers are better than bullets." She said: "There's the idea that they're putting a gym over the Vietnam War. I do believe that's what is happening."[90] Kent State, then, represents an era rather than a single event. William Kunstler spoke in Kent in mid-October 1970; it was, he said, a "symbolic place." Then he voiced a thought that many students have shared in the last twelve years: "Maybe some time in the future historians will say that between May 1 and May 4 this is where it all began."[91]

And yet, May 4 issues, according to Bill Arthrell, have been a "drain" on other political struggles of the Kent State left: "I talk to people and they have a distorted view of oppression because it's looking through May fourth-colored glasses." But, he said, "it's

[89] Gordon to Bills, August 8, 1980.

[90] McAlister statement, *DKS*, May 6, 1975, p. 3; Baez statement, *Record-Courier*, August 22, 1977, p. 3.

[91] *Akron Beacon Journal*, October 20, 1970, p. A5.

damned if you do and damned if you don't. If we don't do something, the University is going to take it away from us. And if we do something, it seems that people get obsessed with it. I've seen some of my friends—that's their life." If May 4 is "where the movement at Kent is stuck," said Arthrell, then perhaps that is the special obligation of local activists. He echoes sentiments of many students, over the years, in his belief that without the regular commemoration of May 4, the event and its symbolism will "get lost in the shuffle."[92]

The First Decade

The emotionalism of 1970, the political and generational polarization over the events of May 4, have lessened over time; but as Mary Vincent notes, the passions are not deeply buried. During the gym controversy, sentiments similar to those of seven years before resurfaced among townspeople. References to "rabble-rousers" and calls for the expulsion of dissident students were seen again in many letters to the *Record-Courier*. All the smoldering May 4 issues were given new life: appropriate remembrance, proper memorialization, and institutional responsibility.

Certainly, there were memorials on the campus before 1977. A small metal plaque listing the names of the four dead had been placed in the Prentice Hall parking lot by B'nai B'rith Hillel a year after the shootings. A pipe-sculpture designed by Alistair Granville-Jackson, titled *The Kent Four*, was placed near the art school for a May 1973 dedication. But it was not a single memorial that was at issue; instead, the point of contention was how the University should preserve or nurture a May 4 "tradition."

In 1978, national media attention was again directed toward Kent State when the University administration refused to accept a memorial sculpture, created by artist George Segal, which had been commissioned for the school by the Cleveland-based Mildred Andrews Fund. The sculpture, titled *Abraham and Isaac*, depicted a knife-bearing father facing a kneeling youth whose hands were bound in front of him. President Golding, remarking on the University's rejection of the artwork, stated: "It was thought inappropriate to commemorate the deaths of four students and the

---

[92] Interview with Bill Arthrell, November 15, 1980; conducted by Bills.

wounding of nine on the campus with a statue which appears to represent an act of violence about to be committed." Segal, in a 1981 interview, commented on his decision "to make a structural image of a metaphor of Abraham and Isaac": "I found that sculpture interesting to do because I could deal with a literary metaphor. I could deal with poetry. I could deal with very complex layers of interpretation of what seemed to be a loud, blunt, clear political event that I thought was far more complicated than it appeared on the surface."[93]

Robert Dyal cites the controversy over the sculpture as a further example of administrative insensitivity to the issues of May 4; others, however, have supported Golding's decision by emphasizing that the University was not obligated to accept the sculpture. Donald Hassler, for instance, a faculty member in the Honors and Experimental College, wrote in 1980: "When the interests of ambiguous,

[93] Golding statement, *Akron Beacon Journal*, August 29, 1978, p. B3; Malcolm N. Carter, "[Interview with] George Segal," *Saturday Review*, May 1981, p. 30.

Candlelit memorial marker, May 3, 1980. Through the efforts of a special faculty committee, chaired by Prof. John Ohles, this marker was placed in the Prentice Hall parking lot for the May 1975 commemoration. The earlier marker, a metal plaque, was stolen in 1974.

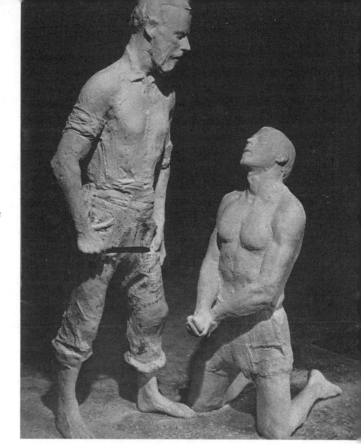

Plaster casts of the George Segal sculpture.

enigmatic art . . . clash with the interests of a forthright and very public institution such as our University, then the art must be set aside to survive on its own terms."[94] *Abraham and Isaac* was later placed at Princeton University, but the controversy stirred in Kent over its symbolism and substance well illustrated the continuing vitality of the May 4 debate.

There are, however, a number of ways in which May 4 has been "incorporated" more firmly into the official past and present of Kent State. The May 4th Commemoration Committee, established in May 1977 by the Board of Trustees, was commissioned to study how the University might appropriately recognize the significance of the events of 1970. The committee was chaired by Raghbir Basi, then director of the Center for Peaceful Change. The final recommendations of the committee, issued in January 1978, are often referred to

[94] Donald M. Hassler, "The Poet and the Republic After May 4," *Left Review* 4 (Spring 1980): 43.

Allison Krause
1951–1970

William Schroeder
1950–1970

as the "Basi Report." The report advised that "a brief historical statement" with regard to May 4, 1970 be included in University catalogs and that a "descriptive brochure" be prepared for distribution at the site of the shootings. The committee's definition of the "site" was identical to that of the May 4th Coalition, and the recommendation was made that "no further surface alterations" take place. The report continued: "The Committee feels that all the programs around May 4 each year should be planned with a view not to propagandize but rather, to provide inspiration and stimulation for people to think and reflect on their own. What happened here was tragic, but we need to move forward in a reaffirmation of the human prospect." Regarding commemoration activities, the report urged continuation of the candlelight walk and vigil and the May 4 program sponsored by the May 4th Task Force. Classes should be suspended from noon to 6:00 P.M. on May 4 each year, and the day should be declared one of "observance." The committee also proposed the strengthening of the CPC as the appropriate "lasting memorial."[95]

[95] "Report of the May 4th Commemoration Committee," January 19, 1978, Box 56, M4C, KSUA.

Jeffrey Miller
1950–1970

Sandra Scheuer
1949–1970

Some of the recommendations were implemented. Beginning in 1978, short statements appeared in undergraduate and graduate catalogs, noting that May 4, 1970, was a "pivotal moment" in the institution's history. A factual brochure was prepared by professors Glenn Frank, Jerry Lewis, and Thomas Hensley, and its distribution at the site began in 1980. Classes were cancelled for the entire day of May 4 in 1978 and 1979. In 1980, May 4 was on Sunday. In 1981, the University administration and the May 4th Task Force agreed to class cancellation during the period of the commemorative program only; and in 1982, because of a shift in the academic calendar, May 4 was part of a pre-final examination "study day." In the Center for Peaceful Change, photographs of Allison Krause, Jeffrey Miller, Sandra Scheuer, and William Schroeder hang in the main office. The same photographs appear in the May 4 Resource Room in the University Library. At many points then, students are reminded of the shootings and their continuing impact on the institution. But this is not the "official" acknowledgment sought by the Mayday Coalition, the May 4 United Front, the May 4th Coalition, the May 4th Task Force, and similar groups. The concept of complicity with a militarist corporate state reflects an ideological viewpoint which the University is unlikely to accept. And the fact of the imposition of external control over the University by state and National Guard officials on May 2, 1970, has not encouraged administrative officials to look back and see University culpability in the events that followed.

Kent State in History

In the summer of 1977, in the midst of the gym controversy, the National Park Service of the Department of the Interior initiated a study of the Kent State shootings for the purpose of determining whether or not the campus could be declared a historical landmark. The survey had come at the request of Sen. Howard Metzenbaum and Cong. John Seiberling of Ohio. The final report was written by James Sheire, historian for the Historic Sites Survey Division, and filed in January 1978—well after it had become clear that it would have no effect on the local politics of gym-annex construction. Sheire placed the Kent State deaths within the context of international events, asserting that the shootings were part of a "list of tragedies" associated with the war in Vietnam. He concluded that the shootings had no lasting political effect, that the social impact was too difficult to measure, and that the only enduring significance might be of a symbolic nature.[96]

The symbolism of Kent State 1970 remains pervasive, and it may well endure. When Haynes Johnson of the *Washington Post* reviewed the decade of the 1970s in mid-December 1979, a natural focal point was Kent State—both in terms of the violence of May 4 and the changes which the institution had undergone over the interim years. Kent State's story was America's story.[97]

The events of May 4, 1970, more than any other single moment —fairly or unfairly—have come to epitomize the heights of societal strife engendered by U.S. involvement in the Vietnam conflict. The response to the shootings well portrayed the generational polarization characteristic of the period. People immediately offered explanations of how such an event could occur and who was culpable,

---

[96] James Sheire, *Kent State May 4, 1970 Site*, U.S., Department of the Interior, National Park Service, Historic Sites Survey Division, 1978, passim. The report is a typescript; see pp. 1–2, 26–27, 31, 34–35. The Interior Department did not declare the Kent State campus to be a historical landmark.

[97] Haynes Johnson, "1970 to 1980: Where Have We Gone?" *Washington Post*, December 16, 1979, pp. L1–2.

and they did so consistent with their perspectives on the major issues of the day: the global politics of cold war confrontation and
falling dominoes; patriotism, dissent, revolution, and national
security; rebellious youth and impatient, angry, frustrated parents;
and, paradoxically, the need for national reconciliation. As John
Seiberling—then a candidate for office—remarked on May 6, 1970,
speaking of the slain students: "Their blood was not shed in vain if
we all pull together, if we will recognize that our forefathers gave us
a great instrument of freedom. . . . The system can be made to
work." Or Donald Shook, then director of alumni relations, who
wrote to Kent State graduates, saying that the deaths must be remembered as "a beginning of a turn away from violence, as a tragedy
that must not be repeated, as a starting point for the understanding
we all so badly need."[98]

The rising student protest—against the war, for domestic reconstruction—which cascaded through the late 1960s, came to a halt
after May 1970, in force and spirit if not immediately in practice. It
did so as a result of several factors, internal and external, which
overshadowed particular events. Yet, Kent State revealed the limits
within which an idealistic and exuberant youth movement could
maneuver. And there were now four martyrs: "We remember our
dead," writes feminist activist Bettina Aptheker. "We try to make
sense out of their deaths, to understand why, in the random course
of human events, they died and we did not."[99] Thus it is, to use Ruth
Gibson's word, that Kent State "haunts" us, individually and collectively. For some, it is a very personal remembrance, as Gibson
describes it in her interview: "For a long time after May 1970, I felt
that Allison and Sandy shouldn't have been killed—that it should
have been me . . ."; the dead were surrogates for radical leaders
whom the guardsmen could not reach. And whether we see Kent
State as an accident, a riot, or the logical result of the "insuperable
class contradiction[s]" of American capitalism,[100] we try to make
sense out of it. The memory and visualization of the shootings
provides a tableau by which the emotions and struggles of the past

[98] Transcript, Seiberling remarks to student rally at the University of Akron, May 6, 1970,
courtesy of John Seiberling; Shook to Kent State alumni, May 27, 1970, Box 40, M4C,
KSUA.
[99] Bettina Aptheker, "In Memoriam," *Left Review* 4 (Spring 1980): 3.
[100] The quoted phrase is from Irwin Silber, "Ends and Means: A Class Question,"
Guardian, November 16, 1977, p. 21, and was a reference to Kent State.

are carried into the present. "For a lot of young people in America," said Bill Arthrell in 1977, "what happened at Kent State goes deep into their roots."[101]

The NBC TV-movie "Kent State" was aired in February 1981; it was filmed in Gadsden, Alabama, after Kent State University officials refused permission for use of the Ohio campus because of their fears that renewed, sharp controversy might erupt. The movie provided a dramatic reenactment of the shootings; and Jane Fleiss, the actress who portrayed Allison Krause, subsequently attended and spoke at the eleventh-anniversary May 4 commemoration in Kent. "Allison Krause graced my life," she said, "and through her I understand what integrity is, what vulnerability is and especially what courage is about."[102] Thus it is that the events of May 1970 continue to touch people, and in many unexpected ways.

At the commemoration of May 4, 1982, Chic Canfora proclaimed, and certainly not for the first time: "Kent State University belongs to the world." How "Kent State" belongs to Kent State, however, or rather how much it belongs, was the subject of a 1980 editorial in the *Daily Kent Stater*, titled "10th May 4 Marks Tunnel's End," which read in part:

> The overriding message of May 4 is not just to learn from history, so that we don't repeat it, but to grow also. . . . We now can see the light at the end of the tunnel—a glimmer of hope that the university can reach a level of academic maturity that was stunted 10 years ago. While we must not forget what happened here, we must not be dragged down by it either. . . . We cannot wear the sack cloth and ashes of May 4 forever.

How to remember, how to commemorate: this has been crucial to the May 4 debate. The past lives in the present, but what do we do with it? Lawrence Shafer, the guardsman who had shot and wounded Joseph Lewis in 1970, was interviewed in 1980: "After 10 years," he said, "I hope everybody will let this thing die and bury it." He wanted to get back "to leading a normal Life." Peter Davies, writing in 1979, had already observed that his own life had been

---

[101] Interview with Bill Arthrell, August 12, 1977; conducted by Thomas Matijasic.

[102] Fleiss is quoted in *DKS*, May 5, 1981, p. 3. For a description of the making of the movie, see J. Gregory Payne, *Mayday: Kent State* (Dubuque, Iowa: Kendall/Hunt, 1981); see Jerry M. Lewis, "*Kent State*—The Movie," *Journal of Popular Film and Television* 9 (Spring 1981): 13–18, for a negative review, asserting that numerous "factual errors" marred the narrative.

forever changed by Kent State: "Normal was pre-May 4, 1970, and that life is dead."[103] But it was not only personal lives that were changed and which continue to be changed by Kent State; it was also the life of a nation. And while the fabric of the nation was altered not simply by the events in Kent, Ohio, but by the upheaval which generated those events, it is to Kent State that we look as a marker, as a historical milestone of our discontent.

[103] Canfora statement from author's notes, May 4, 1982, commemoration; editorial, *DKS*, May 2, 1980, p. 4; Shafer statement, *Akron Beacon Journal*, May 4, 1980, pp. A1, A10; Davies statement, personal letter, Davies to Jackson, May 8, 1979, courtesy of Miriam Jackson.

Fact-Finding

"To dispel the rumors"

an interview with MARY VINCENT

MARY VINCENT *was born before World War I in Shellburg, Pennsylvania, near Bedford. She first came to Kent in the fall of 1962 when her husband, Howard, joined the faculty of the English Department at Kent State University. Vincent comes from a strong Quaker background and takes pride in asserting that women have long received equal educational opportunities among Quakers. She received a bachelor's degree from Mount Holyoke College in 1931 and subsequently did graduate work in psychology at the University of Chicago and the Institute of Psychoanalysis. She did research in the area of child psychology at the Salpetriere and other hospitals in Paris, France, during the years 1953–57. Vincent had only limited contact with Kent State students before the spring of 1970; but immediately after the shootings of May 4, she opened her house to meetings of students, faculty, and townspeople in order to promote dialogue and ease tensions within the community. In 1973, she received the Community Service Award from the student government of Kent State. Still a Kent resident, Vincent continues to be interested in community-student affairs and civil liberties issues. The interview was conducted on November 10, 1980.*

What *do you remember first?*
My husband came home and told me, "They've shot four students. They've killed them." And we just stood looking out the window. We saw knots of people standing on the sidewalk. It was a complete shock. Later that day, I had to go down to the post office to mail a letter, and down on the corner of our street was a jeep with four soldiers with guns. Of course, I had no idea that they were loaded. I went down to Main Street, where there were sheriff's deputies and more jeeps, then down to the post office where two young National Guardsmen ran out and told me I couldn't go into the building. I said, "I've got a letter that has to be dated today, can I drop it in?" And one of them said he would do it for me. But I asked whether I

could, and so I did. But the stores were closed; everything was closed. This was about two o'clock. The National Guard just took over the town. The things I always remember were the helicopters, their noise, the way the searchlights came down; and they went day and night. In some ways, we were like a Vietnam village.

After the shootings, there were a great many rumors that quickly passed through the town. What things that you heard do you still recall?
The main rumor I heard was that communists and their agents were infiltrating the University and town. The rumor that was so completely unbelievable—but some people believed it—was that communists in National Guard uniforms had shot the students. I was told that people on the automobile end of town took their cars out of the display windows because they thought the students and the communists were coming to wreck them. A woman in a laundry said to me: "My husband is sitting up at nights with a shotgun because we think they'll sneak up to burn our house."

Were there a lot of people sitting up at night?
This is just what I heard. But there seemed to be quite a few. In fact, I think there were more than most people realize. People didn't know what would happen next. The town got afraid, angry. I was in a business office that week, and people were talking about the shootings. Suddenly a woman stood up from her desk, raised her right arm straight in the air and said: "I'm 100 percent American and a Christian and I say they should have shot more." Other people said the same thing in letters to the *Record-Courier*. The one thing that townspeople trusted was their churches. Otherwise, they didn't seem to know what to believe or what to do. Neither did most people at the University.

You began meetings between students and townspeople. What did you set out to do?
When I went downtown the next day, I met some students walking around looking just stunned. The townspeople had cut themselves off from them. These students were the ones who had rooms here and jobs and had not been bused home by the University administration. And so I spoke to them and asked them if there was any-

thing I could do, and what I gathered from several of them, including a couple big football types, was that they would like to talk to responsible people in the town, to keep it from happening again. So I said I'd try to find some. I began to hunt around, calling friends, asking who would talk to students, and Lu Lyman was suggested. I called him and he said, "Come right over." So I went over and we talked about it for two hours and I said, "I've invited some students to come to my house tonight to see if we can discuss what can be done." He agreed to talk; also the head of a bank and two very prominent real estate men were invited. I arranged for different evenings with different people with the help of John Looney, the area head of the American Friends Service Committee.

Some faculty were present, including Ottavio Casale—whom I am very indebted to. He was straightforward, his approach was commonsense, and he was reasonable; I mean he talked to students as one reasonable person to another. But he was also very truthful about what would happen if they took certain actions. And we had students in with headbands and feathers. Lu Lyman had said, "I'll talk to them, but I want them to come in and be polite." I said, "I think they will, the ones I've been talking to." And then I went down to a student house, where two or three of them were sitting around— one was looking rather dazed—and I said: "Now you're to talk to a prominent car dealer who used to be Republican party chairman of Portage County, and I'm sure you'd make a better impression if you came with clean shirts on." They looked at each other and one of them said, "I think we can do that to make a point." And when they came that night, they were immaculate. So that was a way to dispel the rumors of their always being dirty. That was one of the rumors that went around: how dirty, filthy, and drug-ridden they were, the students who were shot—and others as well. Generally, the students here were *not* dirty, and the ones in the ambulances were simply reacting physically to tremendous shock.

Did you have the meetings at your house?
Yes, right here. There was a curfew, which we tried to observe. People just sat on the floor. We had two requirements: one was that if you thought something was very important, you said it, just giving information, *not* as a confrontation. And the other thing was that if you wanted to know something you felt was important, you would ask, but not as a matter of contention, asking for information only.

And by and large, the discussion was very reasonable. I do remember an army officer, or rather a former army officer from the Second World War, shaking a cigar at one of the students and saying why did you do thus and so in Washington, why do you carry the flag upside down? And this little thin student, who was working his way through school, stood up and said, "Well sir, we see it this way: we think things are upside down in this country, and we think you haven't seen that, so we're holding the flag that way to show you."

So there were confrontations anyway?
No. I mean that was the closest we came. But the student was polite and there was just silence after he spoke.

Had some of the students who came to your house been involved in campus antiwar activities?
These were just students who were left here after the general exodus. They were living here and had jobs here. They weren't always the same ones either. Some were high school students, and one girl did not appear a second time. A friend of hers told me that when her family found out that she had been here to a meeting they confined her to her room for a week. Yet we had prominent townspeople; it wasn't simply a student gathering. We did our best to observe the curfew, but there was so much to say. One townsperson later told me that when the police checked the license plates of the cars outside my house or recognized that some of the local establishment leaders were here, they drove on by.

What kinds of points were raised at the meetings?
There were discussions of how the police and National Guard had behaved. The students gave better marks to the state police and to some of the town police than they gave to the sheriff's deputies. At first, it was mostly confusion: what do we do? One night there were stories of vigilantes on the outskirts of town. Many people simply told what they saw, and they were trying to figure out what kind of committee they could set up and whom they could talk to. Students kept saying, "We want to talk to townspeople." But in general the townspeople did not want to talk to students. The role of the University authorities was not discussed really. The students saw the matter as a town thing, and the town—this is my impression—saw it

as a student thing, although there were criticisms of the University administration and faculty. The students talked also about the war, of course, and "its effect on society." But most talk was town-centered.

Your short-term goal was to defuse tensions?
Yes, I thought that if townspeople realized how really innocent these students were, they wouldn't be so hostile, this sort of thing would not happen again. We were groping around, trying to know what to do next. And of course the students wanted to know when they could come back to classes. You might say from the student point of view that it was very self-centered: their careers at the University. The fact was that they couldn't understand why it had happened, why it was done to them. They were greatly shocked by the tragedy. But at the meetings, no one suggested politics as the reason for the shootings.

Did the townspeople at your meetings understand what happened?
To a great extent they held the students responsible. The town saw it as self-defense on the part of the guardsmen. I remember two years later I was talking to the head of one of the local banks; it was after a May confrontation. He said, "Well, you know they broke a couple windows in our bank." And I said, "Who did?" He responded, "The students." And I asked, "Do you *know* it was the students? Because a lot of rough people come into town for these things." And he waited a minute and then he looked at me and smiled: "Well no, I don't." But the reflex was "it's the students," mixed up with communism. That was what townspeople saw.

What was the general reaction when the National Guard arrived on Saturday night?
Great relief and thankfulness. They thought they were being saved—the townspeople, that is—that's what I kept hearing. I knew the mayor had sent for the Guard. I mean everybody seemed to know that immediately. I didn't think it was necessary. After the shootings, one businessman told us: "With the vigilantes outside of town, we're lucky to have the police and the Guard to keep them out there." But it was real hysteria. The town really suffered: the parents who panicked on May 4, afraid they couldn't reach their young

children at school; local residents caught outside Kent who couldn't get back through police barricades; the parents who couldn't find out whether it was their son or daughter who had been shot. It was the town that was hysterical, not the students. The students were stunned, they were sad, they were frightened and confused, they couldn't believe it. They had no idea of the way the town saw it. I remember two students at a meeting chaired by Rev. Bill Jacobs over on East Main Street: they were so shocked at the local hostility that they heard there that we never saw them again. But I personally never heard any student make a threat against the town or the Guard.

What community feelings so shocked them?
Talk of vigilantes, guns. The hostility. Parents who said, "If you were mixed up in this, don't come home again." The whole thing. *They couldn't understand why.* KSU had been largely—for under-graduates—an apolitical campus.

How would you evaluate your role at that time?
What I set out to do was to get the responsible people in the community to see what the student situation was. I was looking at it as a parent, and I felt that there would be some community people who would be willing to find out the facts. We were fact-finding. What finally emerged through University, church, and other efforts in town were committees of concerned people, which included faculty and students, a few townspeople, and some ministers. The ministers split, really, over this issue. Some were throwing open their churches to help the students and faculty have classes. Some would meet with students and talk things over with them. Others, I was told, did not want to be publicly involved in it. When you asked what we set out to do, we just wanted to make things better; it was as simple as that. And to keep it from happening again—people kept repeating that.

Have the attitudes of townspeople changed over the years since 1970?
I think there's a bigger group of people now who have the facts. There was so much hysteria and rumor at the beginning. There is a much larger group who know what went on in Vietnam, and that has helped too. Even Watergate has helped. I think a lot of things

have made a larger group of informed or inquiring, and therefore more reasonable, people. It's certainly not focused just on the students like it used to be, and I think that's a great improvement.

Do people still think about the shootings?
Oh yes. They certainly do think about it. From the purely financial point of view, some people realized it was very bad for business to have this happen here and that it would reduce the student body. That has been expressed to me by people who were not unfriendly to students; they meant it was a fact of life. Secondly, there was a widespread feeling that it was unfair and a disgrace to the town, to *their* town. Oh, I met this again and again. People didn't want to talk about it; they wanted to put it behind them. They kept saying, "Why bring it up? It's over." Which meant that they missed entirely what was the cause of the shootings. They took it as their town's personal disgrace. They couldn't see why it had to happen here, in Kent. And of course, the students—now this is where a university education proves itself—the students wanted to get at reasons. But the town wanted to walk away from it. It was painful, much more painful for the town, I think, than the country as a whole realizes. The town did not see then that the shootings had international as well as national implications. I've been asked about this in France and England, wherever I've traveled.

Is the great emotionalism generated in 1970 lessening over time?
It is. Townspeople now are not so frightened as they were. In the last couple of years, they've been saying things like "oh well, they'll have May 4th," referring to the student commemorations, and they have been putting it aside. Before, they felt intensely involved in the issue: I've noticed that difference. "Oh well, let them have their May 4th." They're getting on with their lives. But talk to them about it for a little while, and the emotions begin to rise again.

Do you think it's good for the town to remember?
They should face it and know what caused it, and then they would feel better. The thing that you bury back is always going to hurt. If you bring it out and look at it, and get the facts—I don't think you can be healed unless you know the truth.

Town in Crisis

"It's life, liberty, and property"

an interview with LUCIUS LYMAN, JR.

LUCIUS LYMAN, JR., *was born in 1911 in Akron, Ohio. He attended Harvard University for a brief period during the Great Depression but was forced to discontinue his studies and return to northeastern Ohio to work for his father, who had the Chevrolet dealership in Kent. In the spring of 1946, after returning from military service, Lyman became the owner of the car dealership, which he retained until 1975. Recalling his wartime experience, he says: "One of the things that I got to thinking about overseas was what a mess I was in and how the politicians had really created the mess." After returning to Kent, he became involved in local political affairs and points happily to a time when the Republican party controlled the city administration. Lyman ran for mayor in 1963 and was defeated. "My opponent's plurality," he recalls, "became the biggest in the history of Kent." Shortly before the campus upheaval of May 1970, Lyman worked with a campus ministry group to assess "town-gown" relations, which he found to be "adequate and improving." Regarding the local political situation, he remembers: "I had the feeling that things were pretty calm." He is still a Kent resident. The interview was conducted on September 23, 1980.*

How did you feel about the antiwar movement and student protest during the years 1969–70? Was it your feeling that there was not a great deal of such activity in Kent?
My appraisal was that there was not an inordinate amount. There was a natural resistance to the war, and it was increasing. This was being reported in the national magazines that I was reading and also in the local paper as well as the *Akron Beacon Journal*, which I read because we are a satellite of Akron.

Were you concerned?
I didn't feel that we were in danger of any revolutionary threats. I thought that the Democratic convention of 1968 in Chicago was a

manifestation of the anger of the students and the so-called hippie group. But I didn't have any sense that there was a chance of an over-throw of the government or an overthrow of the capitalistic system.

Then you weren't expecting significant disruption?
No. And I'm aware that when I was a kid, there was an antiwar movement, in the eastern colleges as an example. I did not partici-pate in these movements, but I was sympathetic to them. As a result of this feeling, my position before the war, right up to December 7, 1941, was that of an isolationist. Now, of course, I see the folly of that position.

When unrest began on campus and in the community following the president's speech of April 30, 1970, what was the reaction of the townspeople?
Well, I can tell you what my own reaction was and that of my wife. We lived within a block of the University. I got up early on Saturday morning, May second, and took a shortcut to my business on the west side of the town. I was completely unaware that there had been any disturbance downtown until I got to the office, at which time I was told that there had been a riot and a lot of property damage. This gravely concerned me, because this was an indication that things really had gotten out of hand. I went downtown, and the amount of damage I saw at that time—and this was probably eleven o'clock in the morning—was not as great as I anticipated it to be, as it had been painted to me by my colleagues at the dealership. It's true that there were some windows broken and there were other damages, but it was not nearly as extensive as I thought it could've been or as it was depicted to be. But you have to understand, in a way that maybe you don't, how important property is in the men-tality of those of us who are in the system. You see, it's life, liberty, *and* property. And the deprecation of property as part of this pro-cess still astounds me, because from the time I was born, I and all my peers aspired to be property owners. I don't mean only real estate, but also property such as automobiles, property such as decent furniture—to all the things now such as automatic washers, dish-washers, and so forth. And the destruction of property had a great impact. And I think my feelings about this were sharpened as a re-sult of my experience in the war where I saw millions and millions of

dollars worth of property destroyed. And what a waste it was. So even though the damage downtown was slight in my opinion, it alerted me to the seriousness of the situation.

When the National Guard arrived, were you pleased to see them?
Yes, I think it calmed the community and the campus. It was May third when the Guard's presence was known. It was a Sunday, and I remember driving, after church, along Summit Street to what at that time was the backside of the campus and seeing the National Guard there and how secure I felt as a citizen. The night before, the place had been pretty noisy and pretty traumatic. The destruction of the ROTC building was fresh in my mind, as well as the attitude of the students toward the destruction of the building—some of the students.

Were you surprised then, on Monday, after the shootings? I don't know where you would have heard about them, maybe on the radio?
I was having lunch down on South Water Street, at one of those restaurants, with a colleague, and the sirens coming up Route 43 really got our attention. We wondered what the cause of it was. I thought at first it was probably a big fire. But then after lunch, which we ate leisurely—we didn't feel any sense of tragedy or catastrophe —we got into the car and turned on the radio and heard what had happened. Then I thought that all hell was about to break loose, and I went immediately to Lyman Chevrolet. I felt a need to do what was necessary to secure the property and the well-being of my colleagues at the company. The first thing I did was to instruct everyone to go home, which they did. I'm pretty sure they went home. My objective was to get home too, but I stayed at the company. I got there about 1:15 or 1:30 and stayed until about 4:30. I bet I answered the phone a hundred and twenty-five times. We had four lines, and all of them were busy.

People wanting information?
People: spouses, mothers, parents, everybody wanted to know about my colleagues, where they were. The community was really scared. One of the things that aggravated the fears were the terrible rumors that were floating around. The rumors were not only coming across the radio but were being communicated to me on the phone.

What kind of rumors?
Well, that the high school was going to be burnt down. I think that
Mary Vincent should tell you about some of the rumors. Make a
point of asking her, because one of the services that she rendered
was to void the rumors that really aggravated the situation.

*When I spoke with you before this interview, you mentioned that
you were interested in talking about a "story that hasn't been told."*
The story—and in my opinion it never has been told—is first about
the students. I still have some question in my mind as to who the
students were, whether they were in fact students at Kent State
University or students from all over; and this was one of the rumors,
that they came from all over. I've read Michener's book, and I'm not
sure that he got the full story. I'm not sure that anybody will, and I'm
certain that if you got former mayor Leroy Satrom to talk about it,
for example, he'd give you a point of view that would not square
with mine. It's just that I don't think anybody really knows who the
so-called students were. It's awfully easy, as I've heard some people
say, to insist that these students were communist-inspired. Personally, I don't believe that. I think there were some high-flying radicals
involved, and I have the feeling that some of them came from out of
town to take advantage of the University. I am influenced somewhat
in this opinion by Michener's book, which made the statement, if I
remember correctly, that there was a radical element that descended
on Kent. But what even Michener didn't cover was the terrible crisis
that the townspeople of Kent thought we were in. The national news
didn't tell the story right that the downtown had been damaged.
Didn't tell about the ROTC building being burned down. Didn't tell
about how the students slashed the fire hoses, threw rocks at the
firemen, and in every sense of the word blocked any kind of orderly
procedure for the elimination of destruction. And the fire is going,
you could look up into the sky and you'd just have to believe that
many people in this town thought their houses and their property
was going to be next. I remember so well my wife's personal fear for
our safety. Remember that we lived within a block of the University.

How did people react to this fear?
Some of them reacted in a very vehement way, damning the students, blaming the students, speaking out and saying that the stu-

ROTC building ablaze on the night of May 2, 1970.

dents who got killed and wounded got exactly what they had coming to them. I would say that if I had made a survey of the people in Kent, the townspeople, that the vast majority—and I don't mean fifty percent plus one but the vast majority—would have said that the students got what they had coming to them.

How did you feel?
Well, of course I was terribly disturbed. I remember it perfectly. We had some guests from Akron and we were playing bridge; May second was our wedding anniversary—our thirty-fourth anniversary—and for twenty years of that time we had these same people over or had dinner with them someplace. Well, this night we were playing bridge and we could look right out the window and see what looked like a vast conflagration, and it was scary. But I remember saying, "Well, calm yourself." After all, I had seen these kinds of fires during my war experience. Nevertheless, I did feel some sense of . . . relief, and I want to tell you why. I think this is very important for the story. Immediately after the killings, not three or four days later, Kent was as calm as it ever was. The National Guard stayed. There weren't any students on the street; they'd all been sent home, and the University was closed. There was a normalcy in the community, in sharp contrast to what it had been on the days before. Sharp contrast. Let me tell you the other things I thought. What a

tragedy it was to attain this calm, to have the killing and wounding of students, the use of firearms. And it became obvious to me that if there was any role for me to play in this thing, it would be the role of quieting the situation. Mary Vincent and a colleague of hers representing the Society of Friends came to see me. They recruited me to participate in the calming of fears. The other thing I want to tell you is that I soon found some other persons willing to put their foot into the situation.

Who were they?
The guy who turned out to be the most forthright and effective leader was the pastor of my church, Bill Laurie. He was also connected with the campus ministry, so he had a particular rapport with students because he had worked with them so long. But he was following his Christian conscience, and I must tell you that the church had a great influence on my own concept of this. It's a hell of a way to treat people, shooting them. And Bill Laurie was a leader in the community, both town and gown. The people he recruited to work with him, to assuage the anger, really did a powerful job. And there were other groups that came into it too. I remember a meeting at Davey Junior High School, and sometimes the rhetoric got pretty blue. It was townspeople and University people. I remember attending a meeting over at Mary Vincent's house with some of the student leaders of the University. They didn't want me to talk, they wanted to talk. Of every thousand words spoken, I might have gotten in two. But this was therapeutic. The fact that here was a businessman, an actual representative of the economic establishment, that they could talk to him and he would listen was, I think, terribly important to them. And you know that some of the stuff they were proposing was not easy for me to take: some of their revolutionary ideas, some of the things they were standing up for.

You felt the dialogue was important?
Very important, especially to the students. Much more so to them than to me.

But the differences didn't heal immediately?
Oh, it took a long time and some of the differences aren't healed today. I want to tell you one more story though. In 1970, in July,

there were six of us that went camping along the Pickerel River about two hundred miles north of Toronto, Canada. There was one minister in the group, a professor from Wayne State University, two members of the Kent State faculty, one businessman from a Ravenna company: there were six of us in all. One evening, as we were cooking supper over a grill, I saw a boat coming down the river, and the fellow was paddling the boat. He had a motor on the boat, and so I figured that he had run out of gasoline. He had his son with him. I'd say this man was forty-five years old and his son about sixteen. Actually, as it turned out, he had gasoline, but it had water in it. So we immediately emptied out the water and we had enough gas to accommodate his needs. We got his motor started almost instantly. And it turned out, in a natural way, that he asked where we were from. He was from Cleveland. This was his first time on the river, camping on some nearby islands. "Where are you guys from?" he asked. I was the leader of the group, so I answered that we were from Kent, Ohio.

"You mean Kent, Ohio," he said, "where they had those goddam students? They got exactly what they had coming to them." And he picked up the paddle, shaking it over his son's head, and said: "I want you to know young man that if you ever went away to college and did what those goddam students did down there at Kent, *I'd kill you!*"

In my travels around the country, and they have been extensive, this was a typical attitude. Let me tell you about how I feel about it: this is an event that will last in history because it changed the world.

Chain Reaction

"A series of mistakes"

an interview with LEIGH HERINGTON

LEIGH HERINGTON *was born in 1945 in Rochester, New York. He received his bachelor's degree from Kent State University in 1967, after transferring from Alfred State College in New York. As an undergraduate student at KSU, Herington worked on the staff of the* Daily Kent Stater *as both sports editor and business manager. He enlisted and served in the U.S. Army for ten months during 1968 and 1969; he was discharged because of an eye injury while in Officer's Candidate School. Herington then returned to Kent State to work on a graduate degree and became assistant sports information director at the University, a position which he held from the spring of 1969 to May 4, 1970. Shortly after the shootings, he was appointed assistant director of internal communications, which included responsibility for operating a rumor control center through the fall of 1971. Subsequently he was appointed assistant director of alumni relations. Herington received his master's degree in business administration in 1971 and began law school in Akron in 1972. He worked also as public relations director at Walsh College in Canton, Ohio, and later as director of communications at Hiram College. Herington received his law degree in June 1976 and began a private law practice in Aurora, Ohio, in the spring of 1977. In 1978, he became a partner in the Aurora law firm of Christley, Minton & Herington. Herington's wife, Anita, is currently director of alumni relations at Kent State University. The interview was conducted on November 9, 1980.*

What were you doing on May fourth?
Shortly before the shootings, I walked down from Merrill Hall, which is where the News Service office was located, to the burnt shell of the ROTC building. It was cordoned off—actually there was nothing there—and there were guardsmen all around it. The public information officer of the National Guard was standing there with Don Shook, our alumni director. As we stood there, we watched this bizarre scene of military men trying to push these kids around a very

About noon, May 4, 1970, National Guardsmen begin moving from the Commons toward demonstrators grouped below Taylor Hall and on Blanket Hill at right.

large area of the Commons. That didn't make much sense to me. It appeared that some of the kids were having a lot of fun, although there was tear gas going off. I felt it was a serious confrontation, but many people there did not grasp the significance and importance of what was happening. At any rate, we watched the guardsmen go across the campus and up over behind Taylor Hall where we lost sight of them. When they came back up, we saw them come up to the top of the hill and we saw them turn and kneel. We then heard the firing and saw the smoke. I looked at the PIO and said, "Isn't that dangerous to fire blanks that close?" He turned to me and said, "To my knowledge, no blank ammunition has been issued." Having been in the military, it nearly knocked me over that they were using live ammunition. My second response was, "Wouldn't it be dangerous to shoot live ammunition over their heads?" And the next thing I saw were the ambulances. I actually never got to the site because at that point I knew that I was going to be needed up in the News Service.

A few days later, you visited John Gilligan, a candidate for governor; why was that?
That following Sunday, Anita Dixon, who was to become my wife, and I visited John Gilligan at his home. We asked for that opportunity because we were so upset at what happened. We did not want him to make the same mistakes that others had made. So many people took such incredible sides regarding the shootings. There were people who were writing and saying that they should've shot more students. And of course there were the people on the other side who precipitated the whole action, beginning with the destruction Friday night downtown. But my real feeling about it is that the person who overreacted most was our governor. I think it was an unfortunate circumstance that Robert White was out of town, because I believe he was a capable president. Whether he would have been able to deal with the situation any better if he had been here I don't know; I'm not so sure that any academician, at that point, could have had any control. But when James Rhodes came to Kent on Sunday for the meeting at the fire station with local authorities—when the media showed up—he began to pound tables and put on an act. I have always felt he did that for the benefit of the Senate primary the following week.

Do you think his remarks had much effect?
More than anything else that happened, I believe the governor's remarks on Sunday, May third, had the most significant impact on the subsequent shooting of those four students. He made it very clear, as chief executive of the state, that he was going to be in charge. He said on the one hand that he wanted to keep the University open, but he also stated that there would be no demonstrations, peaceful or otherwise. I think those statements had a most volatile effect on the whole situation. It made a number of students who were just passively involved, and a number of people who weren't even onlookers, extremely angry. I think if he would have had an understanding of the students, he would never have made those kinds of statements. I believe he felt that if he could make a strong show of force that weekend, he was going to win the Senate primary. I also, however, want you to understand that I feel there were a lot of mistakes made by a number of people. There were mistakes made by the students, who didn't understand what they were getting into.

There were mistakes by the aggressive students who didn't comprehend the consequences of their acts, and by the students who were onlookers who had no idea how much their involvement would precipitate further confrontation. And there were mistakes by the University administration because they did not understand that they were in such a tough situation. There was overreaction by the residents of the town, although I think, in some respects, they had a right to overreact with windows being broken and the destruction that was being done.

How did you feel about the arrival on campus of the National Guard?
I had mixed feelings about it. When I went into the army in 1968, I was passively against the war in Vietnam. Ten months later, when I came out, I was actively opposed. In fact, the first thing I did was to march in an antiwar demonstration in Cleveland. But I had a decision to make. I received an offer for a job at the University that was an administrative position. I was very concerned about the system and what was happening. I decided to go to work for the system and try to see what impact I could have from inside, as opposed to actual involvement in the protest movement. So I looked at the arrival of the National Guard both from the perspective of a graduate student and a junior administrator who was concerned about the University. As I recall the situation on Sunday, it seemed fairly calm, almost festive. The image that keeps coming back to me is the image that comes back to other people: the daisy in the gun barrel. And I don't think that was an isolated incident. I believe that the campus generally thought it an unusual situation, but it was not an instance of great hate between the National Guard and the students.

Did you expect a confrontation? Did you feel the Guard's presence was an appropriate response to the situation?
I know that it was an inappropriate way of dealing with the situation, though that is, of course, hindsight. But when the Guard came in, with the kinds of problems downtown and the burning of that building, something had to be done, especially with the destruction of University property. I guess my feeling was that the local police and the sheriff's department could have handled the problem. But you have to keep in mind that my feeling about the Guard at that

point was that it was just a preventative measure, that it was just a way to calm the problem, to try to get the campus back to normal. On Monday morning, when I looked at the guardsmen standing around the burnt remains of the ROTC building, I thought it was ridiculous. When I saw fifteen of them go on line to try to disperse that crowd of several thousand students, I could not believe it. I think Governor Rhodes, without realizing it, challenged those kids to be out there on the Commons and question what he had said the day before. Another dimension of the problem that related to Governor Rhodes had to do with the fear of snipers. Something was said by the governor about snipers, and I am sure that those young guardsmen—and I truly feel that they were victims—were influenced by it. I wore protective [gas] masks several times when I was in the army; you can't breathe and you can hardly see in them. To be wearing them in that kind of situation, with thousands of kids circling around you, was a bizarre circumstance. Also, those troops had just been through what I'm sure was a tiring, frustrating, and threatening situation in the Teamsters' strike in Akron.

What was the reaction you had, knowing they were not blanks being fired?
The first reaction was probably the same as everyone else: one of extreme sadness, grief, shock. But my job was to help facilitate the communication of the facts to the world, and immediately we had all the major networks and national and international media representatives on the campus. Though the University was shut down, the News Service began working fifteen to twenty hours a day. So part of my response was within this framework of trying to help the University deal with this problem the best it could. That was my job. Anita and I decided to talk with John Gilligan because of all the mistakes we felt had been made. We saw the tragedy as a series of mistakes on everyone's part: a chain of events that incredibly led to the shooting of four students on a college campus in the United States. It was our feeling that a number of things could have been done to break that destructive chain. We did not want Gilligan to use the matter in the same way that Governor Rhodes had used it. And there is just no doubt in my mind that I would never have gone to law school and would never have been an attorney had it not been for May 4, 1970.

Is it something you think about?

I think that the community in general has kind of forgotten about the intensity of May 1970. And I think maybe the human mind does that, to avoid remembering the bad things, the painful things. I think that Kent residents have, on a day-to-day basis, forgotten the shootings, and frankly so has the University community except that the memory keeps rearing its head every spring with the commemorations, or as it did with the gym controversy in 1977. As a graduate, with two degrees from Kent State, I am troubled about the fact that this keeps coming up, and I'm afraid that it is going to be with the University forever.

Should the shootings be commemorated?

Oh, I think there are a lot of reasons why people ought to remember Kent State. The kind of military action that took place should never have happened on a college campus, and hopefully it will never happen again. I believe that our military should have as a constant reminder the problems inherent in dealing with public demonstrations, ones that clearly do not warrant the type of military force which the National Guard and the army are prepared to deliver. And I think that young people ought to understand that we have a just system of government that has been developed over a long period of time. We are living under a constitution that has weathered the test of time. If you want to have a real voice for change, whether you are concerned about war or poverty or discrimination, you can have much more of an impact by trying to improve the system that exists rather than dropping out of it or trying to destroy it. And I think that is an extremely important lesson to be learned from the tragedy at Kent State.

After May 4

"Kent State haunts you"

an interview with RUTH GIBSON

RUTH GIBSON *was born in Wheeling, West Virginia, in 1948. She began her freshman year at Kent State University in June 1966 and, as she recalls it, became rapidly "politicized." She served as chairperson of the Kent Committee to End the War in Vietnam during 1967 and 1968; when this group was superseded by the Kent chapter of the Students for a Democratic Society (SDS), Gibson remained politically active but not primarily in a leadership position. She withdrew from classes in the spring of 1970 and left the Kent area shortly after the May 4 shootings. Gibson was among the "Kent 25" indicted by a special state grand jury for charges stemming from the May demonstrations; but those charges were dropped in late 1971. Gibson received her bachelor's degree from Kent State in 1978, and she is currently completing work on a master's degree in history at the University of Akron as well as attending the University of Akron School of Law. This interview transcript is a composite produced from two separate interviews, the first on November 4, 1980, and the second on February 3, 1982.*

What *drew you into the student movement?*
The war, like most people. I had a friend from high school who had enlisted in the army and had been sent to Vietnam by the summer I was starting college. His being there made me think about the war. He wrote me letters with descriptions of the country, and I started to think about the American role there. Then one day I stopped at a literature table in the student center, and I gradually got to know the people involved with the Kent Committee to End the War. My girlfriend supported the war and believed in the domino theory and so forth, and we used to have some pretty good discussions about what was going on. I guess that she and I radicalized each other over a period of about six months. I convinced her to oppose the war, and once she got to that point, she was more critical of the government

than I was. I didn't tie things together as well as she did; I mean, I was a theater major and eighteen and I hadn't really thought about things too terribly much. So she made me think about a host of other issues besides the war. And then meeting more and more people— people who were really impressive, people getting advanced degrees or professors who were against the war.

And the movement was better than any sociology class could ever have been, being around people with varying life experiences. There was one person from VISTA, another who had been in the Peace Corps. This guy was saying one time that the VISTA volunteers could do anything for the Mexican-Americans in southern California, where he had been sent, except help them form a union —which was the only thing that would make any difference in their lives. So I started becoming very suspect of anything that was "official," that was "U.S. government" in any form.

I guess after the antiwar issues, the first thing I started to become aware of was the black power movement. It opened up my mind to domestic issues; it made me realize that there was some kind of relationship between what the United States was doing in Vietnam and the way that minorities were treated in this country. It made me focus on what was wrong with the internal workings of our society. After that, in close order, I began to look at union issues, women's issues . . . and I came to realize that women were never leaders in anything: women always did the secretarial work. We made the leaflets and handed them out, but we often were not on the committees that wrote them. I was an exception; I was a leader. I did write leaflets and dream up the ideas for things to do and very often had to fight it out with different men to get my way. But I don't mean to say that I was always a central figure.

What was the campus political climate in 1970?
There was a great deal of leftist activity. When I had first come to Kent State, the mood was apathy, total indifference. But the antiwar movement changed a lot of things. The Kent Committee to End the War was replaced by SDS in 1968; and SDS was denied the right to organize in a very harsh and high-handed fashion by the University administration after the arrests at the Music and Speech building in the spring of 1969. It was smashed then, though many people had supported the organization. By the fall of 1969, most of the SDS

leaders were in jail or going to jail; some people had left the area altogether; some had become disillusioned and quit school; a few had made up their minds not to be "political" anymore; and things like that. I got kind of disillusioned with SDS after Music and Speech. I realized that any one organization would come and go, but the movement was still going to be there until the goal was attained, at least the one goal of ending the war.

What were the goals; what did you see coming as you looked ahead in the fall of 1969 or early 1970?
Oh, the red revolution, of course. I was just absolutely sure that within five to ten years the student movement would become a much broader social movement, one that would encompass many elements and would be stronger and more explicitly socialist. I thought that the movement would unite all the dissident elements—blacks, Mexican-Americans, workers, etcetera—and was just going to topple the government. The government could no longer relate to or express the will of the people. It was an oppressor, a tyrant government; how could it stand?

What would happen?
I thought that there would be an enormous civil war: a class war, a revolution. A Marxist government would come to power in the United States—not a Soviet-type government, but one which would be responsive to the will of the people, one that would direct the ownership of all major industries by the representatives of the people: the nationalization of all industries. The people would take over the factories.

What about the universities?
Pretty much the same thing. I thought that in the future the administrators would be reduced to something like the medieval level: it would be the professors and the students, as equals, who made the decisions: the professors having the scholarly commitment and the long-term interests of the institution in mind, the students having a more immediate but equally important interest in how the university was run. The university would no longer be a place for doing military research, for developing chemical and biological warfare

weapons. Basically, the domestic counterinsurgency would cease. That is, there would no longer be any organized force to intervene in labor struggles or to try to subvert the black movement. There'd be no more spies trying to infiltrate the SDS or other student organizations on the campus. All that would stop. Well, this was on my good days, when I was really exuberant, when I was feeling really positive about everything that I saw going on and I wasn't depressed about the repression that was coming down. Then I'd get this vision: *this is how it could be*. It seemed like we had the expertise in the movement to run a country.

Was there an active antiwar, radical group at Kent State in the spring of 1970?
No antiwar group, no. But a movement nonetheless. We had seen for two or three years that anyone who was a leader got smashed. This happened over and over again. So finally in the spring of 1970 there weren't any leaders. The University had succeeded in defeating the organizational aspect of the movement by just sending so many people to jail, arresting so many, sapping all the financial resources. But in doing so, the administration created a repressive atmosphere which fueled the movement. The campus became a microcosm of all the reasons why people were against the war. SDS had raised peoples' consciousness to the point where they felt well justified in criticizing the government and being against the government's policies, which had not been the case in previous years. The antiwar movement had been hammering away at University complicity in the war, at the presence of ROTC on the campus.

You were scheduled to graduate?
No, I withdrew. I registered and started to attend classes that spring, but I felt that the classes were meaningless in many respects and were out of touch with reality. The most important thing in the world, as I perceived it, was the international role of the United States, and the University was not related to that except in a sinister way. It was as though Hitler had just come to power and you were in a university studying poetry. It was a very intense kind of time, and I felt that the University was not the place where I could have the most positive effect.

What was your reaction to the April 30 announcement of the Cambodian incursion?
Tremendous anger. I felt that I just couldn't live with that. It made a liar out of Richard Nixon, for everything he had been doing since he became president. I thought this was another part of broadening the war and turning the rest of Southeast Asia into a garrison, the same way the United States was trying to do in Vietnam.

What about the window-smashing downtown—was that political?
Oh, I think it was. If you look at the kinds of places that had their windows smashed, they were banks, rental agencies, home loan associations, and things like that. They had their windows broken and some goods taken out of the store windows; but people weren't going into the stores, fires weren't set in the stores. Most of what happened was, I think, symbolic of rage. I mean, what do you do when you are just so outraged with things which you cannot control? It was not like a mass psychosis, although there were thousands of people, literally thousands, involved in events that spring. The most recent time before that when I remember such large numbers of people demonstrating was in the spring of 1969 when about three thousand students spontaneously marched around campus to protest the treatment of SDS—and these were many times the number of students actually involved with SDS. These were mostly people who had never had any contact with the organization except reading about it in the student newspaper or maybe seeing a demonstration or knowing someone on their dorm floor who went to a meeting once. But thousands of people came out and walked in the rain on a pretty cold day because they were concerned about the lack of democracy. Where is democracy if you don't even play by your own rules and regulations, which is what the administration was doing?

What was the feeling on campus the first days of May 1970?
There was such broad dissatisfaction. I perceived that everybody felt like they had been personally attacked and ripped off by the Cambodian invasion. It looked like many more men were going to be drafted. I think that was on the minds of a lot of students. The ROTC building was a natural focus for dissent. It was on the only area of campus where people could gather in large numbers.

How did you feel when you saw it burning?
I felt pretty good about it. I didn't really feel gleeful in particular, but I understood why the building was burning. It was a symbol in everybody's mind of direct oppression: the direct threat of having to go into a war that you didn't believe in, that you didn't want, that you didn't think your country should be involved in. Right there was a tangible symbol of the military inflicting itself upon us, with the campus being used for the purpose of recruitment, for funnelling young males, for garnering support for programs which were not in the best interest of people in this country.

Were you on campus when the National Guard arrived?
Yes, I was. It was a very surreal experience. It looked like a movie, if that makes any sense. I'd never been around military people very much, but I had of course seen war flicks and pictures of troops. They were getting out of their vehicles and so forth and it looked more like a movie than it did real life. I had to keep reminding myself that everything that had happened was real.

Were you afraid?
No, not at all.

Did you anticipate the confrontations that would follow?
No, I didn't. But a friend of mine did and became very alarmed, and I had the good judgment to listen to his assessment of the situation and we left Kent.

Were you on campus for the noon rally on May fourth?
We got there shortly after hearing about the shootings. I think I was probably more afraid then than any other time. But I had never believed that what happened would happen. My friend's opinion had been that Governor Rhodes would do anything to get elected and that Nixon would back him up. He kept saying over and over: "Someone is going to get killed. Someone *is* going to get killed." He was absolutely sure of it. We had the car radio on as we approached the Commons and heard the report that guardsmen had been killed; we left immediately. We didn't know who had been shot or under what circumstances at that point. We didn't know who would be

next. A lot of people don't understand that there were thousands of people facing off against the National Guard. The same scenario had been playing all weekend. And the students who got shot were up over a hill behind a building. There were many guardsmen deployed to the campus, but only a handful did this crime. A lot of people don't realize this. They think that the guardsmen were being overwhelmed by hordes of screaming, long-haired radicals who were absolutely tearing those guardsmen limb from limb. And that is not at all what happened. Quite the opposite. I think the shootings were a very calculated move, designed for certain specific political, not military, purposes. It was, "We're going to get out there and win over these hearts and minds because we're going to scare the shit out of these people. We're going to make every college kid in the country think that they are going to get shot dead if they demonstrate against the war." I think that was a lot of the purpose of it. At the time, I didn't see Kent State as ending anything; I thought that it was raising things to a new level. With Jackson State happening right on the heels of it, it seemed to me that it was a very clear message to the radical left—the main support of which came from university students: "If you keep opposing us so vocally, we are going to kill you."

Then you left the area?
I immediately split from Kent and I left the state of Ohio. I left with very little money and very few things; I was truly scared to death.

When did you hear about your inclusion in the "Kent 25" indictments?
The indictments came out sometime in October 1970. I was living in California at the time. Somebody let me know about the indictment, even though they were supposed to be secret. I came back to Kent in January 1971 and turned myself in to Portage County authorities.

How was the matter resolved?
The state prosecutors later said that they had no evidence and asked the court to drop the charges and the court agreed. This was in November 1971. It was an incredible period of time. It was nearly a year and there was incredible pressure. I really felt that given the prior experience of students in Portage County, all it took was the testimony of any kind of informer, any kind of disreputable person

or any cop to be put in jail. I didn't think there was any way I could avoid going to [the women's reformatory at] Marysville, Ohio. I came back to fight the indictment but with the full expectation that I would go to jail for maybe seven years. I didn't regret it at the time —maybe I didn't think deeply enough about it, but I made the decision. I don't regret it now. I felt that I represented a group of people who were being indicted for opposing the war, who were being indicted for opposing militarism in this society and the marriage of big business and the military. People who oppose the system tend to get smashed, and that is what we all found out. But there was a lot of support for us. Locally, for about a year or so, we were like minor celebrities. Other people handled that better than me; I tried to avoid the public eye as much as possible. I had been arrested before, for an antiwar action in which I had written in chalk on the library wall, then was handcuffed and taken downtown. I was almost nineteen years old at the time.

Was that at Kent State?
Yes. I was writing, "Strike Against the War April 15." It was the spring of 1967. I was the first person in my family that I knew of to be arrested. I never want to go through it again. I've been arrested four times altogether for activities at Kent State, and I never want to go through it again. It got worse each time. It was always more humiliating than the time before, more confining. You lose your dignity when that happens to you. And there was a whole history of trivial arrests of antiwar activists at Kent State before May 1970. And in spite of that repression, a movement developed.

After charges were dropped in connection with the "Kent 25," did your politics or your political notoriety continue to precede you?
Yes. Kent State haunts you in that way. Before I came back to answer the indictment, for instance, James Michener had visited Kent. I never met Mr. Michener and never regretted not having met him. He was gullible, and he wrote a book in which he just printed any old kind of thing. Many people read it, and that book shaped people's attitudes toward me. I went to visit a friend of mine about eight months after the book was serialized in *Reader's Digest*, and her mother would not let me into their house because she had read about me and was not sure that I was a nice person. Finally, my friend's

dad came home and let me in, and he was certainly no radical. He said, "What is this? Do you believe everything you read?" But I couldn't get a job anywhere. I'd show up to apply for a position— something like chambermaid or waitress—and they'd find out that I was Ruth Gibson and there wasn't a job anymore. The job had already been filled, but the next day I'd read the same ad in the newspaper.

But more important were my feelings about myself. For a long time after May 1970 I felt that Allison or Sandy shouldn't have been killed—that it should have been me, that I was more the guilty party, that I more deserved death because I had been a leader. They weren't leaders; they hadn't asked anyone to come out there that day. I felt like they were surrogates for me, that really what those guardsmen were trying to do was to kill anybody they thought was a leader; they were symbolically firing at all the people who disagreed with them. The people who died were relatively innocent; their activism was minimal. Not that they were culpable and deserved death or that any of us did, but internally I just felt that somehow my worth was lessened, that somehow they should've lived and I should've died in their place—and that would've been more just. Afterwards, I didn't feel like there was a place for me anymore, that I could do anything.

I guess that's what it did to me, that's how it haunted me: it made me feel bad about myself; it made me feel bad about the fact that I was alive. It was five years or more before I started to feel, "Hey, my life is passing me by; there's got to be some fulfillment in life, it can't all be bitterness." I don't know how Allison Krause's father feels now, but I know he was powerfully bitter at the time, consumed by his bitterness and *rage* at what happened. And I felt that too, but I also felt like I was culpable—and I knew objectively at the time that I wasn't, that I didn't pull a trigger, that I didn't plan a murder, that I didn't have any part in bringing it about.

The fear that the Kent 25 indictment and other arrests will hurt me is still there, but I don't think, for the most part, that it would be the individuals who were around in 1970 who will condemn me. It's going to be the idiots who were twelve years old at the time, who only remember what their parents told them was the right way to think and screamed: "They should've killed some more; I'll never let you go to Kent State and become one of those radicals. And if you do, I hope you get shot too." I don't think history is going to condemn the students; I think it will see us in a humane perspective. We weren't successful in bringing about the great revolutionary change; but we had it in our hearts that day, and I think there are many of us still who have that in our hearts. Maybe we're the true patriots— though I hate to use that word. Maybe we're the real lovers of our country and our people and the real lovers of freedom and democracy—not the people who just wave the flags on the right days. I think that we're very much veterans to be honored, the same as the Vietnam veterans. Of course, the Vietnam veterans didn't get any honor either. So maybe we're all in the same boat after all. I never conceived of our troops in Southeast Asia as my enemy; I saw them more or less as a captive army: captive civilians made to wear the uniform. I never saw them as killers or professional hired guns. They were not the enemy any more than the Vietnamese were. And certainly the students weren't the enemies of democracy: the government was and probably still is.

The Ones They Missed with Bullets

BILL ARTHRELL *attended Kent State University from 1968 to 1973, when he received his bachelor's degree. In October 1970, he, like Ruth Gibson, was among the twenty-five people indicted by a state grand jury investigating the shootings of May 4. Since that time, Arthrell has remained active in annual commemorations, and he played a prominent role in the May 4th Coalition in 1977. He is currently a teacher in the Cleveland Public Schools. This essay describes his thoughts and feelings in the fall of 1970.*

"The ones they missed with bullets, they got with indictments."

Kent 25 maxim

The Revolution had arrived. It headlined leaflets passed out in front of the Student Union. It was in the conversations about Angela Davis in the cafeteria at Tri-Towers dormitory. It was the relevant topic for discussion in a sociology or political science class. It was satirized by Yippie smoke-ins at the University Auditorium and by radical bullhorns on the Commons. It was debated at the literature tables of the Young Socialist Alliance and the Vietnam Veterans Against the War. It was scrawled on the bathroom walls in the library: "Nixon, the only dope worth shooting." It was celebrated in song by the Jefferson Airplane at Memorial Gym while slides of student rebellion flashed behind them.

We listened. For four days in May, the streets were ours. We turned the Nixon invasion of Cambodia into an unprecedented student response at home. But the National Guard had responded too. Among the bullhorns, leaflets, and rallies, and right around the corner from the draft resistance table, point blank from a sign that declared *Free Bobby Seale*, was the hill. Clamoring around it was a

University galvanized by the spirit of the Revolution. At its crest was a quiet spot that only knew silence by contrast. The wind that blew through the grasses on Blanket Hill had been shattered five months before. The Revolution of the fall of 1970 was a response to the repression of May 1970. The National Guard had put us up against the wall and pulled the trigger. Four of us lay dead. James Rhodes had called us the "worst elements we harbor in America." Nine were wounded. Vice President Agnew termed student leftists "effete snobs" and referred to a lone man who shouted at him at a rally as "an agent of the North Vietnamese." Twenty-five would be indicted. Nixon concluded: "When dissent turns to violence it invites tragedy." Repression had arrived.

I walked past *Free Bobby Seale*, across the practice football field on my way to a meeting of the Kent Medical Fund at the student center, which had been nicknamed the "Hub." Of course, the same state that shot thirteen students would not reimburse them for their astronomical medical bills. So student activists were raising the money in between going to classes and protesting the war. The wind had returned to the grasses on this crisp October night. I thought of James Taylor doing "Fire and Rain."

I remembered a woman in Fletcher Hall that I was falling in love with. I thought of Crosby, Stills, Nash, and Young singing "Ohio," a song that had so well captured the emotions of the past spring, its militance and sadness: if you had seen the deaths at Kent State or had been moved by them at a distance, how could your life be the same?

There was a voice behind me: "Arthrell! Stop!" I had been stopped before by the campus police. They would routinely frisk me, put me in the back seat of a squad car, question me about my purpose on the campus, then turn to me matter-of-factly and ask: "Hey, Bill, could we see your ID?" It was petty harassment, but it was effective. Sen. Stephen Young of Ohio had charged that fifty FBI agents were enrolled at Kent State as students. In a secret FBI file lifted in Media, Pennsylvania, J. Edgar Hoover had pronounced: "We are out to create an atmosphere of extreme paranoia on the campuses—as if there's an FBI agent behind every mailbox." There was no mailbox on the Commons, but I ran anyway. "Arthrell!" The sound of my name got closer. It breathed down my back.

I knew it wasn't a cop then. Too fast. It was my friend Greg

Haley. I turned and grabbed him by his pony tail and tussled him to the ground. We wrestled for a moment on the Commons. But his grip on me was not feigned. "Arthrell," he said, looking as paranoid as Hoover wanted him to, "don't go in the Hub. The cops are in there, and they want to arrest you."

"Paranoid—you're paranoid, Greg. And you know what? You're not the only one who's paranoid." We turned the other way. Our frolic became a mad dash to Tri-Towers.

Kent State had acted out the paranoia in Buffalo Springfield's "For What It's Worth." There were uniformed police in the dormitory lobbies. They had videos in the hallways. Periodically, cops checked the bathrooms for "subversive" activities. When two thousand students marched on the Administration Building on October 16, 1970 to demand an end to ROTC and the dropping of the Kent 25 indictments, President Robert White was unavailable. The state legislature joined the assault on civil liberties. It passed a bill making campus "disruption" a crime but never bothered to define the term. Thus, any dissent could be deemed disruptive. Finally, James Rhodes, the same governor who had called in the National Guard, convened a special grand jury to study the killings. The state attorney general predicted that no guardsmen would be indicted. When his prophecy came true, the special prosecutor for the state, Seabury Ford, said: "They shoulda shot all the troublemakers."

This same grand jury was about to indict me. And so the police checked my apartment when I was in class, checked my classes when I cut them, and were searching the Hub when Greg Haley ran me down. Yippie Jerry Persky called the indictments the "Academy Awards of the Revolution." Jodie Zahler claimed that people who weren't called before the grand jury had "subpoena envy." Our contemporary Voltaires had done everything they could to defuse the explosiveness of the Kent 25 indictments. But no matter how humorous they were, it was a reign of terror that swept the campus.

Colin Kruchetch and Debbie Cohen joined us in Greg's room in Tri-Towers. "It's ironic," I said as I remembered the old quote from Malcolm X: "The system makes the murderers the victims and the victims the murderers."

"Here we are," I said, "harassed by police, indicted by a grand jury, denounced by the president, spied on by the army, infiltrated by the FBI—and we were the ones who got shot." The grand jury report had not only exonerated the National Guard but also berated students for going barefoot, decried professors for not saluting the flag, and condemned the KSU administration for allowing the Yippies to meet on campus. It hardly seemed to notice that four students were killed. In a literary sense, it *was* ironic. In a personal sense, it was frightening. Politically, it was entangled in the whole web of repression that began against the black movement in the 1960s and then zeroed in on the student movement. It was a system trying to perpetuate itself abroad in the name of peace and justify itself at home in the name of democracy. But democracy at home had become as vacuous as peace in Vietnam. Truly, the war had come home, and we had become the enemy.

Vietnam was not as remote as the thousands of miles that separated Kent State from the Mekong Delta. Four of us had died protesting the same government that was killing thousands in Southeast Asia. And the war wasn't over yet.

That night as we drove Greg's Volkswagen out of the Tri-Towers parking lot, a cop pulled us over for a "routine" check. "Colin, you'd better get out of the car," he said. Greg was wearing a red-and-white t-shirt that read: "Kent Police State University." Colin got back in the car. "Let's get the hell out of here. These cops are like spiders, not pigs. They're everywhere." The police had enlarged their dragnet to searching Volkswagens and other "leftwing" vehicles. "Good thing they didn't bother to search the car," I said. We followed Route 43 north to the turnpike and then headed east toward Pittsburgh.

I was wanted in Kent for second degree riot, stemming from May 4, 1970. It had been a day on which, according to the Scranton Commission, there was no riot. The charge was a misdemeanor, and I could not be extradited across the state line from Pennsylvania. Colin made a joke about me not being able to throw a brick straight enough to be a first-degree rioter. A year in jail for a joke. Like a knife, paranoia cut the humor in half.

Nearly four thousand students had rallied for the Kent 25 just days before our departure from Kent. The featured speaker was Craig Morgan, the student body president, who was the first to be indicted. It was as if the grand jury wanted to indict the whole campus. Morgan wasn't even a radical. He was a member of the same ROTC which many students abhorred. As if the local authorities were dishing out a smorgasbord for a famished executioner, they indicted a diverse enough group to satisfy his terrible appetite: a left-liberal sociology professor named Tom Lough, several former SDS members, a couple pacifists, a nonstudent or two to prove the "outside agitator" theory, and even two students who were wounded by the National Guard. The latter were apparently guilty of getting in the way of bullets.

Then there was me: nineteenth in a dragnet that included about one or two arrests a day. The elongated, methodical process made everyone stop and ask: "Am I next?" People had plenty of time to ponder their fate. Thus a reign of terror was unleashed on the campus. Ken Hammond, Dave Adams, Jerry Rupe, Mary Helen Nicholas, and others were arrested. The repression set in like an ice age. There was little break in its rhythm. We were in the throes of a constitutional crisis long before Watergate.

The grand jury declared itself irreproachable. An injunction was issued which prevented people who had testified before the grand jury from criticizing its findings. One man in Kent who tried to prevent the entire Bill of Rights from being suspended was Glenn Frank, a geology professor. Perhaps because of his conventional air, he was totally appalled at the official censure of dissent. He called the injunction "an aberration of justice" and was subsequently arrested for that statement. It was only an ice pick against the north pole, but it was a challenge against repression by a respected teacher and a bonafide nonradical. If he could see the war that the establishment had declared on the political left, then maybe justice would not be completely lost.

These thoughts were chilling to me as we came full upon Pittsburgh early one October morning. We had arrived. I had gone underground. I was outraged at the magnitude of injustice and humbled by the vulnerability of being the next victim.

It was an overwhelming time to be alive. It was, that is, for those of us who were still alive. Four of us hadn't made it at Kent State. That same infamous spring, six blacks were gunned down during racial strife in Augusta, Georgia. A week after Augusta and nearly two weeks after the deaths at Kent State, the next of us were sent reeling from gunshot wounds: on May 14, blacks at Jackson State College in Mississippi acted out an age-old conflict between themselves and the local police. A barrage of gunfire greeted protesting students. When the smoke cleared, Alexander Hall, a student dormitory, was riddled with bullet holes. James Earl Green and Phillip Gibbs were dead.

June graduation in 1970 was not the joyous occasion it was designed to be. The deaths of that spring overwhelmed the class of 1970. Nearly half of the two million graduates from the nation's colleges and universities simply refused to participate in the ceremonies. Many who did wore black armbands on their gowns. The sense of personal achievement had been replaced by a national sense of horror. Jesse Jackson implored Oberlin College graduates to emulate Fidel Castro and Mao Tse-tung and use their education to topple the system. Even Nixon's conservative attorney general, John Mitchell, called this commencement "the most tragic graduation in American history." The *Cleveland Plain Dealer* depicted the "Class of '70" as a black-shrouded specter receiving a Kent State diploma.

For those of us who returned to college in the fall, a dark cloud still loomed ominously on the political horizon. Pensively, we returned to our campuses in much the same way a GI might return to Omaha Beach. Indeed, Kent State seemed a similar battlefield, and we were now veterans of domestic wars. We didn't have to listen too hard to hear the anguished cry of another war going on half-way

Bill Arthrell is arrested with 192 other protestors at the site of Tent City on July 12, 1977.

around the world. In Vietnam, few had a chance to graduate. Nixon's "Vietnamization" program meant turning American casualties into Vietnamese casualties. "Protective reaction" strikes were code words for bombing North Vietnam. The "strategic hamlet" program uprooted peasants and moved them to areas where they could be more closely proctored for Viet Cong sympathies. The president's claim that this was "pacification" had nothing more to do with peace than the Kent 25 indictments had to do with justice.

Still the war went on. Still I was indicted. We approached a collective of radical lawyers in downtown Pittsburgh. Like many others of my generation, my feelings about Kent State were inseparable from the Vietnam War. Rennie Davis had called us the "most important generation in American history." We were not only the largest, but also probably the only generation that had such a sense of itself and its own mission that it fashioned a revolution in that image. College students, high school kids, disenchanted hippies, even disillusioned GI's. Had all America been young in 1970, we would have been the spearhead of a revolution instead of the object of repression. But America wasn't young. It was old men sending young men off to war. It was old corporations looking for new foreign markets. It was a generational gap that pitted "The Times They Are A-changing" against "America right or wrong."

I was twenty-one years old as I walked up the stairs to the law firm's offices. Reading Marcuse, admiring Che Guevara, I was a card-carrying member of the 1960s generation. I held Debbie Cohen's hand as we opened the door. I was scared. I was young and felt the burden of the world on my shoulders. So did we all. I was a legal virgin and had gone underground to avoid losing that virginity. I looked at Debbie Cohen and thought of the lyrics that wafted over the Commons the night before. The anger of spring returned to my soul, replacing the fear and anxiety of October. Confidence flushed my face. Debbie caught my look in her brown eyes. As I introduced myself to an attorney, I had a thought that would guide me through that fall and through the end of the Kent 25 trials more than a year later: the indictment was my "red badge of courage." I would not shrink from that responsibility. We returned to Kent a few hours later, where I proudly turned myself in. I had known Sandy Scheuer. If she couldn't live, then I knew I would try to live my life in such a way that war abroad and injustice at home would never again afflict a Sandy Scheuer, or a Debbie Cohen.

I didn't know whether I would be convicted or absolved of a crime I didn't commit. I knew that I wasn't returning to Kent just to be another casualty of an arrogant establishment. I was returning to Kent to find my way to a justice that might take a lifetime in attaining. Perhaps I was just naïve enough to believe that I could expose a system by becoming a temporary victim of it. The car radio repeated the haunting lyrics of "Ohio" as our VW reentered the state. I knew too much, and in Nixon's America, there was nowhere to run.

The Frustrations of a Former Activist

by KENNETH R. CALKINS

KENNETH R. CALKINS *is associate professor of history at Kent State University, where he has taught since 1967. He was involved in the drafting of the "Statement of 23 Concerned Faculty," which was released May 3, 1970, and he was present on the University Commons the next day when the shootings occurred. Calkins served as chair of the Portage County branch of the American Civil Liberties Union from 1973 to 1974.*

The militant movement against the war in Vietnam which swept through American colleges and universities over a decade ago dramatically revealed to many sympathetic faculty members the full complexity of their relationship to their radical students. Those of us who were teaching at Kent State University in May of 1970 are fully aware that the quandaries which we faced in this regard were in many respects far from unique. Nevertheless, the violence which occurred at Kent State and the emotions and soul-searching analysis which that violence inevitably engendered may have disclosed some of the more problematical aspects of this relationship more forcefully and perhaps, therefore, more clearly to us than to our colleagues elsewhere.

Undoubtedly, one of the primary reasons for the sense of confusion and perplexity which many of us experienced in 1970 was that we had too easily assumed the existence of a natural affinity between progressive faculty members and students which would assure not only that we would be permanent allies but also that we could confidently expect to be turned to if not for leadership at least for sage advice during any crisis which might develop. We were well aware of the fact that by teaching our students to think critically we had fostered the cast of mind which encouraged political activism, but we were surprised and perturbed when some of our most able protégés began to turn their developing talents against the institutions which provided us with our status and livelihood—and even against ourselves, their mentors. As fellow members of the academic community, we had taken it for granted that they shared with us a fundamental commitment to the virtues of rational debate, and we were nonplussed by efforts to shout down exponents of rival points of view and by blatant appeals to passion and attacks upon the subtleties of normal intellectual discourse.

Moreover, not a few of us had been activists either as students or as younger faculty members and felt that we deserved respect for our involvement at a time when assaults upon the establishment were far less socially acceptable than they had recently become. In my own case, I much too easily assumed that the fact that I had been one of the founders of the Student Peace Union and had spent a few weeks in jail as a result of a peace demonstration a dozen years earlier would confer upon me a perpetual immunity from the censures of this new generation of agitators. I was not a little discomforted when these ancient exploits were blithely ignored.

Of course, the circumstances which forced us ultimately to reassess our relationship to our radical students did not emerge suddenly in May 1970. I recall that as adviser to the local chapter of the Students for a Democratic Society at Lake Forest College, where I taught before coming to Kent State, I had experienced some uneasy moments with several students whom I had helped to transport to Chicago for a demonstration against the House Un-American Activities Committee. They had decided to cross police barriers in order to invade the chambers in which the committee was holding its hearings. I had no ideological objection to their doing so; after all, I had engaged in similar activities not too many years earlier. But I was certainly troubled by the fact that I was in some sense responsible for them, and by my own reluctance for personal reasons to join them.

It was not long after I arrived in Kent in the fall of 1967 that I participated in my first antiwar activity on the University campus. In this case, our "demonstration" consisted of an extremely modest vigil, and, as I recall, a large proportion of the two dozen or so participants were faculty members. In fact, I was informed at the time that earlier, similar efforts had met with an unfriendly, even threatening, response on the part of groups of patriotic students.

Within the course of the next year, however, antiwar and anti-Establishment sentiment grew rapidly at Kent State, as it did elsewhere. A militant chapter of the SDS soon replaced the ideologically radical but rather proper Young Socialist Alliance as the most visible group on the left and began to attract some of our brightest and most socially concerned students. The Black United Students also emerged as a force to be reckoned with, and in November of 1968 these two groups jointly occupied (in a rather quaintly segregated fashion) a campus building in an effort to disrupt recruiting efforts by the Oakland Police Department. I remember experiencing at the time my first real feelings of incompetence, even irrelevance, as I watched a massed body of the SDS, led by one of my favorite students, salute with raised clenched fists a contingent of black students as they marched off campus at the conclusion of that demonstration.

These feelings became still stronger in the course of a new confrontation the following April between the University administration and the SDS. On this occasion, a complicated series of events led to what in my opinion was a deliberate attempt to entrap and arrest a large number of SDS members and their sympathizers in the Music and Speech Building. By this time, other sympathetic faculty and I were feeling increasingly alienated by the bombastic and naïve rhetoric of the SDS as well as by some of the organization's tactics. But when confronted by the spectacle of several hundred students trapped by police on the third floor of one of our "halls of learning," my sympathies were necessarily on the side of the students. Having accidentally run into a colleague who shared my feelings of frustration and indignation, and who also possessed a key to the elevator in the building, I did not hesitate to join him in a partially successful effort to free the captives. Even this act, however, was marred by ambiguity, for it was clear that our intervention could, in fact, be viewed as serving to help the authorities to escape the full impact of their misguided attempt to crush the student movement. Such disquieting thoughts were reinforced by the fact that when my colleague and I were eventually caught in the act by the police we were not treated like the students, who were being herded under guard into buses for transportation to the county jail, but were instead released after having been held only briefly. There was, to be sure, some satisfaction to be gained from the fact that this bizarre series of events culminated in the creation of a very large ad hoc committee which conducted a vociferous and broadly supported campaign on behalf of civil liberties, but in the long run one could not escape the recognition that more than civil liberties were involved in the struggle that was unfolding.

By May of 1970, therefore, we at Kent State were not inexperienced in endeavoring to cope with student demonstrations and administration provocations. Unfortunately, our efforts thus far had given us little cause for confidence. In fact, many of us had begun to view ourselves primarily as observers rather than actors in the stirring events that were sweeping across the nation's campuses. The events of that fateful May simply, if tragically, confirmed that such was indeed the case.

Nevertheless, when it became apparent that in the wake of the American invasion of Cambodia a new series of demonstrations could be expected, most of us did not hesitate to volunteer to serve as faculty marshals. I am not certain what I expected to accomplish when I donned my blue armband on May 2, but I soon discovered that what I could actually do was precious little. I think that in a sense those members of the faculty who were most sympathetic to the ultimate goals of the student radicals were least likely to have any serious impact on the developing situation. Symptomatic of the weakness of my own position was the fact that soon after arriving on the Commons, near the ROTC building which was soon to be set afire, one of my best students asked me to warn her and her comrades if I should see police approaching. None of these students were concerned about what I thought of their tactics. Because I would not, could not, join them, I had become largely irrelevant. The most that could be said for me, from their point of view, was that I was not likely to assist the authorities against them.

In this, of course, they were correct, but the very fact that I could neither lead the students nor cooperate with their opponents meant that I, along with many of my colleagues, was essentially in limbo. The most that we could do that night and during the next two days was to intervene in particular limited situations, such as in assisting groups of students trapped by National Guard sweeps to get back to their dormitories. The one concerted effort by progressive faculty to alter the tragic course of events, the issuance by some twenty-three of us of a statement protesting the appearance of the National

Guard on our campus, appeared to have no effect at all except to provide yet another excuse for the exponents of "law and order" to castigate the subversive element among the professoriate.

By noon on May 4, we had been reduced essentially to the status of mere spectators. We watched powerlessly as the National Guard marched across the Commons under a brilliant blue sky and listened incredulously and in horror as they fired their weapons at our students. The paradoxical character of my own position was revealed once again when after the troops had withdrawn from the site of the killings I walked down among the large number of students who, not knowing how else to demonstrate their anger and frustration, had sat down on the hill across from the threatening line of soldiers. Only a few years earlier I had myself engaged in such peaceful sit-down demonstrations, even in the face of violent threats, but now I did my best to persuade these students to get up and leave in fear that the Guard would unleash still another deadly volley.

Of course, there were undoubtedly some faculty members across the country who became so fully involved in the radical movement that they were able to exert considerable influence for good or ill. At Kent State, however, and I suspect at most other institutions, the vast majority even of those who were sincerely committed to ending the war and achieving fundamental social and political change shared at least to some degree in the sense of impotence I have described. Moreover, it would appear that the very character of our profession makes it unlikely that we will be able to play a more significant role in any similar future crisis. Although we share many of the same values as our students, few of us enjoy their independence from institutional and personal attachments or their extraordinary freedom to experiment, to act clearly and decisively on the basis of their convictions. Moreover, we are inhibited by our commitment to dispassionate intellectual analysis and by the skepticism which both that commitment and our greater awareness of the past almost necessarily entail. It is, of course, quite possible that in the future either more serious threats to academic freedom or more obvious opportunities for rapid and radical change will alter this situation, but until such changes occur, it is probably best for both students and faculty frankly to recognize the limitations which their differing experiences and roles impose upon their relationship.

A View from Europe

by LAWRENCE S. KAPLAN

LAWRENCE S. KAPLAN *is University professor of history and director of the Lyman L. Lemnitzer Center for NATO Studies at Kent State University. He has been Fulbright Lecturer in American History at the Universities of Bonn, Louvain, and Nice. In 1969–70, he was visiting research scholar and lecturer in History at University College, University of London.*

To have been a teacher of American diplomatic history in Europe in the academic year 1969–70 was by definition to be on the defensive. To have been a Kent State professor in Europe on May 4, 1970, was to be a magnet for hostile attention from academics everywhere. The tragedy on the Kent campus was as much a signal for students throughout Western Europe as it was for American students in the United States to protest against the war in Vietnam. But the sharpness and bitterness of their hostility were a product of years of European discontent with American leadership over issues outside the Vietnam War.

The academic year 1969–70 was the third opportunity granted me to live in a European university community, with ten years separating the first from the third experience. Europe in 1959 had just organized the European Economic Community and had not forgotten the enormous efforts the United States had made in providing the psychological as well as the economic infrastructure for the revival of Europe. NATO was a success, at least to the extent of providing political and military security to Europeans after the Second World War. The popularity of American studies, and of American culture generally, was testimony of appreciation for the new power in the West and for its generally benevolent expression of that power. This was nowhere more true than in West Germany, at the University of Bonn, where young Germans looked to Americans to

shield them from the still lively memories of Nazi bestiality in World
War II. The firmness of John Foster Dulles's stance against the
Soviet Union was a comfort to most Europeans as the 1950s drew to
a close.

Why warm feelings for America seemed to dissipate over the decade of the 1960s is most easily explained by the revulsion felt over
American involvement in Southeast Asia. There was a sense that the
leadership of a nation which could entangle itself in the bog of Indochina was incapable of leading the "free world" elsewhere. Even
more seriously, the destructiveness of American military power
appeared as brutal as any action of World War II, and its object
more absurd or more dangerous. Was it communism or nationalism
that was attacked in Southeast Asia? Was it a pattern of American
politics to support reactionary corrupt regimes such as those of
South Vietnam? These were the questions raised by youths in Europe over that decade. The invasion of Cambodia and the subsequent killings on the Kent campus seemed to justify the charge that
America was a mindless machine incapable of knowing its own best
interests, or an imperialist power seeking to tamp down by force
obstacles in its path to power. Much of the language opposing
American policy was expressed in simplistic Marxist terms. The notion that the Soviet Union was the defensive element in the symbi-
otic Russian-American relationship and that communism was pref-
erable to American capitalism were the motifs in the anti-American
mobilization.

This explanation omits too much. European antagonism toward
the United States has deeper explanations, which should at least be
mentioned here. They range from the natural resentment of beneficiary against benefactor, against the wealth and enormous resources of the New World which could patronize an intrinsically
superior Old World. Inevitably, as the Europeans recovered their
economic strength and political self-consciousness, they would
chafe at the symbols of power which America maintained in Europe:
from American companies which seemed to dominate European industry to the American military presence which seemed to establish
an *imperium in imperio*. Innocent though the intention may have
been, the sight of a Firestone advertisement in English on a bill-
board welcoming travelers to the city of Antwerp in 1959 was an of-
fense to Belgian national sensibilities. Similarily, gas stations in

Germany, advertising in English and reserved exclusively for U.S. forces, were a symbol of extraterritoriality which not even the carefully drawn NATO status-of-forces agreements could erase. (The latter sought to defuse the question of American occupation by placing off-duty troops or civilians charged with crimes under the jurisdiction of the host authority.)

Perhaps the deepest source of difficulty, one that the Vietnam War brought to the surface, was the European sense of the unworthiness of an essentially uncultivated America to assume the leadership of Western civilization traditionally the possession of Europeans. Their ambivalence to Charles de Gaulle underscored this mood. While they might deplore his anti-British prejudice, his nationalist pretensions, and his imperious personality, they were intrigued by his idea of the notion of a civilized Europe as a third force. Independent Europe would spread from the Atlantic to the Urals and serve as a mediator between the barbarians of the West and the East. This vision always appeared to have been a source of satisfaction to Europeans of my acquaintance.

For a generation, America's fallibilities raised doubts about the quality of its leadership. In addition to the continuing fears, exacerbated by de Gaulle, that America might trade off Europe's security in favor of its own as it dealt with a nuclear-armed Soviet Union, Europeans were periodically presented with putative examples of America's incapacity for leadership. During my year at Bonn I was often admonished that the McCarthyism of the 1950s had been a species of Hitlerism. In Leuven, Belgium, the U.S. invasion of the Dominican Republic in the spring of 1965 inspired "Yankee Go Home" flyers which were distributed by Latin American students in my classes. In 1970, the American absorption with the Vietnam conflict united most Europeans in opposition: conservatives worrying about neglect of Europe, liberals concerned with the distortion of containment, and radicals convinced that Vietnam was the latest stage in America's plan for world control.

Throughout 1969–70, I had opportunities from my base at the University of London to speak before many of the university communities in the United Kingdom, trying to place American foreign policy of the 1960s into a historical perspective. Hostility was by no means uniform before May 4. The role of NATO as a guarantor of Europe's growth was more often recognized as a positive feature of

American statecraft. My single most difficult moment was at a public lecture on the historiography of the cold war at University College, London, in March 1970, where students from a number of London colleges interrupted me to assert that American professors presenting a different point of view from mine were summarily dismissed from their posts. The well-known Marxist scholar, William Appleman Williams, was a case in point for them. His resignation from the University of Wisconsin and subsequent removal to the wilds of Oregon State University were interpreted as forced exile. That the decision was voluntary—and that it may have been prompted by too many graduate students taking up too much of his research time in Madison—was not credible to the audience. It seemed to me that many British students were prisoners of an image of America which the Marxist rhetoric of many European universities had successfully imposed over the past ten years. The Cambodian invasion and the Kent State shootings became proofs of the validity of their perceptions.

As shocking as the headlines in the *London Times* were on the morning of May 5, the reaction a week later of University of London students was even more upsetting. The news from Kent catapulted the university into public prominence. Students of the University of London's Institute of Education convened a protest meeting of their Union and invited Prof. Charles C. Chandler, then a visiting member of that Institute from Kent's College of Education, to attend. As a fellow Kent State professor I was invited to speak as well. Both of us expressed our horror over the event, our empathy with the families of the slain students and with our bereaved University community. We concluded by expressing our hope that the intrinsic strength of American society would assert itself and that the stricken University would recover from this traumatic blow. Our somewhat disjointed speeches evoked no sympathy from the audience. They shouted us down, with voices urging not reconstruction of the University, but the tearing down of Kent and all other such tools of a repressive Establishment. American institutions were hopeless, they claimed, and liberal faculty members like Chandler and myself were tools of those who killed and maimed students on our campus. A few defenders in the audience, including a former visiting professor at Kent, had no better success than we had in winning over the aroused audience.

One memory of that occasion remains vivid today: the most articulate and persistent questioner was a young graduate student who seemed to know Kent well and recalled troubles on our campus in 1968 and 1969 with great accuracy. When I spoke with her privately after the meeting ended, her outrage over the killings was not tempered by her apparent feeling that Kent State was not worthy of its martyrdom. I had the impression that the honor of leading American protest belonged to a college such as her own— Oberlin.

Student reaction to May 4 was not confined to England. It was equally intense and widespread on the Continent. Shortly before May 4, I had scheduled a two-week lecture tour of ten German universities for late May and early June, under the auspices of the U.S. Information Service. The subject was to be American foreign policy since World War II, with emphasis upon NATO rather than the Third World. The tragedy of May 4 affected my trip in every particular. First, the subject was no longer European-American relations; it was Cambodia, Southeast Asia, and American politico-military policy under Nixon. Second, the passions of the German student audience were raised by my association with Kent State. As in other nations, Kent was the flashpoint of all discontents with American leadership at this moment, and my academic ties along with the sponsorship of the State Department made comprehensible if not quite accurate the epithet of "paid lackey."

The most immediate reactions were threatened demonstrations at the universities of Hamburg, Kiel, and Munich. These were institutions I had visited during my Fulbright years in Bonn and Leuven, five and ten years earlier, with seeming success. Ten years before, German students were excessively deferential to spokesmen of the one NATO country which was willing to forget the crimes of World War II; five years before, German students felt European enough to evaluate more critically but also more reasonably American foreign policy. In 1970, German universities under sway of a violent radical student movement looked upon Kent State as a red flag to rally others to their cause. In Hamburg a police cordon inhibited a plan to start a riot; in Munich my incendiary "Kent State" identification was replaced with a neutral "University of London" label; in Kiel the lecture was abandoned altogether. In other university cities, however, such as Freiburg, Düsseldorf, Regensburg, and Saarbrücken, the excitement was high but the discourse rational. In each of the above my talk was strongly supported by German colleagues and by students willing to listen to a variety of points of view. Unlike my feelings in London, my mood was high as I accepted the challenge and the response.

The most enlightening time in this tour was a two-day stay at a resort south of Hanover where a symposium, supported jointly by the university and the U.S. Information Service in Hanover, brought together Gymnasium students to discuss all aspects of American society. These were well-educated students of senior high school and junior college level, drawn for the most part from an elite stratum of society. Here there was a chance not only to hear their anxieties about accusations against American policy but also to respond in some depth. They were willing ultimately, I believe, to accept the idea that while I may have been a paid agent of the Information Service, the contents of my talks were not written for me. There was no censorship. I was as free to criticize the behavior of the United States as they were. Whether I was able to wean the students away from a conventional monistic economic explanation of history is unlikely; I would have been satisfied if they had recognized something about the complexity of historical causation, of the origins of the Vietnam War in American virtues as well as in American vices. There was, I believe, grudging acceptance of the possibility that while National Guardsmen shot American students on Kent's campus it did not necessarily follow that either a conspiracy existed on the part of the Establishment or a revolution on the part of students.

I returned to the United States and to Kent a month later to find that some of my spontaneous judgments about May 4 were mistaken, that my early fitting of the event into the larger context of American history did not always square with reality. I had not anticipated the depth of community hostility to Kent students, protestors or otherwise; the generational gulf between town and gown was a surprise. Nor did I foresee the unhappy exploitation of Kent's sorrow by groups with little concern for the university or even for the victims of that day; they worked to keep alive the memory of May 4 for their own political or social objectives. My conviction that a free society can right its wrongs, which I proclaimed to my European listeners, was less firm than I had verbalized.

Some of my fears turned out to be misplaced. Would I be able to return to a campus that may have been radicalized by the deaths of May 4? Would my classes again listen to a "consensus" historian? The answer was yes in each instance. I could go home to share with my colleagues the painful process of rebuilding our University.

In retrospect a decade or so later, the division between students and community appears less formidable. Indeed, the nation's turning away from the Vietnam War was heralded by the student movement. By May 4, the tide had already turned, even if it was not evident at the time. The clash on the Kent campus, like conflict elsewhere in 1970, disclosed the limits of protest in this society and the prices to be paid for it. The deaths at Kent State University might have occurred on other American campuses as tensions mounted after May 1, 1970. But the tragedy did not signify the failure of popular protest in a democracy. In an open society, protest did make a difference. The politicizing of American students marked the influence of a new and important interest group in the shaping of American foreign policy. And, as the Iranian crisis of 1979 suggested, student voices may affect national support of, as well as opposition to, the Establishment.

Random Bullets

"It rains on the just as well as the unjust"

an interview with CHARLES KIRKWOOD

CHARLES KIRKWOOD *was born in Jersey City, New Jersey, on May 28, 1941. He grew up in a succession of Pennsylvania towns—his father was a Mennonite minister and moved frequently. Kirkwood attended Wheaton College in Illinois, where he received a bachelor's degree in political science. He graduated from the Northwestern School of Law in 1965 and moved, with his wife and son, to Ravenna, Ohio, in 1966. He recalls: "I was just someone who wanted to come to Smalltown, U.S.A., and raise a family because I had no roots as a child." Kirkwood practiced law in Ravenna and began teaching a course in business law at Kent State University in January 1968. In 1969, he was appointed assistant prosecutor for Portage County, a position which he held until September 1973. "In a small county," he notes, "there is no competition for the office of assistant county prosecutor; if you're a young lawyer, when it's your obligatory year or two to go over and be in the prosecutor's office and get some trial experience, you go." Kirkwood subsequently became chief assistant prosecutor for Summit County, with his office in Akron, where he remained until the summer of 1980, at which time he accepted a position as visiting associate professor in the University of Akron School of Law. In 1978, Kirkwood was named the outstanding trial prosecutor in the state by the Ohio Prosecuting Attorney's Association. The interview was conducted on February 23, 1982.*

When *did you know that National Guardsmen were on the Kent State campus?*
On Friday night, May first, I was at the annual Law Day dinner meeting of the Portage County Bar Association when word first came through that there was some kind of civil disturbance in Kent and that the Guard was being called in.

And you were on campus the following Monday?
Yes, and it worried me, seeing people walking around with guns. I

was teaching on campus at 7:45 in the morning, in the Business School, and probably half to two-thirds of the students were in class. I talked to them for maybe fifteen or twenty minutes about what was going on and told everybody that if I were them I would get out of town right now. I explained to them that when it rains, it rains on the just as well as the unjust—and that the last thing you wanted to do was to be in a crowd. The guardsmen were tired: they had been out on the road for a week or so in connection with a truckers' strike—where people were shooting at them—and they were simply not trained for this kind of situation. In a sense, it was massive retaliation; but more than that, if you give a person a gun and you give him live bullets—and that's his only weapon for crowd control, then you can end up with deaths. With the National Guard, the so-called weekend warriors, you're not talking about professional law enforcement. You're talking about people who might be called up if there's a war. And crowd control does not require people with the training and the mentality of fighting a war. The military doesn't understand and isn't trained to understand what the local police officer knows: that you get paid to take verbal abuse from a certain part of the citizenry of your community, and you will take it every day of your life.

What did you do after your class?
I drove up to Cleveland—I had been in Cleveland for most of the weekend, at a meeting, and I had something to pick up. It was on my way back—I was at State Route 43 and State Route 14, at the light in Streetsboro, just five miles north of Kent   when I heard the first report on the radio about the shootings. So I drove immediately to the county prosecutor's office in Ravenna. That first report was that six guardsmen had been killed, and as soon as I heard that there were deaths on the campus I knew that within six or eight hours all kinds of federal agencies would descend on us, that there would be pandemonium, and that it was important to hold the line and see that nothing got fouled up until they did come.

I volunteered to go over to Robinson Memorial Hospital, which I did. I went down to the hospital morgue, where the bodies would arrive. I went down and sat in there and lit up a cigarette and waited. Nobody else was there. I heard the sirens as the ambulances were coming in, knowing there were dead people in them. Eventually, I heard the noises as the bodies were being hauled down the hall. The door to the morgue opened, and they rolled in the first body with a sheet over it. I put out a cigarette I was smoking and went over and picked up the sheet and saw a young girl whom I later learned was Allison Krause. I could see that she had been very beautiful in life. I turned her over and could see both the entrance and exit wounds; all you had to do was look at it to realize that it had come from some military type of weapon. That's when I assumed that no one had shot guardsmen, that guardsmen had shot the other people.

Were you expecting it to be a guardsman that was wheeled in?
No, I wasn't assuming anything because I couldn't imagine a situation where guardsmen were going to be shot and no one else was going to be shot. I could imagine a situation in which guardsmen would be killed, but if that were so, there were going to be a lot of other dead people lying around. The reports didn't ring true; so I really didn't know what to expect. Of course, when I saw Allison Krause, my worst fears were realized.

What did you feel when you pulled back the sheet?
I guess it was a feeling of sadness more than anything else, at the waste of life. At the fact that the criminal justice system in general and law enforcement in particular had not geared themselves up for this kind of thing. As the son of a Mennonite minister, I'm not very militaristic, but I don't think you need to know too much about the military to know that crowd control is all based on firepower. The problem in this country in the late sixties, in dealing with crowds, was that a police officer holding a nightstick in his hand had a range of three feet, while a student with a rock—or any human being with a rock—had a range of fifty yards. So what you needed for crowd control was a nonlethal weapon with a range of one hundred yards. That's all.

Where did you go after you left the morgue?
I walked through the campus in the afternoon, after it was cleared. Nobody was there. I wanted to know who the people were who got shot. I had seen them; in fact, I was probably the only one who had seen all the dead bodies. We were finally able to get some names, and I went and located some of the places where they lived. They were

just college students, the ones that got shot, living in college housing.
I remember walking into the house where Jeff Miller lived, talking
to some of his roommates. Who is he? Just a college student. That's
when the enormity of it all hit me. People who have a tendency to
lead these types of demonstrations are not the people that get shot.
The unjust do not get shot in that situation, only the just, who are
hanging around. That's why the feeling of sadness was so great: what
happened was what you expect to happen in a situation like that.
You don't expect it unless you're in law enforcement or connected
with the criminal justice system—then you understand. At Kent
State, a crowd gathered, and random bullets struck. I know it's very
difficult to accept. I probably couldn't accept it if one of my children
had been killed: "You mean to tell me they died because a governor
was running for office and a bunch of untrained people were
brought to a campus run by people who didn't know how to handle
student unrest? This whole holocaust happened because of a
comedy of errors?" Unfortunately, the answer is yes.

Are you comfortable with the yearly commemoration of the
shootings?
My feeling has always been that they should be commemorated,
that there was then less likelihood of this kind of thing happening
again, that it be branded well in the consciousness of the people in
charge of keeping the peace. Civil disorder resulting in violent death
should be discouraged at all cost. Of course, Kent State was different—I don't think there are candlelight vigils and great com-

Signs posted after the closing of the Kent
State campus, May 4, 1970.

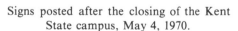

memorative services held in Newark and Watts and Detroit where
there were ghetto riots in the sixties which led to far more deaths.
Kent State is commemorated because it happened on an academic
campus. Nobody holds services in Watts every year, or if they do
you don't hear about it. But when you do something in the setting
of the intellectual community, there's a tendency to remember it
more. Anything that happens in an academic environment is going
to be worked over and picked over and used as a vehicle for so many
theories that it will never be sorted out. Although the causes of the
shootings were somewhat deeper than it appeared on the surface, I
don't think it was anywhere near as complex as scholars and com-
mentators have tried to make it. There was nothing at Kent State
different from a hundred or two hundred other universities in this
country, except that people died here. If it didn't happen in Kent, it
was going to happen someplace else. That was the tragedy of the
whole thing.

Enforcing the Law

"What did they expect?"

an interview with ROBERT GABRIEL

ROBERT GABRIEL *was born on October 26, 1943, in Logan, Ohio, a small town in the southeastern part of the state. He graduated from high school in 1962, worked for several years, and joined the army in April 1965. Gabriel went through flight school at Fort Walters, Texas, and served in Vietnam as a warrant officer and helicopter pilot in the First Air Cavalry from May 1966 to May 1967. Upon his return to the United States, he was a military flight instructor until his discharge from the army in the spring of 1969. He joined the Ohio National Guard shortly thereafter and, upon returning to Logan, worked in various sales positions over the next few years. In November 1969, Gabriel was commissioned a second lieutenant in the Guard, and he was placed on flight status in April 1970. In late April, he flew a helicopter patrol for Guard units stationed in Akron as a result of a truckers' strike; then, "the day they started the Kent State thing," as he recalls it, Gabriel was assigned as a pilot for Lt. Col. Ralph Schwartz, commander of the military police battalion headquartered in Youngstown, a position which involved Gabriel in patrols over the Kent State campus—including a helicopter patrol over the area on the night of May 2, 1970, after the ROTC building had been set afire. Gabriel remained in the Guard after the spring of 1970 and went active as a full-time recruiting officer in 1978. Currently, he is a major in the Ohio National Guard, headquartered in Worthington, near Columbus, and is completing work on his bachelor's degree in political science. He still lives in Logan, where he serves part time as a special deputy sheriff. The interview took place on January 5, 1982.*

You weren't on the Kent State University campus on May 4, 1970, but you had been flying helicopter patrol over the area several nights earlier. Were you aware of what was happening?
Yes, I was fairly well in touch with everything because I was flying the MP battalion commander around. Him being a lieutenant colonel, he attended a number of secret briefings—most of which I didn't get to sit in on—but he would tell me a lot afterwards. I

remember a meeting in Cleveland with representatives from all the local law enforcement agencies: I was sitting across from a guy with long hair and a beard who must've been with military intelligence. "Are you captured?" I asked him. "Are you a POW?" He wouldn't tell me what he was doing except to say that he was "looking around." But Saturday night, May 2—we really got into gear after the ROTC building was burnt—I was flying over the campus; it was lit up very well. We were flying a Korcan War-vintage helicopter; it was a bucket of bolts but fairly good-sized. You could put eight people down in the bay and two up front. In fact, I had been in the bay, where I drew an M-1 and got a bandolier. I remember looking down and seeing groups of people, just running around; there were fires. It was anarchy. I'd never seen anything like that. I did a tour in Nam, but that was different in a military sense than going to what we used to call "the world"—the United States—and seeing, I don't want to say a higher level of people, but certainly individuals who were more intelligent and with a higher lifestyle doing that kind of thing.

What was the impact of your Vietnam experience: what kinds of feelings did it generate toward the antiwar movement, toward American society in general?
Well, generally, I don't think that the American people really knew what was going on. I really don't. You could turn on your TV while you were having dinner and watch a village get blown off the face of the earth and think, "Well, there's the 'ugly American' syndrome again." But from my point of view, that wasn't the truth. Most of the people I served with were just plain old guys like me who were there trying to do a job. I felt that the antiwar movement was working for the other side. I'm sure that a lot of these people weren't hard-core, card-carrying communists or anything like that—I'm sure that they felt they had the best interests of the United States and the Vietnamese in mind. What most of my buddies thought was, "Hey, you don't necessarily have to be with us, but if you're against us, don't make it so damn vocal." Every time the antiwar groups would get on the news, on the TV, the only thing it did was give the enemy a great reason to continue. The North Vietnamese were very tenacious, and they weren't going to give up if they felt that the American public was working for them too. The antiwar people never had the whole

story. But when I was back home, I tried to avoid confrontations; unfortunately, there were some times when I had them—believe it or not—with some of my friends.

Did that surprise you?
I was amazed. If you were in the military, why you were the enemy, you were looked down upon. If you were an American returning home, you were an outcast. I was very angry at some of the stuff I heard. Armed with a little knowledge, people all of a sudden become armchair politicians and shithouse generals. I would hear: "Ah, all you guys did was burn hootches and kill pregnant women." "Look," I would say, "it's not like that." The Calleys were very much in the minority—you're going to find nuts even in the army. But there's a difference between combatting the enemy and murdering people.

But I have adjusted. Something that I think has been blown way out of proportion is the idea that the poor Vietnam veteran can't re-adjust to society. But then again, I wasn't a foot soldier—a grunt—either; I got to fly over it: they had to walk through it. Also, I went immediately back to Logan, Ohio, which obviously wasn't against the war in a big way. It's a small town, with an interlocking society; my parents and most of my friends were supportive. You know, I can look at the division in my life right there: it's Vietnam. Before that, things were different; things were simple. Everybody had the same values that I had: work hard, pay your taxes, obey the law, respect other people's property—and opinions. After Vietnam, it was changed. The feeling that you are a man without a country—that can get to you, especially in this country, because you realized when you got back how free you were and how much of a maternal symbol it is: "This is the mother of my life here." In Vietnam, no one gave a shit whether you lived or died.

When you were piloting the National Guard helicopter over the Kent State campus in May 1970, did you make any connection between that and your flying experience in Vietnam?
Yes, and that surprised me. The whole time you're in Nam, you think: "I hope I make it back to the world." We wanted to get back to the world we knew. At Kent State, I thought, "These are my people. What's happening?"

Did you feel animosity toward the institution, specifically or in a generic sense?

No, because I had been working—and am still working—on my own degree. I didn't think that universities were indoctrinating people, though I felt that some people had been indoctrinated by radical groups and so forth. I thought that the universities at that particular time were very free and open—maybe too much so, maybe not; but when it gets to the place where those who are in the institution can practice lawlessness, then you begin to have a privileged society. I have very strong notions of right and wrong. If someone breaks the law, especially in front of you, and is allowed to get away with it, then you have created a privileged class. Everybody ought to be treated the same. That's part, I feel, of our American heritage. So I'm flying over this stuff at Kent State, and I began thinking: "Hey, why don't they gear up the cavalry, charge down through there, use whatever force is necessary, and pile these people up someplace?" When the National Guard comes into a situation, they should say, "Okay, folks, this is the bottom line. This is the last thing." If the Guard had been hard-nosed when they first came to Kent State, everybody would've known the rules; and I don't think anyone would have gotten killed. I'm not, by the way, trying to make excuses for the shootings.

You were at the Cleveland airport on May 4 when you first heard that students had been shot—what did you think?

The first thing I heard was that guardsmen had been shot, and I thought, "What in the hell is this turning into?" I wasn't even getting combat pay. "If I had been there, there'd have been twenty students lying there"—that was my initial reaction. I had requested, in fact, when I was assigned to Kent State, that I be given a ground assignment rather than fly. But my commanding officer told me: "You are not going to be on the ground because they are not putting any Vietnam veterans on the ground anywhere [in Kent] with any weapons." My assumption was that they figured that a combat veteran would shoot quicker than a guardsman.

Do you think that was right?

No, I think we would have been more cool under pressure. When it got to the stone-throwing and to the confrontation, I think that

Guardsmen on the Kent State campus, May 1970.

veterans would have stood fast. I am convinced that if the platoon that went back up toward Taylor Hall—the one that fired—had stood firm, with fixed bayonets, and stuck some people, the thing wouldn't have happened. But I think they got scared. And it wasn't until maybe an hour after the shootings that I heard it was only students who were shot. My thought was that it shouldn't have gone on that long. It goes back to what I said before: if somebody's breaking the law, and it's obvious they are, then you have the power to arrest. You attempt to arrest. If they resist, you use what force is necessary to subdue them. So who's to say what force is necessary? Obviously, forty guys standing out there with M-1's, shooting at people who don't have M-1's, is unnecessary. But they failed to intimidate the crowd. Let's face it, law enforcement is seeing and being seen; secondly, it is intimidation. Some people don't respect the law for the law, so they have to respect the law for the fear. Fear of being caught, fear of being punished, fear of being clubbed; whatever. The Guard was there to stabilize the situation. Those that refused to allow it to be stabilized, what did they expect?

For a long time after the shootings, the Guard would go places and hear people say the usual, "Kent State nothing, National Guard four," and so on. I suppose I thought that the shootings were a good thing, because they stopped everything right there. Everything cooled down after that. That took the hot air out of the radical stuff in the nation. I don't like to see anyone die for any reason, but I thought, "How could they be so dumb to go up against people with guns in their hands?" If I had been there and seen a platoon of armed soldiers, I would've said, "Well, the fun's over." Maybe it's my military mind, but if someone has a gun I assume it's loaded. I assume that the individual is trained to use it and that if the situation comes up where he feels he has to use it, he will. But there were those students who persisted, walking a tightrope, not seeing that if something volatile happened they would be caught in the middle. And I know there were some innocent people that were killed—and that should not have happened. And it was our fault to the extent that we let it get to that point. If we had gone in and said, "That's it"; gone in there and used clubs, bayonets; butt-stroked them—I don't think anyone would've died. I think there would've been a lot of stitches, a lot of heads getting bumped, but no one getting killed.

As it was though, after the shootings, I thought: "Where is it going from here? If this doesn't intimidate them, then we're going to have an all-out civil war in this country—and we're just going to be shooting people right and left." That was my main concern. I didn't feel sorry for the people who got killed. I really didn't.

Have you changed your initial views much in the intervening years? No, not really. I remember talking to some Kent residents after the destruction downtown on May 1, 1970. They had been glad to see the Guard come. It seemed absurd to me: why would students go downtown and punish local townspeople for something that Nixon had done? Of course, I couldn't understand why we hadn't gone into Cambodia much earlier. The North Vietnamese would come across into South Vietnam from their sanctuaries in Cambodia; hell, they would kill villagers all over the place. We accidentally or on purpose kill one civilian and you'd think the world came to an end. But with Kent State, I guess you could say that I'm hard-core. I still don't understand how somebody feels that a group, for whatever reason, can violate the law and do what they want. I guess that's the basic thing.

The May 4 Disease

by JOHN A. BEGALA

JOHN A. BEGALA *is a lifelong resident of Kent. He received his bachelor's degree from Kent State University in 1972 and was a graduate assistant in the Center for Peaceful Change during 1972–73. He was elected Kent City councilman-at-large in 1973 and completed work on his master's degree in history at the University in 1975. In 1976, he was elected to the Ohio House of Representatives, then reelected in 1978 and 1980.*

There's nothing new to say, in the manner of a conclusion, about Kent State, May 4, 1970. It is a "Middle American cross to bear"; a "tragedy for the families"; a "nightmare for the Guardsmen"; a "pain in the neck" for more than a few local residents who prefer "international affairs" over beer or cocktails rather than something so complex and present in their own backyards. I have no definitive conclusions to offer; the only ones, I am convinced, are the bullet-torn lives.

"International affairs" once included discussion of Kent State (with Jackson State and a couple of others added on, as in "didn't something similar happen at Jackson State or someplace too?"). I doubt if they do now, which is not entirely displeasing to me. I am a little like a lot of other Kent townsfolk who are just tired of talking about, hearing about, and answering about May 4, 1970. I have convinced myself, however, that my reasons for feeling this way are a little different from most. But that doesn't matter to the student of Kent, Ohio. What really matters is this: use care in asking people from Kent about May 4, 1970. They may know less about it than a social worker in Boise, Idaho does.

"Kentites" have distorted views on it; distorted by having lived beside the thing. Some of us have thought we had it all worked out, from time to time, only to find a new angle, a new piece of information or a "new generation of students" wanting to claim this murderous day as their own tradition or heritage. "It," along with the war that drew it to a head in an unlikely locale, made me (like many of my generation) "politically aware." This led me, in turn, down the road to several reinvolvements with May 4 over the last twelve years, which follow three distinct stages in the development of a mass response: the immediate aftermath and early institutional response, the "last hurrah," and the "middle period" institutional response (the present). Below are some of my reminiscences.

The Event

In 1970, some of the graduates of 1967 through 1969 from Kent State's laboratory primary and secondary school, the "University School," were in college. We liked the Moody Blues, relived Woodstock (which none of us attended), hated the war, and hung around on weekends on North Water Street.

North Water Street was quite a bit different then. More bars than now and more shadowy nooks and crannies in which to find a wide assortment of townies, street people, hippies, would-be hippies, radicals, and an occasional liberal professor who was or would soon be divorced. The bars were all on the west side of the street, bounded by more legitimized businesses to the south and the Davey Warehouse and then a couple of dive bars to the north. The east side of North Water Street, directly across from the bars, then as now had a converted house containing Dan's Shoe Repairs and Pandolfi's Barber Shop (Joe Pandolfi cut the hair of Kent's most prestigious jocks), the Eagles Club, a couple of parking lots and, stuck in close between, an old, dirty-windowed house with a porch that is still collapsing, where some reputed radicals lived.

On May 1, I had a date to go to the movies at University Plaza (one-and-a-half miles south of the center of town). We saw *Zabriski Point* and left feeling mildly depressed. Stanley Kauffman reviewed the film in his *New Republic* column as "Phony Antonioni"; *Zabriski Point* was Radical Chic. We drove to my date's home in Cuyahoga Falls (also called "Caucasian Falls" by many in this area) and I returned to Kent. At the Stow-Kent Plaza, to the west of town, however, Route 59 was blocked. "You don't want to go home tonight," I was informed by a helmeted police officer, who refused any details.

I detoured a mile to Graham Road and drove to North Water Street to drink and hang out.

North Water Street, however, was empty. There was debris in the street, some broken glass and a few cars, but otherwise empty. I went to find my brother, who was at Gary Spiker's house and about to go to the Kent Motor Inn. "All hell broke loose," he said. "Go home." Instead, I went with him to the Kent Motor Inn, ate, drank coffee, and listened to rumors at the other tables. Downtown Kent was a mess, local businessmen were out and about past their bedtimes for a Friday night, and City Hall was called the "command post" by a couple of police officers. The Cambodian "incursion" and "outside agitators" were alternately offered as the causes for the riot; revolution and Nixon were discussed together with whether this would mean that the bars would be closed tomorrow night. Nobody talked about *Zabriski Point*.

Over the weekend, things got out of hand. Armored vehicles rolled in at some point, a building burned, helicopters with searchlights roved the night skies; Governor Rhodes was coming, maybe. There was a curfew as well, and people had to drive to neighboring towns to get beer. Access on the main routes in and out of town was limited, but everybody knew how to get around the roadblocks. Kent was suddenly a different home for many. People were scared, yet full of unwarranted confidence that this would pass quickly, order and normalcy restored.

On May 4, I went to morning classes and talked to a couple of guardsmen who were in very good spirits and anxious to go home. "It's almost over with," one said outside Bowman Hall. Yet, inside, there was talk of a rally at noon on the Commons (not "demonstration," but "rally"). I would be at work.

At about 12:30 P.M., just after the shootings, our truck full of books left the University Supply Center for the old bookstore, which was on the western fringe of the Commons. A couple thousand people sat on one hillside. They were being asked by several notable concerned faculty to "please go home." After we unloaded, we wandered into the crowd, where I had two memorable encounters. One was with a guardsmen who pointed a rifle at me and said "move back." Things didn't look like they'd be over so soon to me. But then, we *all knew* that the guns were not loaded. Everybody, absolutely everybody, knew that. So, I figured the guy was just a

cowboy, probably tired from the truckers' strike where, just days before, guardsmen had been shot at with real bullets.

Then, somewhere in the crowd of spectators around the west
periphery of the Commons, I encountered one of my father's
wrestlers—my father was Kent State wrestling coach from 1929 to
1971—who was also a bouncer at the Dome (like my brother, back
then), a fightin' bar that was not on North Water Street. "They just
blew one of the mothers away." he said. "You're full of shit," I said.
"No! Some guy with a gun. Blew the guy's brains out in Kent Hall."
Kent Hall was not near where "the action" was. I thought it was a lie.

It was about two more hours before "the word" was out and
about. WKNT Radio had anywhere from one to four dead (maybe
more) at different times. Nobody knew for sure, except perhaps
those who were right there. We were let off work early. When I got
home, one of my parents' neighbors said, "That'll show the
bastards." He thought the dead ones were "outside agitators." He
had no idea that they were students.

The Immediate Aftermath and the Early Institutional Response

The two years that followed "it" were the times of the Great Division in Kent. There were mainly two schools of thought on the
shootings. One was the they-should-have-killed-more-of-them
school, named for a locally famous statement at the inevitable
public hearings by a female Kent resident whose name does not
(should not) come to mind. The other was the let's-face-up-to-our-
unique-role-in-history school, which included an apparently more
sensitive but ideologically diverse crowd. The former had the
numbers on their side, back then, but eventually lost the "public
debate" to the other. That was the natural outcome, of course; time
is kind to those who argue for a unique place in history.

I was (and remain) part of the let's-face-up school. The first
orders of those days were to "get involved," provide "relevance" in
the curriculum of the University (to some awful, unintended effects,
since that movement has been co-opted by the anti-liberal arts, pro-
vocational movement in higher education), protest war and injustice
in all their forms, and get liberals elected to public office. The
autumn of 1970 brought some changes for the better. A new internship program and the "Princeton Plan," allowing five days off from

classes for campaigning for politicians, were instituted at Kent State, largely because of a wonderful Political Science Department chairman, Tom Ungs. A Committee on Political Education, including a few student members, was formed to guide the programs. Within two years, less desirable but still much heralded reforms came: Introductory Philosophy and the 18-hour foreign language requirements were dropped and deemphasized, respectively. "Relevance," ultimately a mixed success/failure, was winning out at Kent State.

Involvement did better, for a while. Students became a "legitimate" force to be dealt with. Through internships and the Princeton Plan, we worked in campaigns and with students at other schools, helped elect a liberal governor, John Gilligan, and an antiwar representative to Congress, John Seiberling.

The protests continued. For about two years, KSU had frequent demonstrations, like most colleges and universities. As late as 1973, organizers were successful in moving large crowds to raise their voices: against war, against injustice in all forms, for justice against those who murdered on our campus. The demonstrators were in the right and temporarily made believers out of many cynics who were also right in saying that it was all so unrealistic. For a while, it looked as though war and injustice might lose out, that the killers would be condemned in the courts. Even some of the cynics pulled their strings for the right causes. There was also litigation, but I know few people, except for bona fide May 4 junkies, who can recount it all. I can't. It resulted in acquittals for the guardsmen and a statement of regret from Governor Rhodes, who made a successful comeback against Gilligan in 1974. (So much for justice.)

During those years, I jumped into any and all forms of "legitimate activism": a full-time internship in the Gilligan and several other campaigns; student member of the Committee on Political Education; the McGovern campaign in 1972. It was a perfect course of study for a case of May 4 burnout. But that came later.

The Center for Peaceful Change (CPC) was created in 1971 as a "living memorial" to the four who were killed. It was one of the University's better innovations. In the last few years, it has evolved into a broad, interdisciplinary program that is keeping alive ideas about a better, humanistic America. Back then, it was searching for that role. The CPC attracted an odd assortment of devotees. It was directed by Raj Basi, an Indian professor of economics who once consulted in Iran. His main accomplishment was to get approval for a major course of study in "Integrative Change." The program was entitled "Peaceful Change," like the Center at first, but the Ohio Board of Regents found the title objectionable because of the word "peaceful." A more appropriate title was a condition for approval.

"Integrative Change" met universal criticism from those who inhabited North Hall, a former ROTC building and the home of CPC. Basi thought it was reasonable. "It's the same proposal, the same program," he assured us. "We can still call the center 'Peaceful Change.' Only the title of the major was changed." "Peace" was not a popular word among the holdover Regents of James Rhodes; it possibly was unpopular with Gilligan's as well. Still, Basi turned out to be right. Substance prevailed over names, the people at the CPC put together a first-rate program despite their silly-titled major and a purposely low financial commitment on the part of the University administration.

North Hall had only one true inhabitant: Paul Keane. He lived on the floor of his office as often as in his van, which was parked outside. He taught the introductory courses, I think, and had part-time salary. He was a brilliant speaker and a superb writer. One letter to the student paper had one of his most memorable lines, something to the effect that the indoor fountain at the newly constructed Student Center, a winner of some architectural award, looked like Moby Dick urinating. Keane was poetic, outraged, outrageous, and a bit of a sociopath. But above all, he was brilliant and had a knack for exciting ideas. He made Charles Kuralt's "On the Road" news shorts with his creation of Pop's Snow Squad, a group of volunteer snow shovelers who during the winter months made the walk across town easier for an elderly school crossing guard, Louis "Pop" Fischer. It was Kuralt's Christmas story one year in the early 1970s. Keane pleaded to save the john walls in North Hall when it was razed a couple of years later, on the grounds that they had the best grafitti on campus. Keane rebelled against the idiots who inhabited part of the Administration Building. And Keane single-handedly made thousands of students aware of all sorts of things in "their" school and "their" lives.

Keane later left the CPC in anger, an event precipitated by a disagreement he had with the secretary. The last I heard from him was in 1976. He invited me to contribute money through a charitable tax deductible gift to a scholarship fund at an Ivy League school. The fund was to be used to assist him in paying for his studies.

But before he left Kent, Keane also had the idea of establishing a May 4 Resource Room in the University Library. It was to contain all available written materials and records on the event, its prelude, and its aftermath. In the late winter of 1973, the negotiations between him and Library Director Hyman Kritzer and the library's advisory committee broke down. Keane wanted a prominent location; they did not want it at all but would accept it in a cement block cube on one of the upper floors. This and a problem with finding funds for the room brought an impasse.

Keane gave up on the project in frustration and anger sometime after I was assigned to coordinate the CPC-sponsored May 4 activities. (I was then a graduate assistant serving half-time at the center.) It was agreed that I would take on the project, the hope being that we could dedicate the room during the first week in May. Somewhere along the way, I contacted the KSU Foundation about the possibility of receiving a private gift to finance the room. Dan Newcomb, the Foundation director, found an interested alumnus in Victor Buherle, an Akron rubber manufacturer. There would be strings attached, though. Buherle wanted prominence, which was helpful; but he also wanted the room dedicated to Father Junipero Sera, the explorer-priest of Spanish California. His motto was to be part of the room: "Always go forward, never turn back."

Nobody at the CPC was enthralled with this. But the offer was too good to forget. With this legitimizing element and the financial assistance, there was no rational basis (on their terms) for the library people to say no. That May, the room was dedicated in a prominent area on the library's first floor. By that time the library people were more enthusiastic about the idea. The room has attracted many users since then, and the library's commitment to it has grown over the years. It was a kick in the teeth when a frustrated Peter Davies decided to give his abundant collection of materials on May 4 to another school. He meant it that way, I understand.

The most stable and rewarding program in the CPC's early years was the internship program overseen by the Committee on Political Education, Tom Ungs's creation. It was merged with the Center in 1972. The coordinator was a graduate assistant, Mike Turner.

Mike's quiet ways were also successful ways. He placed and eventually supervised scores of for-credit internships in government and political campaigns. He was also a constructive activist in the community. Together with another CPC devotee, Doug Fenske, we organized the Kent Community Center (now defunct) and operated a curbside newspaper recycling program for the Kent Environmental Council on the west side of town. Mike's contributions to the CPC were many but subtle; above all, he brought stability to an office of brainstormers. After five years, though, he finished his Ph.D. and went to teach at Findlay College in western Ohio. Findlay is the home of Marathon Oil, although it could be argued that I've got that backwards. In any case, it was no place for a person of his intellect and capabilities. A few years ago, he moved to Langley, Virginia, to take a job with the Central Intelligence Agency.

After the May 1973 activities, I caught the disease. May 4, 1970, the reelection of Nixon, and the dreadful state of America as viewed through the mire of May 4 and the annual ceremonies around it put me into mental paralysis. These and the strange discipline of political science, my field of study, became more than I could stand. In the letdown that followed the first week in May activities, I quit it all to go to work and run for city council. I later returned to study history and served three years on the council, where I had a chance to test directly some of the ideas of the day outside of academia, with some success and some failure.

Between 1974 and 1977, the student body completed its first post-1970 turnover. They were years of change everywhere. In Kent, they were years of renewed optimism. Violence no longer seemed possible. Time began to work its magic on memories of May 4, and the possibility of "normalcy" started appearing more frequently.

It was in the spring of 1977, after I had been in the state legislature for several months, when normalcy hit the skids again at Kent State University. Columbia had a gymnasium crisis that started the student movement in the early 1960s. Like fads in fashion and music, which start on the coasts and move inland, the gymnasium syndrome reached Kent late.

The Last Hurrah

Sometime in March of 1977, I got my first indication that something might happen over the addition to Memorial Gymnasium that the University's Board of Trustees had approved the previous November. Mary Vincent, a perennial member of the advisory committee on May 4 activities and commemoratives (and who, with her husband, Howard, a nationally known expert on Herman Melville, were friends of Keane), showed up on the porch one day to inform me of this "atrocity." She assured me that there would be protests.

I thought then (as now) that building anything in the area was asking for trouble, but frankly, I did not see on what rational grounds there should be much objection. I told that to Mary Vincent; she looked disgusted and left. Then she sent me a letter on it. And then she called. And then, a couple of weeks later, there were rumblings. Several more calls came; I was expected to use my position to do something about it, I was told.

It was pretty late to be talking about it, with the design completed and bids requested. And there were few reasons to try in the first place. "Historical significance" I was told. "Cover-up" also crept in along with the ruination of green space on campus.

Only the green space argument washed with me. Of course May 4, 1970, was historically significant. That will never change. Did it make sense to preserve the site on that basis, though? Perhaps, but why stop the project at this late date? Why not a year earlier, during the planning process? "It was kept secret," people said. That is hardly true. The thing was discussed in public meetings for well over a year.

Anyone who has been to Gettysburg has seen a unique manner of "preserving history," for there is preserved the whole battlefield and a few myths, as well as green space. There has also been built a very cheap industry around the gruesome affair. That part of Gettysburg came to mind during the months that followed. I visualized a May-4th-O'Rama, electronic-talking self-tours. I kept my mouth shut about those visions, though. The green space argument, however, was a good one. That, together with a very deep desire to see the University, town, and God knows what beyond avoid another confrontation led me to call Ted Curtis, the University's architect, for details.

A short time later, we walked off the area to be covered by the new building. It would take a lot of trees, but would not cover the spots where the dead students fell. "It distorts the view; it will make it look like the Guard was trapped and had to shoot," I was told later. "It will make it impossible to prove the conspiracy of the huddled G Company over there." Bunk. There were pictures to show those things, and reams of sworn testimony and more reams of written speculation.

Curtis, like myself, was not too pleased with the whole thing. He said that they could take steps to protect some of the trees, and he shortly thereafter worked out a plan that eventually accomplished that. He also mentioned rotating the building away from the site, but that idea developed later.

Things got very crazy in short order. My liberal friends at home and in Columbus started asking about it. Letters to editors started appearing. A tent city on the site was discussed and suddenly appeared. And then, an extended old home week began for quite a few of the antiwar, pro-justice-in-America people from early 1970s Kent State. They were here for a "last hurrah," and confrontation became inevitable. Nearly everybody started choosing sides: "Build the Gym" versus "Stop the Gym." In Ohio, with all its urban poverty, "country justice," low benefits levels for the poor, low subsidies for education at all levels, *and gross apathy on all those problems*, the great liberal cause was stopping a gym. It would have been only mildly disgusting had it not been for the right-wingers' reaction to the protest. They made it significant, with their law-and-order, anti-communist rantings and petition drives. They sided with the guns and bullets and the human fingers on the triggers. Their activism, more than anything, made me get involved.

Some people were looking for something called a "mature response" to the affair. Fay Biles, then a vice president at the University, suggested a new, significant memorial to the dead near the shooting site. That made the papers. In Columbus, Harry Lehman, chairman of the House Judiciary Committee, approached me with the idea of putting together a resolution calling on the KSU Trustees to do that very thing. We put one together, but the idea simply wasn't any good, even though Lehman's general approach of *doing something* put him in a rather exclusive club of legislators who recognized that *something* might be advisable. The memorial idea, however, was not that something. Kent State already had memorials: the Center for Peaceful Change, the May 4 Resource Room, the Granville-Jackson sculpture, a modest marker near the site.

It was then that the idea of rotating the building started floating about. I called KSU President Glenn Olds from Columbus one evening after hearing of some bitter verbal exchanges that had taken place that day. Olds was scared and said so. We discussed "mature responses," rotating the gym in particular. There were problems with the idea he said: it would fail to appease the protestors, infuriate the right-wingers, and cost a lot. I said I would work on trying to get the dollars and talk to the inhabitants of Tent City about practical alternatives. The right-wingers, I thought, could be isolated if we all pulled together. Olds said Ted Curtis was already working on design and costs; with about $750,000, it appeared that the rotation could be pulled off.

It was about 9:30 P.M. when we hung up. I went to consult my predecessor in the House, State Senator Marcus A. Roberto. He said he knew of the cost estimate and suggested that we go talk to House Speaker Vernal G. Riffe, Jr., about his views on getting an appropriation in the biennial budget bill that was then before the House. We went to see Riffe. He thought the project should be completed, but saw the political problems involved for the Democrats who represented Kent in the legislature. Still, though, he was not inclined to do a thing to appropriate money for anything to do with May 4, 1970 (even though he supported the state's appropriating funds to pay Governor Rhodes's legal fees for the civil action brought against him by the families of the dead students).

It was after Riffe had said no for the umpteenth time (insisting now that "this is the trustees' problem") that Roberto jammed his foot in the door: "Look Vern, I haven't asked for much."

"Markie," Riffe said, "Markie, I'll consider it for you. Now, I'll consider it. If the Trustees pass a resolution asking for the money, I'll consider it." He repeated "resolution" and "consider it" several times, to make sure we understood.

We then sought out support for the idea with the Trustees. Shortly before they were to vote on awarding a contract, several of them flew to Columbus to discuss it. We met them in Senate President (Pro Tempore, then) Oliver Ocasek's office. When I got there, Ocasek was gone but had already indicated support for the additional appropriation. They were to talk with Riffe later. Mike Johnston, a Rhodes-appointed Trustee and editor of the *Canton Repository*, wanted to build as planned. We argued. George Janik, their chairman of the board, could see "both sides." I left thinking "maybe."

But the "maybe" was unwarranted. Not too long afterward, the Trustees voted to award the contract and move ahead "as planned."

In the meantime, I had a chance to talk with the Tent City people on "their ground." The rotation idea was not big with them. "There has to be an alternative that will not be too costly." I felt like a broken record on that point. "And you all have to support one, or all this is for nothing." I was told pretty directly what they thought of my "point." Alternatives were not their problem, they said. "It is the Trustees' problem." That line got very old.

With the Trustees' decision to go ahead "as planned," things got worse. Injunctions were sought and won. The contractor fumed publicly. The right-wingers circulated petitions supporting the building as planned. The protestors dug in their heels. News cameras rolled and rolled and rolled. University enrollment projectors got nervous. Security and law enforcement costs skyrocketed. And my telephone rang.

Things looked worse to me than they did in 1970. There were nowhere near the number of protestors, but the pros were there. Four people were shot down after three crazy days back then. There were months of crazy days behind the "last hurrah."

In the midst of this entrenchment, a new idea surfaced. It was suggested that the University School, which was open only to elementary students but once ran kindergarten through twelfth grade, be converted to serve the purposes of the gym-annex. It was close, feasible, and cost effective (it would have cost about two-fifths of the over six million dollars appropriated for the gym project) and ironic. Only two months before, Roberto and I were successful in getting a line item appropriation for the operation of the school incorporated into the biennial budget for the first time. Even though it operated a bit more like a private school than a public one, I thought the support worthwhile, given the quality of the program, my sentimental attachment to it as a graduate, and the strain its closure (a real possibility) would have had on the Kent Public Schools.

I thought the proposal to convert it worthwhile, nonetheless, thinking that it should offend nobody. Even the right-wingers could approve, I thought, since it would save a few million dollars. The contractor would have a beef, but given the full-blown emergency, I thought it reasonable that the legislature act directly to award him the contract for converting the school and even cover his losses if necessary.

What I did not anticipate was the reaction of the local liberals. After I publicly supported this alternative, the parents of University School children held a meeting to object. In the room were more than a few supporters of the antigym protestors. They liked the state-supported, semiprivate education their children were getting. They would put up their own Tent City to protest their children being sacrificed in this manner, they said. One should never mess with a liberal's privileges, I learned. Many notable pro-justice-in-America people had intense anger in their eyes on the evening of that meeting. When they won the battle to keep the school, they also killed the last viable alternative to the gym-annex.

It was only a matter of removing hurdles after that. The University stuck to it, step by step, and broke ground in the early fall. Once the work began, the protest soon disappeared.

There were many other trying and great moments along the way of the Gym Affair: the tragic death of one of the protestors (in an auto wreck); a teary-eyed meeting with several of the parents of the dead students at the Statehouse; a magnificent speech by History Professor Larry Kaplan at the August commencement; another meeting between Roberto, myself, and the Trustees, which most of them boycotted; and much more.

But the Gym Affair was bizarre and crazy, most of all. It was dumb, if not "wrong," to build there. And it was dumb to protest it. What else could one expect? The disease that comes with May 4 broke out and ran rampant during those several months. America was not getting better, even with the war over. America was still not immune to things like May 4 burnout. That has a lot to do with the way we abuse symbols in our causes. A lot of poor kids in Cleveland could have eaten for quite awhile on what was spent on the Gym Affair. A lot of Cambodians too.

The "Middle Period" Institutional Response

Since 1977, Kent State University has entered a new period of institutional response. It is characterized by the low key. With new management under the leadership of President Brage Golding, the University has begun to work its way out of the depths to which it was plunged during the 1970s. He has done a good job in many ways. But there have been some bad turns over the last four years. The Segal Sculpture Fiasco and the Davies Papers Affair inflamed the condition of those with chronic cases of the May 4 disease. There will undoubtedly be more of these as this middle period goes on. I have no idea of how long that will be, but I suspect it will be quite a while before we enter the endless "late period," which will begin with the reduction of it all to footnotes. "Four Dead In Ohio," will be an old folk song by then.

The sad and morbid thing is that something like Kent State University, May 4, 1970, will happen again and again in America. There is so much to be learned from it on which we have collectively closed the book! In 1980, I read in an article heralding the improved enrollment picture at Kent State University something to the effect that the administration was "getting tough with demonstrators." As Albert Camus wrote of the plague, the May 4 disease will linger dormant only to break out again. Somewhere.

A closing note: I wrote the preceding portions of this article two years ago, without the benefit of a crystal ball. Last year, 1981, Kent State University decided to close the University School, over mild parental protest. Then, this year, the Ohio Senate inserted a provision into a prison construction bill authorizing a memorial to Gov. James A. Rhodes, to be constructed on the Statehouse lawn. It came back to the House for concurrence with the Senate amendments on May 4, 1982, where it won final approval.

Events such as these remind us that nature likes to imitate art and that irony is not a bitter palliative—it is no palliative at all.

The Kent Heritage

A Commencement Address Delivered August 27, 1977

by LAWRENCE S. KAPLAN

LAWRENCE S. KAPLAN *is University professor of history and director of the Lyman L. Lemnitzer Center for NATO Studies at Kent State University. This is the text of his commencement remarks, slightly edited for this collection, as they appeared in the alumni magazine* Kent, *July 1977.*

You know that commencement addresses are very much alike. They present a composite of platitudes strung together in such a way as to provide inspiration for the new graduates about to depart the cloistered world of the university for new roles in society. Much is made of the contrast between the joys of the ivory tower—the shared memories of songs, cheers, even the lectures of favorite professors— and the harshness of the real world where college fraternity is replaced by Darwinian competition. The commencement speaker— and I am no exception—frequently regards his task as that of helping the baccalaureate make the transition by noting the difficulties ahead, balancing them with the opportunities, and then softening the awesome prospect with comforting words about the preparation which the University has given graduates to master life on the outside. . . .

A few months ago at the Harvard commencement exercises, the professional amateur George Plimpton offered a whimsical commentary on graduation as commencement of a new life. Essentially, he had one word of advice: "Unpack!" Don't leave the university. Go back to your rooms. The outside is too awful to contemplate, particularly from the perspective of a comfortable Harvard House. Why abandon the shelter of your alma mater for the sorrows of the cruel world if you can find some way to avoid it?

Plimpton's tongue-in-cheek advice was intended to mock the conventional commencement speech, but it serves also to underscore the irrelevancy of such speeches to Kent State University in 1977. There would be no point in urging you to unpack and return to the sheltered life of an unworldly society. There is no shelter here. The experience of the Kent universe has been a microcosm of society at large. The turmoil of America in the last decade was and is an integral part of life at Kent. Whatever our individual preference, this university has been marked as a historical site—whether or not a national commission officially designates it as such. Four students died, and nine were wounded on this campus on May 4, 1970. Their deaths became a symbol of the nation's reaction against the Vietnam war, particularly against the extension of that conflict to Cambodia by presidential action. In the nation and in the world it was a signal for students everywhere to articulate their opposition to the war. This tragic event has since entered most college history texts.

I am not indulging in hyperbole. Living in Europe in 1970, I found myself the center of unwelcome attention when I lectured for the United States Information Service three weeks after the tragedy. My Kent State connection, previously innocuous when not invisible, was an occasion for demonstrations wherever I went. . . . For European students Kent State had become an instant shorthand to define American imperialism or American fascism, expressed in what I felt to be a mindless Marxist rhetoric. But no matter how unfair the charges against Kent, or against America, the emotions were real; the war was real! The dead students became martyrs in the cause of a world revolution wherein students everywhere would tear down the evil old world of war to create a new world of peace.

Seven years later we have not yet achieved the detachment necessary for a definitive judgment of the significance of this event in American history, and I am wary, as a historian, of venturing anything more than a personal opinion. It seems to me that few if any of the students on the Kent campus equated the May demonstration with a stand at Lexington Green inviting a shot that would be heard around the world. The students were not volunteers protecting patriots in Concord. Rather, they appear more victims than martyrs, victims not of a repressive fascist government but of the tribulations the nation was undergoing. The leadership of the country had lost its way; the inspired statecraft of the 1940s, when the United States wisely and courageously accepted the burdens of world responsibilities, was corrupted, perhaps inevitably, by "an arrogance of power" as Senator Fulbright had warned in the 1960s. And college youth played its own unfortunate role as the students expressed justified grievances in unjustifiable ways, refusing to respect rights of others as they demanded rights for themselves.

Living on the edge of campus, I wonder how objective a scholar I would have been if I watched what I had been informed were wild mobs destroying property a few blocks away. Much of the fear of students was understandable even if the irrational hatred that appeared in the wake of violence requires a deeper explanation than I am able to offer at this time. Perhaps the historical analogy that might best fit May 4 was the Boston Massacre of March 5, 1770, an analogy that seemed to have been widely observed a few years ago, and then apparently dropped. But both the incident and the symbol have elements that fit it. Five died, and six were wounded in front of the Customs House on what was then King Street. No one knows who fired the first shot, or who started the massacre. Was it a protest by innocent schoolboys against repression by the British government that led to these shootings in Boston, or were the soldiers goaded beyond endurance by politically motivated mobs? The British officer in charge was later acquitted through the efforts of his lawyer, the future President John Adams. It was not a "massacre," but it was a step in the growing violence between colony and mother country as the links between them were being shattered by successive provocative incidents.

The incident is worth remembering, not as part of Sam Adams's propaganda against British rule, but as one of the birth pangs of a new nation. The Kent State tragedy will be equally worthy of remembrance, in my judgment, as a nation's agony which was to be resolved by the democratic process within the system rather than by revolution against it. What then, of Kent State today and tomorrow? Should it be immobilized by the event? Should it be the site of continuing protests against present or future sins of society? I trust that this will not be the case at Kent any more than it was at Boston.

The site of the Boston Massacre is part of the Freedom Trail, part of Boston's heritage, well memorialized but not a graveyard that has prevented the growth of the dynamic city around it. Life goes on at the busy corner of Devonshire and State streets where Bostonians died in 1770. There are those without interest in Kent, except as a symbol for their cause, who would not have it this way here. While the wisdom of the decision to build an addition to the gymnasium so close to the site is open to serious debate, the arguments for doing so were not necessarily made by people wishing to cover up the site literally or figuratively.

The best memorial I believe that we could make to the memory of May 4 would not be in the form of a tower or chapel or even a revitalized Center for Peaceful Change, desirable as all of these may be. It would be a dynamic university that remembers its past as an inspiration for its future. The spotlight of national attention should include what too many of us tend to forget; namely, that the decade of student activism was also the decade that witnessed the transformation of Kent State University from a small, barely visible, former teachers' college into a place of academic leadership with a reputation broader than that of northeastern Ohio.

When I arrived at Kent in 1954, its title of "University" was largely by courtesy of the state legislature twenty-two years earlier. Despite a student population of 5,000 and despite thriving colleges of liberal arts and business as well as education, the pace was leisurely, the spirit parochial, and the scholarship subordinated to other needs of the University. Research was not scorned; it was just irrelevant (even bad form) as if teaching and research were two separate occupations. It is easy to make fun of the atmosphere of the 1950s, and it would be unfair. While the ugly passions raised by McCarthyism raged elsewhere, academic freedom was fully maintained at Kent. The teachers did their jobs and did them well; Kent alumni filled schools around the state, earning reputations from which KSU still benefits. . . . And life itself was attractive here. My own memories center on a smaller campus where I chaperoned student dances and served as adviser to the class of 1959. Although there were a few students thirsting for ideas from a larger world and there was a small faculty forum debating world affairs, politics was not part of our scene.

The Blanket Hill of the 1950s was just a thickly wooded area above the Commons where activities, conducted by couples rather than by larger units, were singularly devoid of political content. For a picture of another era look at Phillip Shriver's history of the University, *The Years of Youth*, published in 1960, the year of our semicentennial. Toward the end of the Shriver book there is brief mention of a relatively unnoticed act of the legislature in 1959— permission for Kent and Bowling Green to offer doctoral degrees. For Kent this was an invitation to reshape the University into a serious scholarly center.

The changes in the 1960s were swift and dramatic. New buildings transformed the face of the campus here as elsewhere. What distinguished Kent from others was the willingness and ability to implement the mandate to create centers of excellence on this campus. The state's master plan in 1966 ratified what had been under way since 1961: the beginning of exciting new programs, with personnel to man them, in biological sciences, chemistry, education, English, and history. Resources were used to identify other strong, or potentially strong, elements on campus and expand them, rather than spread them so thinly that no one department would achieve distinction. The products of these efforts are with us today. In the physical sciences they are represented by the Liquid Crystal Institute, established in 1965 as a pioneering enterprise in interdisciplinary research. In the fine arts Kent made an early and close connection in 1967 with the Cleveland Symphony Orchestra's Blossom Center. The Kent Blossom programs now range from the Festival School of Music and Kent Light Opera Company to Blossom-Kent Art Program and the KSU Repertory Theater. In the humanities and social sciences the newly created Department of Pan-African Studies calls to mind the early leadership of the University in Black Studies, most notably in black history, led by distinguished scholars from history and sociology. Its success has stimulated innovative programs in other ethnic programs which now include Hellenic, Judaic, Lithuanian, and Rumanian Studies.

The examples I have listed did not exist fifteen years ago. They represent a commitment that has given the University distinction in research which, as one would expect, has reinvigorated teaching. To disseminate this work the Kent State University Press grew to maturity in this period. As the only university press in northeastern Ohio, it is an institution that has distinguished itself by the high quality of its publications as well as distinguishing Kent from most of the universities in the state and the region. But of all the components of the University none has been more important in its evolution than the library. The 1954 catalog lists some 115,000 volumes and 800 periodicals, a respectable number for a small liberal arts college, but less impressive for a school of 5,000 students. Eleven years later, as Kent entered the take-off stage of development, the library had trebled to 300,000 volumes and 3,000 periodicals housed largely in the 1958 addition to Rockwell Library. In 1977 the figure had grown to 1,300,000 volumes and 7,500 periodicals on the Kent and regional campuses, most of them in the twelve-story tower that dominates the campus. Within a dozen years, out of limited resources, Kent achieved a position of significance among American universities in a variety of areas of scholarship.

This preeminence does not go unchallenged. Our sister institutions with stronger political bases have ambitions, understandable if not always logical, to duplicate the accomplishment of Kent. More seriously, our own internal resolution to sustain and expand excellence has flagged too often in recent years, with resulting erosion in the world of the University. . . . In light of uncertain political support and anticipated decline of enrollment it is not surprising that many of us are upset by the present prospects of the University. Yet the damage is not irreparable; the infrastructure built over the years should be strong enough to surmount the challenges ahead.

It is the continuing negative attention to the tragedy of May 4 that has dampened Kent spirits more than any other issue. That attention should be paid to the event is appropriate; that it should be negative is quite another matter. It should not be allowed to destroy what has been built here. May 4 is part of our heritage, as it is part of America's heritage. We should remember that past, not to reopen old wounds or to seek out new villains, but to learn from it and to use it for the building of a greater University. We are a more mature institution now. As a community we have become more aware of the outside world because at Kent the two have merged. Having been touched by a searing experience, perhaps we are better prepared to grapple with the complexities of the past and turn them into opportunities for the future.

Official Violence

An American Tradition

JOHN LOGUE *is associate professor of political science at Kent State University, specializing in the study of American and Scandinavian labor movements. Logue was relaxing on the grass in front of the University of Texas library listening to "yet another speaker" when the news came about the Kent State shootings. "First it was unbelievable. And then, suddenly, the illusion of spring and safety was gone. The guns were loaded."*

> When he went to the wall to be shot
> He went to a wall that was built by his fellows
> And the guns pointed at his chest and the bullets
> Were made by his fellows. . . . Not even
> Those who shot him were different from him.
>
> *Bertolt Brecht*, The Mother

Governmental use of force against demonstrating citizens is no novelty in American history. The shots fired by the National Guard in Kent on May 4, 1970, belong to an American tradition, hallowed by age and honed by use. Official violence, rarely discussed in times of domestic tranquility, has been a standard response to the waves of popular discontent that called into question the sanctity of governmental decisions. It is part of that tradition, too, that those shot were subsequently (and frequently posthumously) declared guilty, while those who did the shooting were exonerated.

The monopoly of the legitimate use of coercion has been part of the traditional definition of government. It is one of democracy's more signal virtues that this coercion has generally rested on prior majority consent, only fitting in an age when the will of the people has replaced the grace of God as the source of governmental legitimacy. There are few, for example, who question the government's right to use coercion in dealing with crimes of violence, with murder, armed robbery, rape, and the like; we would freely agree to those rules prior to the fact of any crime. Likewise, the legitimacy of governmental coercion in responding to property crimes is accepted, where our concern is with evenhandedness, with equality before the law.

However, beyond the enforcement of the criminal code, the legitimacy of governmental coercion is cloudier. The fact of majority consent was not necessarily a redeeming feature in the internment of Japanese-Americans during World War II, or in the systematic use of state coercion in the South to maintain the official, legally sanctioned system of racial segregation. The fear of majority tyranny is well grounded in American political tradition, and it was invoked in the South, when the wider majority prevailed, imposing its norms through federal coercion in Little Rock, at Old Miss, and elsewhere.

But the role of official violence at Kent State and subsequently at Jackson State belongs in a different category and one that is quite rare in Western democracies: the use of the ultimate forms of violence by government to quell explosive popular dissatisfaction with policies widely regarded as illegitimate, to reshape popular attitudes. It is quite common elsewhere, as in the situation that poet and playwright Bertolt Brecht described in the context of the military suppression of the June 1953 rebellion in Berlin:

> After the rebellion on June 17
> The secretary of the writers union
> Had leaflets distributed on Stalin Allee
> In which you could read that the people in their frivolity
> Had lost the confidence of the government
> And could recover it only through
> Redoubled labor. Would it not
> Be simpler for the government
> To dissolve the people and
> Elect a new one?

What the American government sought in May 1970 was to still the rising tide of popular protest, to bring the popular will into accordance with its own, to replace an unduly critical population with a more quiescent, if not more supportive one.

This is not a new practice in America. It was, for example, the typical governmental response, prior to the New Deal, to the waves of unrest that periodically swept the labor market. The violence of the government was not a reaction to political radicalism, for the ideology of the American labor movement was that of a "business unionism" which limited its goals to narrow economic ones. The use of force was not intended to discourage radicalism—indeed, it often encouraged it, turning the 1914 Ludlow strike from an economic altercation between Rockefeller and the miners' union into a virtual civil war in the Colorado coal fields. It was not the (very moderate) goals of the dissenters that were at issue. Of course, demands for wage increases—or American withdrawal from Cambodia—while narrow are not trivial, but they are far from a threat to the maintenance of public authority. It is the very effectiveness of popular protest for narrow goals that seems at issue: the use of governmental violence to reshape public opinion puts a palpable price tag on dissent.

The events of May 1970 are perhaps too sensitive politically for us to see them clearly: we see it as tragedy, as misfortune, as a coincidence of errors, as an accident. Perhaps we can see it more clearly in the analogy to American labor history.

The goals of American unions were limited. Wages and working conditions were at issue, not political revolution. Yet the standard histories of American labor, such as John Commons's classic *History of Labor in the United States* (4 vols., New York: Macmillan, 1918–35), are filled with military metaphors: "industrial battlefields," "conflicts waged," labor losing "its battle of the Marne." It may seem strange to find the language of class warfare in the mouths of liberals—or in the title of George McGovern's *Great Coalfield War*—but it is all too accurate a description.

The industrial battlefields *were* bloody. Sometimes the engagements were with employers' private armies, as at Homestead in 1892. More often, the blood was shed by the state, for the use of police, of state militia (the forerunner of the National Guard), and of federal troops to break strikes was common. Government guns made strike-breaking easy, and their volleys left deaths among strikers and their families in scores of encounters: in Pittsburgh, Baltimore, Reading, Martinsburg, and Chicago during the railroad strikes of 1877; in Pullman, Chicago, and Spring Valley during the Pullman strike of 1894; in the anthracite towns during the strike of 1902; in Lawrence during the textile strike of 1912; in half a dozen towns in the steel strike of 1919; in the textile strikes in the South in 1929 and again in 1934; in the textile strikes in New England, at Auto-Lite in Toledo and Kohler in Sheboygan, on the San Francisco docks, and among Minneapolis truckers in 1934; in the Memorial Day Massacre at Republic Steel in Chicago in 1937, to list but a few of the more notable. It is a litany of heroism, of the unarmed advancing into the sights of the armed, and of illusion, for who could believe that the government would shoot its own citizens for exercising their right to demonstrate? The last words, "Those guns aren't loaded," or, "They won't shoot" could have been engraved on a fair number of tombstones.

It is also a litany of defeat, for it is not surprising that the practice of shooting demonstrators has a chilling effect on the exercise of the freedom of assembly, and the shooting of strikers a chilling effect on the freedom to organize.

Those killed and wounded at Kent State were atypical, for they were college students, a group previously protected by social status from such a fate. The traditional post-game celebration or rites of spring with their concomitant property damage were apolitical. But as the universities have opened, the social backgrounds of their student bodies have changed, and their special dispensation has lapsed.

The demonstration of opposition to government policy in May 1970 was threatening not in broken windows or even a burned ROTC building, but because the massive nature of the demonstrations reflected a shift in the sentiment of a significant segment of the population. Was it the majority view? That question was academic: on the Cambodian question the government's authority stemmed not from popular consent but from its status as government. But the effective, mass mobilization of popular opposition revealed the dubious legitimacy of the policy too clearly. That Vice President Agnew's alliterative invective took on new malice, that President Nixon's incipient paranoia expressed itself in the siege mentality that prevailed in the White House, that Governor Rhodes of Ohio perceived anarchy in the wings and inveighed against "brownshirts," were only expressions of the recognition that certain of the government's actions had ceased to be legitimate in the eyes of the people. It was time for the government to choose another.

Perhaps violence is as American as apple pie, as the adage holds, but its official use and who become its victims are products of political decisions. That is not to allege that the actual shots in Kent were fired because of specific decisions taken, any more than it is to allege that Grover Cleveland ordered Pullman strikers shot; rather, the political decision provided the context within which the shootings of unarmed demonstrators in Kent, as in countless labor conflicts in the past, and the bayoneting of unarmed students at other Ohio universities in those same days, became possible, logical, perhaps even unavoidable. After all, the political process had been set aside; it was not consent to the Cambodian invasion that was sought but quiescence. In the quiet that followed the shots, the government could voice that consent in its enunciation of the will of the "silent majority."

Paradoxically it was the limited nature of the goals of students—and in the past, labor unions—that made them so susceptible to the chilling consequences of official violence. They sought no revolution, no systemic change at all. They were loyal to the American system; they believed in the democratic process. How, then, was it possible for official violence to strike so suddenly? The very incomprehensibility of events was paralyzing.

In the case of the labor movement, the answer is clear: lack of political power made it the object of so much official violence between the 1870s and the early 1930s. It was not that labor had no spokesmen in legislative bodies; it had substantial and, on occasion, eloquent representation there. It was, rather, its inability to influence the executive at those key moments when strikes were general and spreading, when victory seemed within grasp, *not* to intervene with armed force to break picket lines and bring in strike-breakers. The sit-down strikes—factory occupations—of the CIO organizing campaign in the stubbornly anti-union rubber and auto industries in 1936–37 left strikers in possession of the factories and made the use of scab workers and police power more difficult; but the major reason for labor's organizing breakthrough was the reduction in official violence against labor under the New Deal. For the first time in American labor history, the government ceased to be the automatic ally of capital. While employers continued to appeal for the use of governmental force to break strikes, the troops were kept home. The match between labor and the local police was not blood-less, but the outcome was not a foregone conclusion. Moreover, the New Deal labor legislation gave unions the ability to invoke the law against intransigent employers. As John L. Lewis, the head of the miners and the CIO, thundered during the sit-downs at General Motors in 1937, it ill behooved a corporation that chose to violate the Wagner Act to complain of the illegal acts of others in occupy-ing factories. It also ill behooved those who used napalm on Asian villagers to complain of student occupations of administration buildings, much less of demonstrations in violation of official sus-pension of freedom of assembly, but complain they did. Moreover, unlike GM in 1937, they had at their disposal the means to impose their views.

The gunfire at Kent was a product of official response to a general wave of discontent. That the gunfire occurred in Kent was accidental, but that it occurred at all, of course, was not. The demonstration to dissidents was clear: dissent that is successful in mobilizing mass opposition to government policy will not continue without consequence. The government is no "pitiful, helpless giant," but, like Kronos, does not shy away from consuming its children.

Official violence is not particularly discriminating in its selection of victims. Spectators, passers-by, and children suffer the same fate as those active in protest. Kent State was not Ludlow, Colorado, where the state militia killed not only men, women, and boys, but also eleven children under the age of ten, including two infants of three and six months, while machine-gunning and burning the camp of striking miners. There were few small children on the Kent campus that day. It is in keeping with tradition that Sandy Scheuer died because she took a route between classes that brought her with-in range of the National Guard's guns.

The names of the dead at Kent State are as accidental as the names of the guardsmen who shot them. That they died is not. It is no accident that the right to protest is limited only when people make use of it. It is no accident that the government resorts to violence to defend policies its citizens no longer consider legitimate. Perhaps it is fitting that the National Guard came to Kent State directly from its intervention in a truckers' strike, for the link to the tradition is clear enough. But that can hardly be a source of solace to the wounded or the families of the dead. Nor can there be any solace in the fact that those behind the gunsights were much like those in front of them in background, in experience, even—perhaps—in their doubts about the invasion of Cambodia.

There is no monument at Kent State like the one the United Mine Workers erected to its dead at Ludlow. Universities are not like mining communities: their traditions are weaker, their memories shorter, their administrations more responsive to governors. What memorials there are have been erected elsewhere, outside the state. Confronted with the reality of the bloodshed at Kent and Jackson State, the May 1970 demonstrations were the peak of the mass mobilization against the war. The sense of unity on strategy collapsed, for the success of demonstrations had revealed the iron fist of official violence without changing the government's policy. The "law and order" slogan of an administration that would ultimately be revealed as a systematic violator of the law prevailed. The silent majority remained silent while the government interpreted its will. The not-so-silent opposition to the war found itself split, and split again. A few turned to terrorism. Most went home. The wave was broken; the tide of opposition ebbed.

The Burning Question

A Government Cover-up?

by PETER DAVIES

PETER DAVIES *was born in England and first came to the United States in the mid-1950s. In May 1970 he was an insurance broker in New York City. Davies is author of* The Truth About Kent State: A Challenge to the American Conscience *(1973). In 1975, he assisted the Kent State families in their preparation of a civil suit against Ohio Governor James Rhodes and National Guard officers and men involved in the shootings of May 4. Davies's private papers pertaining to the incident and to his subsequent efforts, with Arthur Krause and Rev. John P. Adams, to get a congressional investigation of the shootings, are available to researchers at the Yale University Archives in New Haven, Connecticut. Davies lives now, as he did in 1970, in Staten Island, New York.*

Few incidents have been so thoroughly investigated and analyzed over so long a period of time as was the thirteen-second fusillade of military gunfire that occurred on May 4, 1970. More than three hundred agents of the FBI compiled some eight thousand pages of interviews with witnesses and others. Ohio's Bureau of Criminal Investigation conducted an extensive, but partisan, investigation that indirectly confirmed the U.S. Justice Department's conclusions that the National Guard had not fired in self-defense. A cursory, biased inquiry by Ohio's inspector general helped to underscore these conclusions by revealing, in the statements of some of the principal shooters, an antistudent sentiment bordering on hatred. A presidential commission, chaired by former Pennsylvania governor William Scranton, investigated the incident and ruled that the shootings were "unnecessary, unwarranted and inexcusable." A special Ohio grand jury exonerated the guardsmen of any criminal liability and placed blame for the four deaths and nine woundings on the University's administration and the student demonstrators. All these investigations were completed in five months following the gunfire, and they were only the beginning.

During the next eight years the Kent State killings were dissected and analyzed by lawyers, paralegal assistants, journalists, and writers to a degree that left nothing unexplained or unaccounted for except the one burning question: why did eight to ten guardsmen, veterans of street riots and violent strikes, suddenly wheel around in unison and open fire on students a hundred to four hundred feet away? As one who has been privileged to examine the federal grand jury testimony and pretrial depositions of most of the key figures in this historic incident, I can say, without reservations, that the ROTC fire on May 2 was the work of *agents provocateurs*. Acting on behalf of the Justice Department's Internal Security Division, then headed by Robert Mardian, in conjunction with the intelligence community, whose domestic covert operations had become President Nixon's secret weapon in his campaign to silence dissent, these provocateurs set the stage for the show of force that was to come two days later.

Kent State did *not* just happen. It was the bloody end product of a governmental decision to put a lid on campus demonstrations against America's participation in the invasion of Cambodia. During the last days of April 1970, the most dominant subject of discussion at the White House was student reaction to the invasion and how best to deal with it. A former aide to the National Security Council told me, several years later, that White House anxiety over the expected campus revolt "was almost paranoiac." A disproportionate amount of time was devoted to this one problem because, as he put it, "they were not going to allow students and antiwar activists to do to Nixon what they had done to Johnson." It was from those many hours of discussion that a plan evolved; a plan designed to accomplish two important political objectives: (1) scare the hell out of the antiwar movement in general, and student demonstrators in particular; and (2) give the so-called Silent Majority precisely what it so ardently yearned for from this law-and-order administration: a no-nonsense showdown with the country's Abbie Hoffmans, Jerry Rubins, and Mark Rudds.

That the high-noon confrontation on May 4, 1970, which resulted in the senseless killing of four young men and women, was not intended, I have no doubt; but once done, like the Watergate break-in, the Nixon administration was left with but two options: to act in accordance with the demands of the law, or to cover up responsibility for the incident. As with Watergate, President Nixon opted for a cover-up, a fact indisputably proven by John Ehrlichman's "eyes only" November 1970 memorandum (first revealed in 1978) to Attorney General John Mitchell in which the president's domestic affairs adviser reminds Mitchell of Nixon's order that under no circumstances is there to be a federal grand jury on Kent State. This blatant obstruction of justice on the part of President Nixon was the second act in a chain of events that answers the burning question of why the shooting occurred. The first act was a month earlier, in October 1970, when the Justice Department asked the Ohio grand jury's special prosecutor, Robert Balyeat, to give the department the names of all those likely to be indicted for inciting to riot and for arson in the ROTC fire. Although Ohio law prohibited the disclosure of such information to any agency or individual prior to the actual handing down of indictments, Portage County Judge Edwin Jones approved the request from Washington. Three lists of names were duly forwarded to the Justice Department, and some of those targeted for indictment in connection with the ROTC fire appeared on all three, or at least two, of the lists. When the grand jury issued its report, however, none of those obvious targets for prosecution were among the twenty-four students and one professor indicted. Washington had struck from the lists of an Ohio grand jury its *agents provocateurs*.

Throughout the winter of 1970, the Justice Department repeatedly assured newsmen and the families of the Kent State victims that the government's investigation into the killings was continuing. Ehrlichman, for example, knowing that Nixon had forbidden a federal grand jury, cruelly promised Arthur Krause, whose nineteen-year-old daughter Allison was one of those killed by the guardsmen, that there would be "no whitewash" of the shootings. In reality, the Justice Department was looking for a viable reason for *not* convening a grand jury despite its own summary of the FBI investigation condemning the guardsmen and the Scranton Commission's conclusion that the gunfire was unwarranted. It is, perhaps, the ultimate irony of this political drama that I, unwittingly, provided Mitchell with the vehicle he needed to make public what President Nixon had ordered in secret.

At a May 1971 meeting with Assistant Attorney General Richard Kleindienst, the Reverend John P. Adams of the United Methodist Church and a lawyer representing some of the families of those killed and wounded raised the question of a possible conspiracy amongst some of the older guardsmen to "let the students have it." Kleindienst, to the surprise of Adams and the attorney, expressed immense interest in this suggestion and told them it was an avenue that the Justice Department had neither thought of nor explored. With almost unrestrained enthusiasm, Kleindienst suggested that the Reverend Mr. Adams, rather than his own department with its incomparable investigative resources, submit a report—"substantive in format"—on the conspiracy theory. For the few, like Art Krause and myself, who had fought for a year in the wilderness of fear and disinterest, the Kleindienst invitation was an offer we could not refuse.

By early June of 1971, I had completed my 226-page "Appeal for Justice" addressed to Mitchell and Kleindienst. With the limited evidence available at that time, bolstered by scores of incriminating photographs, I alleged that as many as ten guardsmen, out of the more than seventy involved in the May 4 dispersal of demonstrators, had conspired together to open fire at the students on a prearranged signal. What I did not know then was that those guardsmen were simply carrying out a loosely conveyed order initiated at the White House, passed on to the Justice Department, filtered down from there to Ohio Governor James A. Rhodes, who, in turn, informed his adjutant general, Sylvester Del Corso. This loose order for a show of force was finally translated into understandable instructions when, at noon on May 4, Assistant Adj. Gen. Robert Canterbury brushed aside a professor's appeal for restraint. "These students are going to have to find out what law and order is all about," the general said, and thirty minutes later the students really did find out. For four of them, however, the lesson was moot.

On August 13, 1971, Attorney General Mitchell finally closed the Kent State file by announcing that there would be no federal grand jury. There was, he said, "no credible evidence of a conspiracy" on the part of the guardsmen. Obvious violations of the students' civil rights were conveniently ignored, even though he conceded that the government's findings supported the conclusions of the Scranton Commission. The cover-up of the Nixon administration's role in what had happened was now complete, and so it might

well have remained but for a House Judiciary subcommittee, the unfolding Watergate scandal, and the famous "Saturday Night
Massacre" of October 19, 1973.

For well over a year following Mitchell's announcement, the
Justice Department rejected all appeals to reconsider. Mitchell's
successor, Kleindienst, became visibly irritated by reporters' questions on the subject. The case was closed, period. There was absolutely no basis whatsoever on which to consider federal intervention, and that remained the government's position until August 3,
1973, when Kleindienst's successor, Elliot Richardson, stunned us
all by announcing a dramatic about-face. He had ordered "a new
inquiry" into the Kent State incident to determine if facts brought
to light since Mitchell's statement warranted grand jury action.
What had happened to precipitate this remarkable reversal was the
very real threat of a congressional investigation into the Justice
Department's handling of the case, an investigation which the
Nixon administration had to thwart if its Kent State cover-up was
not to go the way of the Watergate cover-up.

In the spring of 1973, Cong. Don Edwards (D.-Cal.), chairman
of Subcommittee No. 4 of the House Judiciary Committee, initiated
a fact-finding inquiry into our charges that the Nixon administration was obstructing justice by continuing to refuse to do in the Kent
State case what it had done years earlier in the Jackson State incident: convene a grand jury. At the request of Patrick Shea, the
congressman's legal aide, I prepared a forty-page outline of the
history of the Kent State killings and its aftermath. The document,
along with other vital material submitted by the Reverend Mr.
Adams, proved sufficiently compelling for Edwards to have his staff
proceed further, with interviews in Ohio. By June he had a prima
facie case for obstruction of justice by Attorneys General Mitchell
and Kleindienst.

In July, Shea told me that the subcommittee had agreed to investigate the Justice Department's handling of the case and that we
could expect public hearings to begin in the early fall. At the end of
July he confided to me that the first list of witnesses had been drawn
up, and that among those to be subpoenaed to testify were Mitchell,
Kleindienst, Ehrlichman, John Dean,[1] Rhodes, and the two Ohio

---

[1] At the time of the shootings, John Dean was an assistant attorney general at the Justice
Department and a Mitchell protégé.

National Guard generals, Del Corso and Canterbury. It was an impressive list, but our hopes for this long-awaited breakthrough were to be very short-lived. Less than a week later, Attorney General Richardson made his surprise announcement of "a new inquiry," a very clever move that had the immediate effect of forestalling any further action by the Edwards committee pending the outcome of Richardson's intervention. The congressional investigation, which Arthur Krause had publicly called for the day after his daughter was killed, was blocked but not yet torpedoed, and although the families and the rest of us were heartened by Richardson's move, we were also mystified.

For more than three years the government had steadfastly insisted that there were no grounds to justify grand jury action and even less on which to expect successful prosecution. What had prompted the new attorney general to reverse this position was not only the threat of the Edwards investigation but also the knowledge that Nixon's secret order might well come to light. As a loyal administration official, Richardson, who had not been involved in the cover-up, must have been persuaded that disclosure of the "eyes only" Ehrlichman memo to Mitchell would at best be an acute embarrassment to the president, particularly at that time of almost daily Watergate revelations pointing to White House involvement in the break-in and ongoing cover-up. Richardson needed time, and the "new inquiry" into the old evidence was the most effective means of stalling Edwards without committing himself to a grand jury.

Throughout August and September of 1973, Justice Department spokesmen assured keenly interested journalists, like Dave Hess of Knight Newspapers, that the "new inquiry" was continuing. In October, however, the roof fell in when President Nixon dismissed Watergate special prosecutor Archibald Cox and Richardson resigned. When the new acting attorney general, William Ruckelshaus, also refused to rubber stamp Nixon's order, he was promptly fired. His successor, Solicitor General Robert Bork, did the deed, and Cox was gone. The Saturday Night Massacre was, perhaps, the scariest evening this country had experienced in a long time as newscasters reported Nixon's stunning demonstration of presidential power followed by accounts of FBI agents seizing the offices and papers of the attorney general and his deputy. And what of Richardson's "new inquiry" now that he had resigned? For awhile the Justice Department insisted that these dramatic events would in no way jeopardize the probe, but we, and more importantly, Congressman Edwards's subcommittee, were unconvinced. Once again it seemed likely that there would be a congressional investigation, and Shea told me to expect it after the Christmas break.

President Nixon, however, was always one step ahead of everyone in this test of wills. At the end of November he took our breath away by announcing the nomination of Sen. William Saxbe of Ohio to be the new attorney general. Saxbe, a former colonel in the Ohio National Guard, wasted no time in telling the news media that once he was confirmed he would immediately "shut down" the Kent State inquiry and reclose the file. He could not understand why Richardson had reopened the case in the first place, especially as the evidence so clearly showed that "the guardsmen fired in self-defense." We were back to square one, but now we had the subcommittee.

There can be little doubt that Saxbe's remarks about the Kent State case endeared him to Nixon but not to Justice Department officials cognizant of the president's order and the role played by the government in the events leading up to the fatal volley. Saxbe, of course, knew nothing. Acting Attorney General Bork did. As the day approached for the start of Saxbe's confirmation hearings before the Senate Judiciary Committee, Bork found himself increasingly impaled on the horns of an infuriating dilemma: do nothing and hope that the damage from the congressional investigation would be minimal, or handcuff Saxbe by convening a federal grand jury and, once and for all, scuttling the congressional probe forever. The families of the victims were alarmed by Saxbe's negative comment. Art Krause spoke with several senators on the Judiciary Committee. Although there was confidence in Congressman Edwards, the Saturday Night Massacre and the nomination of Saxbe were cause enough for concern about both Richardson's "new inquiry" and our hopes for the congressional investigation.

On December 10, 1973, Senator Saxbe appeared before the Senate Judiciary Committee and was asked several questions about the Kent State case and his remarks on it to the press. He was persuaded to promise that if confirmed he would not interfere in the case—at least that is how it was reported by the media and generally understood by those senators, like Edward Kennedy, who had insisted on this commitment. Careful review of the transcript of the hearings shows that his promise was not what it seemed to be. What

Saxbe actually said was that he would not interfere in the Justice Department's handling of Kent State if by the time he became attorney general "a federal grand jury was convened." This clever phraseology was not overlooked at the Justice Department. Had Saxbe just promised not to interfere, it is more than likely that the "new inquiry" would have been allowed to drag on into the next year whilst a compelling explanation for doing nothing was prepared for the Edwards committee. But Saxbe did not do that, and Bork's hand was forced.

After more than three and one-half years of claiming there were no grounds to justify federal intervention, and only hours before Saxbe was confirmed as the nation's new chief law enforcement officer, Acting Attorney General Bork suddenly, and dramatically, announced at eight o'clock on the night of December 11 that he had ordered a federal grand jury to be convened in Cleveland within a week. It was a stunning move that made little sense at the time, but which later was clearly the only move Bork could make. The stakes were too high to risk a congressional inquiry like that which took place on Watergate, the scene of so many surprising, and, for the president, disastrous disclosures. A grand jury is controlled by Justice Department attorneys, and the strength or weakness of a prosecutor's case, in the event of indictments, can also be determined by the government. As far as the Kent State cover-up was concerned, Bork's decision was to prove to be a bold and brilliant stroke.

On March 28, 1974, after three months of hearing witnesses, the grand jury indicted eight Ohio National Guardsmen for violating the civil rights of the victims. Five of the eight were charged with causing the four deaths. Although on the surface, justice, at long last, seemed to be being done, from my knowledge of the actual shootings it was all too clear that two of those indicted should not have been, and that at least two of the principals involved in triggering the gunfire were pointedly *not* indicted. The last hurdle for the Justice Department to negotiate was the criminal trial of the eight men, and prosecutor Robert Murphy cleared it adroitly by virtually assuring their acquittal during the course of his opening statement to the jury in November 1974.

Murphy conceded before the court that he had no ballistics evidence to show which guardsman had shot which student. Had I been on that jury such an admission would have precluded me from finding any of the eight guilty. The shootings had taken place under confused, almost chaotic, conditions. Even the extensive number of photos available, including several films, cannot show who shot whom. From statements by guardsmen, some of the wounded, and witnesses, it is possible to prove, for example, that Sgt. Lawrence Shafer shot and wounded Joseph Lewis, but as for who killed Bill Schroeder and Sandy Scheuer, there just is not a clue. How, then, could a jury believe that the government had indicted the right killers? Perhaps one of the guardsmen charged with firing recklessly into the crowd had killed a student, and one of those actually charged with that crime had not. My immediate reaction on hearing what Murphy had said was utter dismay. "He's blown it!" I told Art Krause, who was not in the least surprised. He had always viewed the Nixon administration's conduct in handling the murder of his daughter with a jaundiced eye.

As it happened, the jury was not even asked to render a verdict. When Murphy had concluded the presentation of the government's inordinately weak case, the judge stopped the trial and acquitted the eight men. How convenient for the Justice Department that he did not just dismiss the charges, thereby leaving open the possibility for further legal action by the government. By acquitting them—and there is no question that some of the eight did indeed kill some, if not all, of the four students—the Justice Department and the White House were finally off the hook for good.

It is this remarkable chain of events, from July through December 11, 1973, that helps explain so much about Washington's involvement in those first days of May 1970 at Kent State University in Ohio. If what happened was simply the local tragedy it was claimed to be, why was Washington so anxious to know the names of likely targets of state prosecution for arson and inciting to riot? If what happened on May 4, 1970, was in no way planned, why were the same three units marched over the same routes and terrain on May 2 in what amounted to a dress rehearsal? General Canterbury testified that he was unfamiliar with the terrain, and that had he known of the long fence skirting the practice football field he would never have allowed his troops to march into such a situation, yet he was there Saturday night along with General Del Corso.

The shootings at Kent State, like the break-in at Watergate,

Peter Davies stands a vigil for William Schroeder, May 3, 1975.

were a political operation with specific political goals. It was not, however, intended that any students should be killed, any more than the Watergate burglars should be caught red-handed. In the case of Kent State, a few guardsmen used the opportunity to vent their anger and hatred by aiming and shooting deliberately at the backs of the fleeing students. In the case of Watergate, carelessness triggered a chain reaction that did not cease until the president was forced to resign. It is hardly surprising then that in both incidents there was a massive cover-up designed to conceal the government's role. That the Kent State cover-up succeeded is due more to the country's general animosity toward its youth, and the steadfast silence of the Guard and Ohio officials, than it is to any artfulness that was lacking in the Watergate affair. It was also successful because our news media failed to realize that what had happened was not the tragedy they repeatedly called it, but the inevitable, deliberate act of an administration that consistently put its political survival above all other considerations.

A Phoenix Reaction

Peace Studies at Kent State University

DENNIS CAREY *was a graduate student in the Department of Psychology at Kent State in 1970 and was among those observing National Guard efforts to disperse demonstrators on May 4. He subsequently served as a member of the Commission to Implement a Commitment to Nonviolence, appointed by President Robert White in the aftermath of the shootings. Carey is currently the director of the Center for Peaceful Change.*

During the summer following the events of May 4, 1970 at Kent State University, an incredibly complex judicial process was just beginning to sort out the implications of the deaths of four students at the hands of the state. That process was not to approach conclusion for almost a decade. Even then a sense of closure was not achieved for many who felt justice was never truly served during the myriad courtroom maneuverings. Moreover, the innumerable formal and informal discussions carried on during the summer of 1970 in homes, committees, churches, and the media provided precious little satisfaction on the matter. Arguments were made endless by the fixed ideas each person had on exactly who among many possible culprits was to blame for May 4 and what ought to be done in retribution. It was only with the coming of fall, and the imminent reopening of school, that the realization struck that there was a future to be faced by the community and the University.

It is not unusual in these circumstances for people to exhibit what I shall call the "phoenix reaction." Somehow, even following the shock of a disaster like May 4, a time comes when life must go on. The real question becomes how to make it bearable. The mental health of individuals, organizations, and societies alike requires mechanisms for coping with catastrophic events. One such coping mechanism is the creation of a memorial to those who suffered, freeing those who survived to get on with life while not seeming to forget the loss. Better yet, create a "living" memorial, something which is active and can represent a rebirth out of the ashes of tragedy. It was under this motivation, in my opinion, that Kent State University established its peace studies program, which came to be known as the Center for Peaceful Change (CPC).

With the passing of more than a decade it is necessary to review the history of the CPC and assess its effectiveness as a phoenix reaction. This is called for not only because those who established and supported the program over the years deserve such an accounting, but also because, in a broader sense, these kinds of institutionalized reactions to human agony represent the history of adjustment and change in communities and need to be studied.

Expectations and Reality

One of the problems attending the creation of a "living memorial" like the CPC is that the depth and intensity of the emotions which drive the effort often result in unrealistic expectations. Initially, the CPC was supposed to "study the role of higher education in creating nonviolent social change." This charge lacked the kind of specificity and concreteness necessary for realistic job descriptions and behavioral objectives. Among the first tasks, then, was to begin to define the actual functions such a center is capable of performing and to hire a staff adequate to those tasks. Unfortunately, this was to prove very difficult from the outset. Such a practical approach threatened the psychological dynamics of the phoenix reaction which the Kent State community was experiencing.

Students, professors, administrators, and townspeople could all embrace the concept of a Center for Peaceful Change and enjoy what it offered as a living memorial in response to their need for healing and doing something positive. But they could embrace it only so long as the idea remained at the level of noble but ambiguous sentiments. As soon as the small but eager staff of the newly inaugurated (1971) center suggested that their work should fall under the traditional university functions of teaching, research, and service, endemic conflicts arose among supporters. Letters to the editor in the campus newspaper as well as direct communication with the various constituencies revealed during that first year that each sector of the public had strong biases operating.

Students, for example, felt that the CPC should focus its energy on social action. The idea seemed to be that, through the Center, the University could express ideas regarding social and political changes in a society involved at that time in a questionable war. Townsfolk, on the other hand, emphasized the need to have an agency on campus which could influence student protestors to remain "non-violent." Colleagues teaching in other departments at the University saw an opportunity to design research on such topics as social movements and organizational violence. Courses might also be constructed, but they must clearly not be in serious competition for enrollment with existing departments. Finally, the administration of the University, in its unavoidable quest for an ever more conservative fiscal policy, pushed for designing the Center in ways which would not permanently commit support resources.

It is understandable that each of these groups, given its own particular perspective, saw its approach to the CPC as the obvious choice. The challenge for the staff of the new center in that first year was to put together a program which went at least part way in meeting the diverse needs of each of these constituencies. After considerable research on the matter, it was decided that the closest thing to a design which could satisfy some of these requirements was to be found in the field known as peace studies. Coincidentally, during the period 1970–71, the field of peace studies was coalescing under what was to become the professional organization for teachers, researchers, and practitioners: The Consortium On Peace Research, Education, and Development. The CPC moved quickly to become a charter member of that organization and has maintained an active role in its development. More will be said later about the growth of this relationship. At the time, however, the advantage gained by joining this very dynamic group of innovative Irenologists (the name coined to designate this emerging discipline) was twofold. First, Kent State could announce to the outside world that it was taking a step as an institution to react to the events of May 4 in a way which it hoped would be acceptable to a public deeply polarized by the tragedy. The Consortium was national in scope, with many international ties, and Kent's notoriety at that time was sure to draw attention to its entrance into the area of peace studies. Reactions were bound to be very positive across the country, especially at other universities with similar programs. The second advantage in joining the Consortium was the help it provided in suggesting which academic or nonacademic activities were being successfully employed at other schools in their own peace studies programs. It should be noted that one of the most surprising discoveries of that first year for the CPC was that Kent State was not the only school to begin a peace studies program in response to May 4, 1970. As the media coverage of the days immediately following the shootings so graphically depicted, over 300 colleges and universities closed. The phoenix reaction at these institutions resulted in the initiation of many programs very similar to that of the CPC.

The decision to design the work of the CPC along the lines of Irenology was an attempt to meet all or at least some of the particular preferences of the various constituencies. The Center was committed to active mediation of conflict, in the role of consultant, during protest and "social change" activities as was the wish of the student faction. Community groups seemed responsive to the idea that here was a university activity devoted to communicating to students the wisdom of nonviolent versus violent means of creating change. Faculty participated in the excitement of creating new interdisciplinary courses focusing on such esoteric topics as Ghandian philosophy and tactics while not feeling particularly threatened by competition for enrollment. And, last but not least, the administration could be gracious about assigning money and personnel to the program, having the reassurance that peace studies programs at other schools were found to be run primarily on soft funds through grants and contributions. In any case, as one administrator put it to me after only six months had passed, "Centers like this can always be dismantled easily enough when all the excitement over May 4 dies down."

It should be said, for the sake of accuracy and perspective, that it is my best estimate that only something on the order of 10 percent of the University population and significantly less of the general community were even concerned with the CPC, much less involved in its inception and design. This is important to realize because it reflects the fact that the phoenix reaction, at least as it occurred at Kent State, is limited to only a small portion of the total population.

More important to this discussion, however, is the fact that approximately 90 percent of those which the Center was being asked to serve most directly were probably unaware the Center existed, knew of it but were uninterested, or were actually opposed to the whole idea. The only retort to the natural conclusion that the Center lacked enough support to deserve birth is that research tells us that most organizations are, in fact, the result of an active but small group of supporters. This certainly was the case in the early as well as the later history of the CPC. Expectations of the CPC, then, ranged from outright involvement in social protest actions, to classroom and research publication activity, to remaining as inconspicuous as possible in order to avoid the risk of awakening opposition. It seems reasonable to say that expectations of the Center were sometimes contradictory. This incongruity of expectations on the one hand and organizational realities on the other has continued over the years to bear bitter fruit, at times threatening the very existence of the CPC. It is, perhaps, inherent in the very nature of the phoenix reaction that people invest great hope in an organization born out of severe tragedy and that it never is able to function up to that level of expectation. The discussion from this point on is intended, however, to suggest that inordinately high levels of expectation could probably be borne if only the expectations were made less idiosyncratic.

Achievements and Shortcomings, 1971 to 1980

Regardless of the somewhat disconcerting expectations and realities surrounding its conception, the CPC viewed its primary task as that of providing a positive, concrete institutional response by Kent State University to the devastating events of May 4, 1970. It was decided that designing, implementing, and certifying an academic program should take first priority. After great hesitancy by the various committees and boards through which such programmatic matters must pass, the CPC was ratified by the Ohio State Board of Regents as a degree program under the College of Arts and Sciences. John Begala's essay has already described the Regents' reluctance to accept "peace studies" as the title for the academic major within the Center's program. The subsequent title, "integrative change," was, apparently, sufficiently vacuous to reassure the most conservative of Board members. It must be noted, however, that this compromise, which was seen as a necessary expedient at the time, has not been without consequence. Naming the peace studies major "integrative change" has resulted in some negative repercussions. Students are sometimes confused by the term and tend to dismiss the possibility of taking courses in the Center because it sounds too esoteric. Some have even said they were not interested because it sounded like a program having to do with busing to achieve racial balance.

A more serious criticism of the way in which the CPC went about constructing its academic program has to do with the choice to establish the program as an independent unit within the University structure. One alternative would have been to utilize faculty and resources of those departments most closely related to the field of peace studies: political science, psychology, sociology, and so forth. This would certainly have reflected an interdisciplinary approach and would have helped to involve more people in the active life of the Center. Instead, the Center chose to acquire its own staff, facilities, and monetary support base. The reasoning behind sacrificing the richness afforded by combining the backgrounds of scholars from a variety of fields has to do with the basic dynamics of the phoenix reaction as it impinges on the complex matrix of institutional politics and economics.

First, support by the original group of people who initiated the idea of a living memorial to those who suffered on May 4 simply stood no chance of being sustained over time. The reasons are both numerous and obvious. This group represented a small minority of the population of the institution and its surrounding community. Of this number, given our highly mobile society, only a very few remain in the geographic area. As time goes on, the very dynamics of memorializing work against the survival of the memorial itself. That is, as was stated earlier in this analysis, memorializing allows people to go on with their lives secure in the thought that the tragic event is receiving proper attention. They generally do not perceive the memorial, even a "living memorial," as needing constant nurturance and protection in a resource-scarce environment where competition is high. Therefore, it was reasonable to conclude that the Center would not be able to depend on a significant support base being generated and constantly renewed through the merit of the original motivations. As the years pass, memorials such as the CPC must gradually begin to assume the responsibility for their own support.

This subtle but pragmatic reality led to another conclusion, namely that such self-support would not be built upon staff and material resources provided by University departments which were becoming hard pressed even to support themselves. Higher education was facing an increasingly hostile economic picture. Moreover, Kent State University was encountering a massive decline in enrollment because of the adverse publicity surrounding May 4, 1970. The effects of that enrollment problem resulted in particularly difficult fiscal problems for the University quite apart from and in advance of the depression felt by all other schools in the nation. Threatened with cutbacks, academic departments began to retract any and all extraneous involvements of their faculty.

Hence, today the Center for Peaceful Change stands as an independent academic unit within the structure of Kent State University. It teaches its own courses, promotes and tenures its own faculty, and produces income which covers the direct costs of the program as well as a significant portion of its indirect costs. On the surface this may seem rather cold as a design for the support of a unit which was meant to be an all-university memorial. It must be remembered, however, that the decision to create the Center as a "living" memorial meant that it was to be more than a statue or marker on the graves of the slain students; it had to be designed to "do" things. It was also meant to be an institutional response. Institutions are, by their nature, impersonal creatures; however, they do have one advantage over individuals when it comes to memorializing an event like May 4. If care is taken and the right structures are put in place, a program like the CPC can have a reasonable hope of growing into a permanent function of the University.

Within this framework, the CPC has attempted to build into its design as much interdisciplinarity as was reasonable. Faculty have come from as broad a background as funds allowed. Hence, the CPC has employed professors of philosophy, psychology, business management, communications and rhetoric, history, and international relations. In this manner, the Center has established its independence while maintaining the ideal of involving as many sources of information as possible about the nature of social change.

Service: The Candlelight Vigil, Conflict Mediation, and the Gym Controversy

In addition to the academic program just described, the CPC has also tried to take seriously its community service obligations. One of these obligations is to remind the public periodically that the work of the CPC is done as a memorial to May 4. To accomplish this, the CPC conducts an annual Candlelight Vigil to symbolize its origins and to bring people together to rekindle that emotional sense of loss which gave rise to Kent State's phoenix reaction.

One of the most dramatic opportunities for the CPC to perform a service which went well beyond the vigil was the mediative role it played in 1977 during the gym controversy. The protest itself is detailed elsewhere in this book, and it is the purpose of this discussion only to analyze the particular activities of the CPC during the protest period to determine if it was able to fulfill people's expectations as an institutional response to May 4 by helping to prevent a repetition of that violence.

Early on, the CPC was asked by the organizers of the protest—the May 4th Coalition—to become involved in the strategy meetings of the group. I agreed to assume the role of mediator/adviser, but only with the understanding that I would also be participating in consultations with the administration, whose members had asked the CPC to become involved. Thus, the Center would follow one of the basic principles of mediation and establish a communication channel between the adversaries in a controversy. It was clearly explained to all parties that any discussion judged by either group to be privileged and not to be shared should be so designated, so that a level of trust could be maintained.

The situation was particularly complicated for the CPC because the focus of the conflict was, in a sense, too close to home. The proposal to build the gym on the site of the May 4 events created the impression that the CPC, as a memorial to that tragedy, should certainly stand on the side of the protestors. This obviously would have invalidated its role as mediator. In addition, certain elements of the administration had just placed the Center under a severe threat of being dismantled. That decision was only reversed through the happenstance of the protest and the need for a mediator, combined with the efforts of a sympathetic president on behalf of the Center. For these reasons, the CPC's role should not be taken as a typical example of mediation by those in the peace studies field. Normally, mediators are asked to help as unbiased and unthreatened consultants whose function is to try to encourage continued communication and provide an environment where compromise can be reached nonviolently. This was to prove extremely difficult in the case of the gym protest at Kent State; sometimes it became literally impossible.

Over the months that the protest was in progress, representatives of the Center were present during hundreds of hours of debate and discussion within and between the protestors and the University administration. At particular times, the administration began to ask the mediator to abandon his role and simply tell the protestors to stop what the administration viewed as unwarranted interference with its legitimate powers. At the same time, the protestors were arguing that the Center should carry their non-negotiable demands to the administration and bring back the response. A good example of this sort of impasse occurred when it was decided that the protestors' "Tent City" would be removed. The administration concluded that the kind of negative publicity they were receiving from the press and public for allowing the encampment to continue to exist had begun to outweigh the possible benefits of continued negotiation and a possible settlement. At that point the role of the Center as mediator was reduced to working with both sides on the details of carrying out a nonviolent protest with civil disobedience and arrests. The action resulted in what must be called a classic example of cooperation between law enforcement personnel and the leaders of the protest. Over one hundred and ninety people were arrested without anything like the kind of violence present on May 4, 1970. The police did not wear guns, and the protestors made an absolute commitment to nonviolence during the process of being arrested. For many this was their first experience with actual civil disobedience. This was as true for the police as for the demonstrators. Moreover, since the protestors decided to lock arms and legs, meaning that they would have to be pried apart before arrest, a great deal of physical contact was necessary, including the use of controlled force on both sides. Again, it is a tribute to both parties that injuries were held to an absolute minimum. I would like to think that the Center for

Peaceful Change played a useful role in insuring this outcome. However, the fact that the situation deteriorated to the point where only civil disobedience was left as an option is a good indication of the untenable position in which the Center was placed. Much of the leverage that mediation might otherwise have made available in order to maintain negotiations was lost through the claims made on the Center's allegiance by each side. The University expected loyalty from one of its own units, and the students expected commitment by the CPC to the cause of a protest born of a sense of moral outrage.

The outcome of the gymnasium protest is, by now, well known. The gym was built, and the protestors were left with the modest but deserved recognition that they had fought the good fight. Both the administration and the protestors could lay claim to credit for the nonviolent manner in which most of the action was carried out. However, as with the academic role of the CPC, the various constituencies of the Center made its role as conflict mediator during the gymnasium protest very difficult to realize. For one thing, it is almost impossible to say that any one discussion or negotiation or compromise resulted in the avoidance of violence. One does not know for sure that violence would have occurred on any particular occasion, with or without the Center's mediation. Thus, if violence had occurred, the question would have been asked, where was the CPC when it was really needed? But, when violence was averted, credit for the work it took to assure a nonviolent action was assumed by each adversary and rightly so. The CPC served as a facilitator and, as such, could only really succeed when the participants came to see themselves as capable of using nonviolent tactics. Normally, this is just what the conflict mediator would be looking for. But, with the Center involved in a conflict within its mother institution, it is easy to see the dilemma which arose.

Two conclusions can be reached concerning the long-range effects of the gym protest on the CPC. First, from the standpoint of the CPC as a conflict mediation agency, it must be said that the Center achieved at least modest success since it did play an active role in mediating a controversy which could well have resulted in serious violence. Unfortunately, what will probably be remembered by the participants is the intransigent position taken by the Center in its refusal to compromise its stand as a mediator by taking sides on the issue itself.

Developing a Research Model

Having discussed the CPC as a teaching and service program, it is necessary to review the research activities of the Center in order to complete this assessment of the institutional response to May 4, 1970. As with its teaching and service designs, the CPC's research program was aimed at taking a practical approach to the original charge to the Center. A concrete and usable model for researching nonviolent social change had to be identified. Again, the survival of the Center as a memorial was at stake. Almost from the first day of its existence the CPC has encountered skepticism about its place at a scholarly institution. The attitude was one of cynicism concerning the rigor and respectability of doing research on such a seemingly ephemeral topic. Many of those who were willing to support the Center at the level of its general charge were embarrassed by bringing the idea of studying nonviolent social change into the same scholarly arena in which the rest of the social sciences compete. They could not be blamed for this reticence as very few had any real experience with the work which had been done at other institutions in the field of peace studies.

It took almost the entire decade for the Center to begin to familiarize the Kent State community with peace studies research. However, at this point, a significant number of faculty throughout the University have responded favorably to the record of publication and professional activities accomplished by the CPC staff. It is interesting to note that, once again, the phoenix reaction in and of itself could not have supported the existence of the Center as a memorial in the minds of those who make up the research community at Kent State University. For them, any unit must eventually merit sustenance through credible performance in scholarly endeavors.

Fortunately, the CPC was able not only to produce such research through the individual efforts of its staff, but also has become a recognized program among other universities with peace studies departments. Recently, the Consortium On Peace Research, Education, and Development relocated its headquarters to Kent State University and is looking forward to a mutually beneficial relationship. In addition, the Center was chosen as the new site for the scholarly journal *Peace and Change* and has assumed managing

editorship. The point to be made is that, even with recognition outside of the Kent State community, the CPC would stand little
chance of survival if it had not moved quickly to translate that
recognition into meaningful terms for home consumption.

The preceding analysis has attempted to relate the institutional response by Kent State University following the May 4 tragedy to the
phenomenon of the "phoenix reaction." The experiences of those
who worked to make the CPC a success reveal that the intensity of
an event such as May 4 creates a dynamic but short-lived base for
such an institutional response. It is dynamic because the feeling was
acute, immediately following the tragedy, that the institution must
have a dramatic rebirth. Something must be created which was
lacking in the old institution, something which can help prevent the
situation from occurring again. This base is short-lived, however, in
that people cannot long maintain the energy created by the emotional reaction to tragedy, especially in an institutional setting. The
Center for Peaceful Change, like other living memorials, had to assume responsibility for its own maintenance. This it has done
through the implementation of its academic, service, and research
programs. That the Center has had to go through this process does
not mean that this particular method of memorializing our losses is
flawed by the fickleness of the human character. Rather, it would
seem to be due to our need to depend upon our institutions to lend
permanence to our feelings.

The Candlelight Vigil

"A way of participating"

an interview with JERRY M. LEWIS

JERRY M. LEWIS *was born in 1937 in Oak Park, Illinois. He first came to Kent in 1966 and was appointed assistant professor of sociology. He received his doctorate from the University of Illinois in 1970. Lewis was an opponent of American involvement in Vietnam and served as adviser to several student political groups. Looking back at May 1970, he recalls: "I was one of the leaders of the faculty [peace] marshals that weekend, and as a result of that I was in the Taylor parking lot when the National Guard fired. I was in the direct line of fire." In the years after the shootings, Lewis has become the principal figure associated with the candlelight vigil, which begins in the evening of May third each year. Students, faculty, and others who wish to take part, make a candlelight procession around the perimeter of the campus and then conclude their walk at the site of the shootings. Small groups of people then stand a silent vigil through the night. Lewis has published extensively on the Kent State shootings as well as other topics, and many of his articles appeared in a book co-edited with Thomas Hensley in 1978, titled* Kent State and May 4th: A Social Science Perspective. *Lewis is currently professor of sociology at Kent State University. The interview was conducted on November 17, 1980.*

The candlelight vigil has become one of the most distinctive characteristics of the annual May fourth commemoration. It was begun by you and a few other people in the spring of 1971; how did it come about?

I was talking with Michelle Klein, who was a student of mine and was on campus in May 1970. We were talking about an appropriate commemoration and decided the best thing would be a vigil, where students, faculty, and whoever wanted to could stand at the spots where the four slain students had fallen in the Taylor parking lot. Independent of us, another student, Jeff Auld, had proposed that there be a march around campus. We got together, and the march and vigil were combined, which has become known as the candle-light walk and vigil. It was really a two-pronged sort of thing. The initial response of the University administration was very negative. President White, I remember, wanted only four or eight people on the entire hill. I recall turning to one of his representatives and saying, "Well, I think there are probably going to be about two thousand people on the hill, and there's not much you can do about it." He blanched and said, "Oh, okay." And so they didn't bother us. But now, everybody starts calling us and encouraging us; the candlelight walk and the vigil have become really the cornerstone of the commemoration.

Officially though, the walk and vigil are sponsored by the Center for Peaceful Change. That's now its one commemorative event. The way it usually happens each year, Dennis Carey, director of the Center, calls me in late March and we start working on it. Generally, I pick up two students from the CPC and they work with me through the spring to organize the whole thing. A number of agencies must be dealt with: the University police, Parking and Traffic, the press, and so forth.

Has the program been effectively institutionalized?
No, not really. It's been too much institutionalized around me. To the degree that it has become identified with the Center for Peaceful Change, I think that's good. But I still want to see it become independent of me, and that is one thing I hope to achieve in the next few years.

What is the broad purpose of the vigil?
One of the things that I think is so unique about the vigil—and if I've had any stamp on it, it's been in this area—is the effort to keep it a personal thing for the people who attend: students, faculty, towns-persons. Over the years I have had to really, and sometimes nastily, resist people who wanted to say prayers or play music, or do some other thing. I've tried to keep it simple. It's not been easy, and there have been prayers read; one year a trumpeter played taps. The vigil itself means several things. For one kind of person it is a historical reenactment of the event: people are in fact placed where the four students fell. When freshmen particularly come up, they are amazed at the distances involved. So it's really a teaching device. People learn about the dimensions of the protest that went on during that

day in 1970. Some people of the political left have tried to have their own perspective put forward at the vigil but considerable pressure was exerted against that. I remember once when members of the Revolutionary Student Brigade marched with red flags and chanted. But the ideological aspect of it is broken up because people see it, and they should, as a personal statement.

The vigil serves also a humanitarian purpose, broadly defined. Many people, independent of historical reasons or any kind of ideology, just think that an injustice was done.

What are the dynamics of the vigil?
It has evolved over the years, but basically the candlelight walk and vigil begins about 10:30 on the night of May 3. There is a procession around campus, which usually takes about forty-five minutes. There is no significance to the route followed; it's really just for convenience. There are a couple points where you can look back to see the row of candles behind you. The walk starts from the Victory Bell on the Commons and ends at the Taylor parking lot. What we've generally done is to have people who are associated in a strong way with the shootings stand the first vigils: the parents of the slain or wounded students, often members of the May 4th Task Force. All the vigils are half-hour segments, through the night until the beginning of the commemorative program the next day on the Commons. What has evolved recently is that the people standing the last four vigils and I walk to the Commons about 12:15 on May 4 to mark the transition to the other commemoration activity.

Are the half-hour vigils always filled, year after year?
No, we've had some problems with that, interestingly enough. The first year was no problem. But we often have trouble signing people up for the period between three and five in the morning, though something like a thousand to twelve hundred people usually attend the candlelight walk. Somebody always stands the vigil of course; some people will stand for several hours.

Since 1970, there has been a marked difference, which has perhaps increased over time, between the vigil of May 3 and the more political commemoration of May 4. How do you explain that difference?
I don't know. I have struggled with that. The vigil has not changed that much. It's really the same thing year in and year out. That may

be the attractiveness of it: so clear and consistent. Everybody knows the proper behavior. I think that's the first reason that the vigil has been so successful and the political rallies so unsuccessful. People just don't know what's going to happen at the rally. The second reason is that the political rallies have been terribly narrow; that is, some of the viewpoints have been so esoteric that people don't want to sit through it. I think that the activists have failed to see that. The general run of students wants to go to the rally to hear some statement about what happened on May 4, 1970. Plus, I think there is a general lack of political interest in recent years.

How do you respond to comments that the vigil is not the appropriate commemoration, that the political rally is closer to the real meaning of the shootings?
I can understand that sentiment, and I guess that I respond that you can make a political statement by attending the vigil.

What is the political statement that you make by going to the vigil?
I think that you say there was an injustice done here ten years ago, and that you should never forget it. That's what mine would be. But

Candlelight vigil, May 1972.

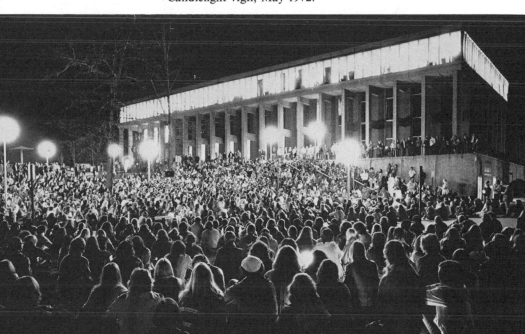

I understand those people who say it's phoney, it's maudlin. Someone was very angry with me in the spring of 1977 because I wouldn't let him make a speech against the gym. I just think that the vigil is so many things to so many people that if we began to politicize it too much, people would be driven away.

Do you think the vigil's appeal is enhanced because it has become a ritual?
Yes. It's a nice warm glove to put on; it's a way of participating on a campus that doesn't have much tradition to it. To some, it may be a ritual to be attended because it's there. I don't mind that. I think if we're trying to reduce militarism in our society, and if one way that militarism survives is through ritual, then we might find alternate rituals to give people. Rituals are important. They give people a sense of meaning, tradition, and continuity—and I think that's important.

Do you see the vigil as something that will go on indefinitely?
I hope it does. I guess I have to answer that on two levels. At the personal level, I'd sure like to see it continue. As a sociologist, I suspect it won't. I think that there has been a great sense of closure after the tenth-anniversary commemoration. There will be a vigil as long as I'm here. I made that promise to Mrs. Scheuer several years ago.

How useful is it to continue the commemoration?
It was very useful in a functional sense early on, to help people work through their pain. Now I think it's useful in an educational sense, for people to learn about what happened. And it's probably useful to a school which has limited traditions. Of course, the Kent State controversy went on, as many people have said, until January 1979; so it made all kinds of sense to have the commemoration until the final settlement of the civil suit. The functionality of the commemoration in terms of the pain and the personal statement has certainly diminished, but the whole sense of a humanitarian perspective and an opposition to injustice will continue. I see it now in students who were ten years old in 1970. I suppose what I will find most interesting is some young person attending the vigil who was born after 1970. Certainly as long as I'm here, there will be a vigil, even if I have to stand alone. But I don't think I will have to stand out there alone.

The Kent State Legacy and the "Business at Hand"

by MIRIAM R. JACKSON

MIRIAM R. (MIM) JACKSON *was a freshman at Kent State University in 1970. She joined the antiwar/anti-Guard demonstration on the Kent State Commons just before it was dispersed on May 4, 1970, and heard the shots fired from the crest of Blanket Hill soon thereafter. In May of 1982 Jackson received her Ph.D. in American Studies/History from Purdue University. Her dissertation, which concerns both Vietnam and Kent State, 1970, is entitled: "We Shall Not Be Moved: A Study of the May 4th Coalition and the Kent State University Gymnasium Controversy of 1977."*

> "Kent State" has meaning around the world.
> Vietnam, Cambodia, Kent State. People struggling in the United States and Asia against the hegemony of American capitalist power.
> Orangeburg, Kent State, Jackson State. Savage military repression of young Americans.
> Kent State, Watergate. Cynical obstruction by overt class-interested state action.
> Yet in Kent one is still asked, "Were you *here* in 1970?"
>
> *Nancy Grim, KSU '77, "The Politics of History."*[1]

As May 4, 1970, fades more and more into history, it becomes both appropriate and necessary to put it in perspective with past, present, and future needs and realities. This is so not only because we did not achieve justice for 1970, but also because the national conditions which produced the events of 1970 continue to cause widespread suffering today. Kent State University would have preferred us to make May 4 simply a day of mourning. It has always felt most com-

---

[1] Nancy Grim, "The Politics of History," *Left Review* 2 (Fall 1977): 8.

fortable with the quasi-religious candlelight vigil the night of May 3–4, and least comfortable with the somewhat contrasting atmosphere typical of May 4 itself, an atmosphere which has tended to encourage reaffirmation of the necessity and justifiability of dissent. Confining a commemoration of 1970 to mourning for "The Tragedy" would conveniently freeze "the past into particular situations and . . . [would show] . . . the present blameless."[2] This, however, is precisely what the University has tried to do with respect to 1970. Kent State cannot admit that its handling of student unrest on May 2 and 3, 1970, was remarkably inept, or that its delivery of campus control to the hands of Governor Rhodes and the Ohio National Guard helped pave the way for the May 4 confrontation. Nor can the administration, given the role it played that long weekend of attempting to ban the scheduled May 4 rally, admit that those of us who insisted on exercising our First Amendment rights by peacefully assembling on the Commons that day may have been justified in denying the subsequent dispersal orders of the National Guard. How much easier for successive Kent State administrations to classify the shootings as a "tragedy" and concentrate their annual blessings on the May 3 vigil, an event, according to former Kent State President Glenn Olds, "in which all concerned persons may participate, reflect and silently commemorate the meaning of these events without distractions of any alien, partisan, or political interpretation."[3]

In May of 1971, the administration created an institution meant to function as a "living memorial" to the dead of 1970. It was, revealingly, named the Center for Peaceful Change (CPC), reflecting both apparent administration conclusions concerning the shootings: that social protest was neither conceivable nor justified unless it was peaceful, and that the four students had died because the May 4 protest had not been peaceful. Neither conclusion has ever been acceptable to those of us who, throughout the 1970s, sought explanation and accountability for Kent State. Only the Ohio National Guard, after all, was actually violent on May 4, 1970. Many of us, therefore, regarded the Center for Peaceful Change as an administration attempt at compromise between two groups: campus radicals who wished May 4 to be memorialized in an entirely political

---

[2] Grim, "The Politics of History," p. 9.
[3] Letter from Glenn Olds to *Daily Kent Stater*, April 28, 1977.

manner and conservatives from both campus and community outraged at the idea of May 4 being memorialized at all. The CPC was a way of safely institutionalizing the events of 1970 without having to analyze the real causes of them. It has operated, in fact, throughout most of its existence, as only the tamest and most neutral of "living memorials." It played a partisan, political role during the spring and summer of 1977 (when it supported the May 4th Coalition with everything from verbal encouragement to key aid in arrest procedure training for Coalition members) only accidentally and rather out of character.

We at Kent State have, in many ways, been spoiled this past decade. This fact becomes only too apparent when we compare our experience with demanding accountability from government and society for causing the four deaths to the experiences, for instance, of the black victims of Orangeburg and Southern University. No one paid much attention, nationally, to the latter set of campus shootings—after all, was it that unusual for blacks to be shot, particularly in the Deep South? The killing of two black students at Jackson State on May 14, 1970, produced some national reaction only because it occurred within ten days of the killings at Kent State. Deeply ingrained racism has placed Orangeburg, Southern University, and Jackson State outside the mainstream of national attention; clearly, neither the American government nor most American citizens have ever cared about or questioned the causes of those tragedies. Kent State has gotten the lion's share of attention because mainstream America—and the American government—could not display with such impunity the same degree of indifference toward victimized white students that they had traditionally displayed toward victimized black students. National indifference about the killings at Orangeburg, Southern University, and Jackson State has, thus, translated into national ambivalence about the events at Kent State.

This country apparently suffers from a permanent case of schizophrenia about May 4, 1970. It did not like the idea of materially comfortable white college students demonstrating and causing "trouble," but neither could it justify the fact that troops acting in its name had shot down its children—unless and until those children could be portrayed, like blacks and Native Americans, as "subhumans" and "undesirables." And, in fact, this is exactly what happened. By 1977, it was still being claimed that the responsibility for 1970 lay "entirely on the shoulders and conscience of those students, professors and outside agitators who planned and carried out the riots on [*sic*] Kent."[4] Students trying to plan a peaceful march through Kent as part of the commemoration that year were characterized by a Kent public official as mere "rabble."[5] In 1970, Vice President Agnew's "effete snobs" became President Nixon's "bums" and, finally, Gov. James Rhodes's "brownshirts." Once we had been classified as a problem to be "eradicated," we became a new form of "nigger" subjected to a type of lynching the following day. As author Peter Davies has noted: "In retrospect it is hardly surprising that the guns did fire, that thirteen of 'the worst people we harbor in America' were shot, four of them fatally."[6]

Unfortunately, the views of student activists expressed by the president, vice president, and governor served both to reflect and to manipulate broad public opinion (certainly public opinion in Ohio). A Gallup poll taken shortly after the shootings indicated specific majority support for the guardsmen's actions at Kent State and disgust and hostility toward students in general. "If for a great many campus moderates, the shootings were inexcusable," wrote Davies in 1973, "a majority of their parents felt that the resort to lethal force was long overdue."[7] What had happened to the "tradition" of toleration in America?

A *Daily Kent Stater* columnist, searching for the meaning of the shootings on the occasion of their third anniversary, suggested that an appropriate social cause might be found, as a legacy of 1970, in efforts to eliminate the dynamics in American society that allowed "some to be treated as subhumans."[8] And that focus, really the central issue of May 4, 1970, remains the central issue today. For very little in the fundamental structure of this country that produced the armed suppression of dissent has changed in a decade. The American economy has deteriorated greatly; but the American war ma-

[4] Letter from Richard Larlham to *Kent-Ravenna Record-Courier*, June 13, 1977.

[5] Editorial, *Daily Kent Stater*, April 19, 1977; quoted in Thomas D. Matijasic and Scott Bills, "The People United: A Tentative Commentary on the Kent State Struggle, 1977," *Left Review* 2 (Fall 1977): 15–16.

[6] Peter Davies, *The Truth About Kent State: A Challenge to the American Conscience* (New York: Farrar, Straus & Giroux, 1973), p. 22.

[7] Ibid., p. 141.

[8] R. F. Livolsy, "Tragedies Like KSU Deaths Not New to 'Black America,' " *Daily Kent Stater*, May 4, 1973.

chine, the potential and actual machinery of domestic repression, the use of anticommunism, anti-intellectualism, and racism to confuse and divide students and workers, blacks and whites, stands intact and largely unchallenged over a decade after 1970 and seven years after the end of the Vietnam War.

American society was faced in 1970 with the reality of a seriously deteriorating capitalist system, one which sought, particularly through such government agencies and projects as the CIA, the FBI, and COINTELPRO, to perpetuate itself by imperialist adventures abroad and by domestic repression. This crisis has only worsened in the past decade, though the spotlight may alternately focus on Iran, El Salvador, or plant closings in Detroit and Youngstown rather than Indochina, the Black Panthers, or student protestors. There was something terribly wrong with a society that could kill its own children in 1970 for exercising rights of speech and assembly which those children had been taught were inherent in the American Way. There is still something terribly wrong with a society that looks away from the Vietnam War rather than admit that it lost a battle for domination of a foreign, nonwhite, "underdeveloped" people. It is a society afraid to confront, openly and honestly, the fundamental issues raised by the repressive realities (as opposed to the progressive myths) of past and present American conduct toward emergent peoples all over the world struggling for self-determination.

During the 1970s, those of us who had been involved with the events at Kent State in May 1970 and all others who, after the shootings, chose to struggle with us, undertook both a quest for justice for the victims of May 4 and an effort to define and carry on the positive legacy of 1970. Each May 4 we returned to the Commons to continue the rally forcibly dispersed in 1970; to analyze the connections between 1970 and the current economic, political, and social situation; and to pledge our continuing efforts to prevent the repression of 1970 from recurring.

Unfortunately, the annual speakers were too often vague about the specific causes of past and present injustice and vague or contradictory as to how the future was to be made better. It was said that it had been an outrage for people to die in an atmosphere of dissent. We, however, were still dissenting, demanding a better society. If we expected, at some point, to force a basic social confrontation with our oppressors (who were by no means always as clearly identified as, say the Fortune 500), it would, perhaps, have been only honest and realistic to have predicted many more deaths before the "final victory." After all, liberation fighters were being killed every day in struggles all over the world—why should we have felt we would be spared?

Somehow, such rhetoric encouraged us to believe that we could avoid a repetition of 1970 with better planning and a stronger movement, that we had paid the price of dissent with our four deaths. Exacerbating such naïvete were the contradictory strains of liberal and Maoist thinking among us. The liberals viewed 1970, like Vietnam, as an isolated act of mistaken interference and repression on the part of a government and society needing some alteration but essentially open and democratic. The Maoists seemed to believe, on the other hand, that the 1970 shootings, like Vietnam, were a simple, logical outgrowth of the needs of American capitalism and could only be avenged by a transfer of power at the point of a gun.

We were very isolated, as well, from the concerns of workers and blacks on campus and in town. We gave time, each May 4, to discussion of mass national and international issues such as foreign intervention, inflation, unemployment, and racism; but too often our annual impulses to reach beyond Kent State to other and broader struggles died at the end of the rally. The "May 4th Movement"—if one could call it that—had not yet moved beyond Kent State; we were unified, in fact, only in our desire to attain accountability for the shootings and by a general agreement that the United States needed a great deal of social change.

In 1977, the struggle to prevent the University from using part of the May 4 site for construction of a gym-annex returned the events and issues of 1970 to the forefront of national attention, sandwiched between the New York blackout, the Johnstown flood, and the sudden death of Elvis Presley. Extreme reactions surfaced again: myths, delusions. Some area residents repeated their abusive judgments of 1970: that demonstrations were un-American in general and that protesting Kent State students in particular were rioters who deserved to be shot. Some May 4th Coalition leaders claimed, on the other hand, that all students caught in the Guard's line of fire that day had consciously been protesting war and repression. (Never mind that Sandy Scheuer, one of the dead, had been quite a-political and had simply been walking toward class when a bullet hit her.) According to these leaders, "the masses" who had risen against the war in 1970 would rise again to aid us in 1977, this time to prevent KSU from building a gym-annex deliberately planned to "cover up" the site of the shootings. This rhetoric emanated mostly from the Coalition leaders associated with the Maoist bloc, although it did not come exclusively from them. The "conspiracy" theory of annex construction was accepted by a wide range of Coalition members, both Maoist and non-Maoist radicals and moderate/liberals.

Local and outside reactionaries claimed that the Coalition was an organization composed primarily of "outside agitators" who cared not about honoring anyone's memory (not that they thought the memory deserved to be honored anyway) but about "taking over" the University for their presumably communist purposes. This view was only encouraged, during the late summer and fall of 1977, when an alliance of two Maoist groups, some of whose members had come into Kent from places like Chicago, did indeed usurp control of the Coalition, no doubt in part to gain more credibility for themselves on various campuses.

Some of the concerns of 1977 were constructive extensions and expansions of the concerns of 1970. If May 1970 can, in a national sense, be viewed as the climax of the student movement and the mass struggles for peace and civil rights (especially when one recalls the fact that Cambodia and Kent State produced the biggest student strike in American history), the gym struggle can be viewed as an inheritor of these movements. The lifestyle of Tent City, for instance, echoed the communalism and antiwar feeling of the 1960s in its insistence on participatory democracy and nonviolent behavior. The "official song" of the May 4th Coalition, "We Shall Not Be Moved," came straight from the days of Martin Luther King, Jr. and SNCC during Montgomery, the sit-ins, the Freedom Rides, and Selma. (That it has also been and was originally a refrain of the labor movement was perhaps not so widely recognized.) The Coalition reflected the emphases of the 1970s as well, however, particularly in its concern for the environment.

For those of us who were politically active on the left at Kent State in May 1970, the central issues were the American government's policies of foreign intervention and domestic repression. For those of us active on the left at Kent State in 1977, the issues were campus problems unresolved since 1970 (such as administrative insensitivity toward the whole subject of May 4), new campus problems (such as the immediate threat to the May 4 site), and campus reflections of current national crises (such as land-use policy). The May 4th Coalition fought to protect the May 4 site from partial destruction both because the land was beautiful and because the Coalition members wanted the site recognized, at least henceforth, as an honored American battlefield. The comparisons to Gettysburg were not accidental. Nor was it accidental that a tree formed part of the official Coalition insignia. Much symbolism (encouraged by Native American supporters) was attached to a very old oak tree on the controversial site, and the Coalition knew it had truly lost its battle to preserve that land when the tree was finally removed in September 1977, just before gym-annex construction began.

The antiwar protests of 1970 demanded respect for national self-determination and for human life and liberties. The protests of 1977 demanded respect for honorable memories, for the legal and educational need for historical visualization, and for the idea that beautiful land should be appreciated, not exploited. All these feelings were present, to one degree or another, in the hearts of those who wrote letters, debated, rallied, picketed, lobbied, and went to jail that spring and summer to save Blanket Hill from the mercies of the courts and the bulldozers.

Kent State was, in one sense, an event unique in American history. Although any thorough examination of that history reveals a long tradition of suppression of serious dissent, May 1970 was the only occasion on which armed troops actually attacked and killed, without warning, unarmed white, middle-class college students on their own campus. For this reason, many Americans have found it difficult to come to terms with 1970: we must become rioters or the victims of a cosmic tragedy to be analyzed comfortably. Most Americans cannot face squarely the events and implications of 1970 because they are unable and unwilling to admit to themselves that their society produced such a monumental violation of rights. And if it became clear that Kent State represented not an aberration but an extension of traditional American behavior, the discovery would surely prove overwhelming to those who thought they knew what their country stood for.

Tree-and-Pagoda logo of the May
4th Coalition.

It has often been said at Kent State, during the past twelve years,
that it is time to "get away from" 1970; that it is time to forget about
it and get on with "the business at hand." And, in a way, this is true.
It will never be time to forget about 1970, but it is surely time to put
it in perspective, make a progressive definition of "the business at
hand," and make the losses suffered at Kent State in 1970 a link in a
chain of solidarity with all others struggling for social change.

Those of us concerned with Kent State 1970 can no longer strive
for direct accountability. The out-of-court settlement of January 4,
1979, resolved that question. The victims of 1970 received some
financial compensation from the state of Ohio. They also got a
signed statement of "apology" from Governor Rhodes, the guardsmen, and the other defendants in the Kent State civil suit—a statement promptly disavowed or qualified by all of its prominent signa-
tories. In return, of course, the victims and their families agreed to
drop their suit—which virtually ended any possibility that what
really led to May 4, 1970 would come out in an open courtroom—or
anywhere else, for that matter. Many of us who had hoped for a
clean breast of the case in court felt both betrayed and disappointed
by the settlement, although we were thankful that the victims had
succeeded in squeezing money and regrets from the state of Ohio.
We also knew a fair trial would have been unlikely. Preliminary

jury surveys indicated that public levels of hostility toward students, dissent, and the "rioters" of 1970 were still very high nine years later.

The energies, in any case, of those who struggled for almost a decade to place legal responsibility for 1970 where it belonged—on the shoulders of the state of Ohio and the National Guard—are sorely needed elsewhere now. Such people must break out of the isolation this unfortunately narrow fight has produced and work with organizations concerned with truly mass issues, locally and nationally: decent housing, price controls, jobs, health care, affirmative action, and the environment. They need to work in an organized manner both here and abroad for peace, national liberation, and a new international economic order. The task for those of us associated with the struggle on behalf of the victims of Kent State ought to be to link the mourning of the vigils and the reaffirmation of the May 4 rallies to much larger issues. We must link 1970 to the great questions of the past two decades—none of which have diminished in urgency—and honor its memory by pledging ourselves to expose and alter the general conditions that produced the specific tragedy of Kent State.

Sensitivity to an Image

by D. RAY HEISEY

D. RAY HEISEY *is professor of speech (rhetoric and communication) and coordinator of that division at Kent State University. He came to Kent in 1966 and was serving on the Faculty Senate and on the Executive Committee of the Faculty Senate in 1970. The first part of this essay is a condensation of a paper titled "University and Community Reaction to the News Coverage of the Kent State Tragedy," which Heisey presented at the Central States Speech Association Convention in Cleveland in April 1971.*

Images are created in peoples' minds, but they often carry the force of reality. In fact, images often become reality. The May 4 tragedy, as interpreted by the media, quickly produced images that had to be dealt with as realities. These images were not so much of the killings themselves, but of the victims, of students, of the University and its administration, of the National Guardsmen, and state officials. The images were created and carried by the media and evoked considerable reaction from readers and listeners. This essay deals with that reaction and the response by three successive University administrations.

The responses to the events of May 4 may be seen in the news coverage of those events and are as different as the many people reacting. However, definite patterns developed and can be described. An examination of the letters to the editors of the local newspapers, and of the letters on file with local broadcasters, shows that community readers and listeners (defined here as non-University persons) generally reacted negatively to the reporting of the tragedy because they perceived a student sympathy in much of the news coverage.

The local Kent radio station, WKNT, received scores of phone calls and letters during the crisis. The station's letter file reveals two pervasive types of comments: first, that the station should be commended for its fair and continuous coverage and, secondly, supported by more people, that the station was biased, making the guardsmen look like murderers and the demonstrators appear to be innocent kids. One listener charged that WKNT was "adding flames to the boiling pot" by broadcasting the term "Kent massacre." Over two hundred angry Kent residents supported a neighbor who wrote a lengthy letter to WKNT as well as to other news media which said in part: "So far, we have heard very little or nothing from the news media with statements from the National Guard foot soldier, the policemen or the firemen who had to feel stones, sticks, shouts and screams from a mass of humanity worked into hysteria by professional agitators, undoubtedly communist trained."

News items were perceived as either pro-Guard or prostudent, which served to solidify further the opinions already held. When the Justice Department's summary of the FBI investigation was published July 23, 1970, calling the shootings unwarranted, students cheered and townspeople found it difficult to believe. When the Portage County grand jury report was released on October 16, blaming the University and students, students wanted to hold a protest and townspeople felt that their side had been vindicated.

Probably the greatest criticism from the community was directed at the *Akron Beacon Journal*. In the letters to the editor which commented on May 4 coverage, and particularly on the newspaper's special report on the shootings, 67.5 percent condemned the newspaper as "yellow," "irresponsible," "garbage," "idiotic," "too sensational and dramatic." For their special Kent State report, published less than three weeks after the shootings and which won the George Polk Memorial Award for national reporting, the *Beacon Journal* acknowledged that criticism outweighed praise. One reader wrote: "I would like to say congratulations for . . . 30,000 words of unprecedented, slanted journalism. It is obvious that your newspaper has a closed mind on all the facts in favor of the National Guard." The newspaper's publication of the FBI findings brought the worst reactions. "A Great Cry of Anger," formed a special feature on the editorial page. Excerpts from several of those letters reveal the intensity of that anger:

God in heaven, to what lengths you have continually gone to excuse or cover up those bums that started the trouble.

Are you sure you are not one of those longhaired rioters? I have never seen such bias, untruthful and bad reporting as has appeared in the *Beacon Journal* lately.

I'd like to know how many Communist parties are paying you off for your stories about Kent State. Why didn't you put the pictures in of the four darlings as they really looked when they died? Your paper is nothing but a scandal sheet.

On July 29, 1970, the *Beacon Journal* indicated it had received in excess of nine hundred letters. The editors were concerned about the paper's credibility, for it was becoming quite clear that people thought the paper was contributing to the cause of the "revolution-aries." The next day the editorial staff felt obliged to publish its own statement along with angry letters from readers. The *Beacon Journal* "does not pretend that it has been able to tell 'the whole truth' on this or any other matter," said the editorial. "Truth is not just 'two-sided,' or X-sided—it has an infinite number of sides."

Even nine months later, the *Kent-Ravenna Record-Courier* was accused by a KSU parent of applauding students who lowered the national flag on campus at an antiwar rally in February 1971 by picturing on its front page the three hundred students at the rally instead of the 18,700 who "were either in class or the library or in their rooms studying." She continued: "I firmly believe there would be no more demonstrations, no more riots, no more marches, no more sit-ins, if our newspapers, radios and TV newscasters would wake up to the fact that they are giving this segment of our society exactly what they are after—front page of newspapers, prime time on TV and radio newscasts." A prominent business leader in the Kent area described the attitude of his average customers: "If the papers would quit publishing today the KSU problem would be all over."

Students and faculty, on the other hand, generally felt that the news coverage was fair and accurate. An examination of the letters to the *Beacon Journal* reveals that about 50 percent of the favorable ones were from people associated with Kent State University. Faculty members obtained extra copies of the special *Beacon Journal* report to send to friends. One professor wrote: "Whatever

the outcome of the legal problems associated with the May disturbance, at least journalistic justice has been done. It is a rare thing
when, in the face of what must be and have been enormous
pressures—political, financial, and so on—a newspaper and its
editor demonstrate so graphically a commitment to informing its
readers. It is not an overstatement to say that without your dedication Kent might not have survived." A number of students who
claimed to be eyewitnesses to the events in May wrote in the face of
much criticism to support the newspaper's version of the Kent State
tragedy.

In general, then, the reaction of the community to the news
coverage of the Kent State tragedy was largely unfavorable, that of
the University was favorable. The news media, by keeping the interpretations and opinions about the tragedy before the public eye,
contributed to image polarization. The media created a universe of
discourse, disclosing the extremes of opinion. And, of course, the
judgment that the press was either objective or biased in this case, as
in most cases, says more about the public's view of the events than of
the press. As Walter Lippmann wrote: "The theory of a free press is
that the truth will emerge from free reporting and free discussion,
not that it will be presented perfectly and instantly in any one
account."

The emergence of the "truth" about May 4 events and the image
of the University in the public mind in the years that followed 1970
created numerous and recurrent problems for the administration.
The three University presidents who have had to respond to the May
4 image have all implicitly recognized the public polarization
surrounding the event. It goes without saying that a state institution
must be sensitive to its constituencies and that a president has an
obligation to see that the institution fulfills its commitments. The
manner in which sensitivity to May 4 events is expressed by any
president will necessarily be determined by his background, his style
of leadership, his views on the nature of the University, and his
interpretation of the needs of the University constituencies.

Throughout the year that President Robert I. White served in
office following the May 4 tragedy, many decisions were made
which reflected a high degree of sensitivity to the public image. The
unfavorable press received by the University was responsible in part

for the "closed" nature of many campus events. The administration could not afford to allow events that might get out of hand, that might bring newsmen and cameras, that might create additional negative images in the minds of the public. Although the administration spoke out strongly against the Portage County grand jury report and its repressive tendencies, it did not permit the holding of the National Student Leadership Conference at Kent in January 1971 in conjunction with the NSA; it rejected plans by National Educational Television to conduct a TV discussion on campus; it decided to withhold publication of the report of the Commission on KSU Violence since it was not unanimous and its contents might result in libel charges and adverse publicity for the University.

White also rejected demands from certain student groups to abolish ROTC and end the law enforcement program on campus. While he was faced with this kind of pressure on the one hand, he received over 10,000 letters from community people and others whom he said were writing "frightening" things. President White did respond to campus pressure to engage students in question-and-answer sessions and be interviewed on the campus TV program. Nonetheless, he insisted on keeping the first commemoration of the shootings for the University community alone. Gov. John Gilligan agreed, but student body president Craig Morgan announced that he would not participate in the scheduled May 4 activities. He said, "I am tired of the public relations game that the administration is playing in order to please parents and outsiders. By trying to play both sides, the university has confused the issues so much that no one knows what is legal and what is illegal."

In a press conference after the first commemoration, White said that no other university had faced a greater challenge than Kent State and that the main line of defense rested with the faculty and the students. He felt that the survival of the University during this critical period was due to the positive efforts of the campus community itself, not needing the assistance of outside law enforcement agencies. By seeking to close the commemoration to outsiders, he helped to create an image of internal strength for the public, badly needed at the conclusion of the first post-May 4 academic year. Such a position was also consistent with White's personal style, which emphasized a low profile.

Glenn A. Olds, a former clergyman, college administrator, and a diplomat with the United Nations, was appointed in 1971 as the next president of Kent State University. There was much expectation that he would bring the needed personal and experiential qualities for leadership following Dr. White's retirement. The latitude which a new president had in dealing with the May 4 image was considerable since he was neither personally nor institutionally involved in the tragic events. In addition to this advantage, President Olds, in temperament and style, was given to much dialogue in an effort to help bring reconciliation. Whereas President White saw as his immediate goal the restoration of the University, President Olds perceived his as the binding of the deep wounds among students, faculty, and community.

When Olds arrived on campus as the new president in September 1971, he announced that Kent could be a new symbol of the future direction in higher education and that its tragedy could become a symbol of the unfinished task ahead. "I have an impression that there is a new confidence here at Kent," he said. Though refusing personally to sign the petition for a federal grand jury investigation of the shootings, Olds performed a much stronger act in behalf of the student campaign by personally presenting the petitions to the White House. He used this event to proclaim to the nation his confidence and the students' confidence "in the peaceable process, both of petition and assembly, as a principal tool in the achievement of a larger measure of democracy." His remarks, upon accepting the petitions on the University Commons in October 1971, were published extensively in the official University weekly along with a photo of Olds being interviewed by CBS newsman Ike Pappas.

In addition to such public symbolic gestures, Olds talked frequently at student forums on campus. He encouraged the establishment of a lectureship in peaceful change, he announced that the May 4 commemoration would be open to all who wanted to participate, he talked with students at a sit-in staged against the continuation of ROTC on campus, even though he held to a faculty committee decision to retain the military program. President Olds also announced that police surveillance on campus would be stopped and invited George Wald, clearly a recognized leader for change and peaceful protest among students, to be the featured speaker at the May 4 commemoration in 1972.

During the years of his administration, Olds attempted to respond to campus pressure by decreasing the campus security budget and by bringing to the campus such speakers as Peter Davies. He emphasized that the University image was on the "upswing" but began running into trouble with students who wanted classes to be cancelled on May 4 in commemoration of the tragedy. Three times the request was refused, and in an effort to convince students that numerous measures had been taken by the administration to show its concern for proper commemoration, Olds finally wrote a lengthy letter to the *Daily Kent Stater* outlining the various steps that had been taken by the administration.

Glenn Olds had come to the campus advocating openness and dialogue, had spoken to many student concerns, and had taken the initiative in attempting to make May 4 a positive image for the University; yet, in the end, he was accused by some of not being decisive enough on certain matters, of dragging his feet on collective bargaining with the faculty union, and of not being sensitive enough to May 4 issues, such as the cancelling of classes. Olds's final year, 1976–77, saw him taking an increasingly harder stance on class cancellation and related issues, including the gym controversy. There obviously was pressure from the Board of Trustees on such matters. Controversies all grew in size and in momentum and unfortunately could not readily be resolved. In November 1976, Olds announced his resignation.

When President Brage Golding took office in the fall of 1977, he stated the "single-minded goal to keep KSU from breaking out into another eruption," as he put it in an interview with the *Daily Kent Stater*. He was quick to express his sympathy with the student concerns by saying that he would not, in fact, have recommended the approval of the controversial site of the gym-annex, for "it might well have been expected to press upon the sensibilities of a segment of the Kent State—even the national—community." He made it clear, however, that he was not sympathetic to the "outside busybodies" and "professional agitators," whom he identified with the gym protest.

President Golding offered his own twelve-point memorial plan, including modifying the asphalt parking space behind Taylor Hall into areas of greenery, planting shrubs and trees in the area of the shootings, and dedicating the gym-annex to the slain students, the National Guard, and all who suffered in the tragedy. Reaction to his suggestions was positive. The Faculty Senate urged support. A letter to the *Stater* editor said that Golding's points showed "both sensitivity to the tragedy of May 4 and recognition of the unreasonable costs of further delay and debate." Golding also made himself very visible in an effort to listen to students and discuss their concerns with them. He agreed to hold "a great debate" with May 4th Coalition representative Alan Canfora. He used these occasions to make clear to students that decisions were going to be made with which they would not always agree. "KSU is not a democracy," he said. "We can't have a mass meeting every time a minor or major decision is being made."

The new president added strength to his words by going to the Board of Trustees to obtain an "authority" resolution that would grant him power to "regulate" the campus. After the May 4th Coalition staged a large demonstration in late September, Golding charged that 80 percent of the people involved were outsiders. He declared, "I intend to get tough. We were assured it would be a peaceful assembly. I have had enough." The Board granted the authority to "get tough." His new power was viewed differently by different constituencies. The *Stater* cautioned Golding to use his power "wisely," but the student government condemned his use of a court injunction to stop further rallies on campus.

Golding insisted that he was not opposed to free speech and free assembly, but that "they have to be peaceful rallies." In April, he wrote a lengthy letter to the *Stater* outlining his reasons for the decision to cancel classes on May 4. This was a significant move and he did so only after talking with faculty, trustees, and campus representatives. His executive assistant said that the decision was "in direct response to allegations" of administrative insensitivity toward May 4. But it was to be viewed as an act of "conciliation" rather than a direct response to pressure. Golding hoped that plans for the May 1979 commemoration would begin "with a spirit, not of dread and apprehension, but of unity and purposefulness of balance and dignity with the preservation of the University and its ideals foremost in our minds." In an effort to prepare the media for covering this May 4 event, Golding asked them to "consider a more balanced perspective on the events."

During his second year, Golding rejected George Segal's design for a May 4 sculpture. This brought considerable reaction, but the

administration insisted that the idea or theme was "inappropriate."
The Abraham and Isaac scene, it was felt, might even be the cause of
an incident, were it to be placed on this campus. A public relations
firm was employed to assist the University in building a positive
image—the "Kent State Difference." This was an important decision with regard to Kent's image, because many people felt as did
Prof. Lawrence Kaplan, when he addressed the campus on May
4, 1978, that "despite all the publicity of the past year . . . we
should not forget that the major missions of Kent State University
are being served—served very well." In the next academic year, the
positive approach paid off as an influx of new freshmen surprised
University residence staffs and even created space problems. The
commemoration on May 4, 1980, was marked by a faculty convocation and a program by the May 4th Task Force, without incident.
President Golding was very pleased with the result and remarked
that the University had now reached the turning point, for "it was
the first truly peaceful May 4 in 10 years."

In summary, each of the three Kent State University presidents
during the last twelve years has expressed a sensitivity to the events
of May 4 that shaped the manner in which he responded to pressures
and proposals. President White wanted very little publicity: he kept
the campus closed to outsiders at the first commemoration in order
to keep the University under control and open. He rightly predicted
that the effects of the tragedy "will be with us a long time." Glenn
Olds engaged in extensive discussion to keep open the lines of
communication and provided a favorable climate for students and
faculty who cared about how the commemoration was to be observed and what directions the University should take. Though it
could be argued that he sided too often with students, as opposed to
the public at large, resistance to students on several fronts eventually
played a major role in his departure from Kent State, though other
factors were also involved.

President Golding was most concerned with fiscal soundness for
the University. Like Olds, he sought a positive image for Kent State,
but he accomplished it by different means. He took a tough stand,
acted decisively, and provided explanations to students and faculty
for his decisions both in person and in writing. He continued the
openness in the form of dialogue but took some calculated risks to
bring direction to the substance of the discussions. The risks paid

off. He had some help, of course, from the 1979 out-of-court settlement which put an end to May 4 litigation. With no incident to mar the tenth-anniversary commemoration, according to a *Stater* editorial, the University had seen the "light at the end of the tunnel."

It was a troubled period, which saw responses by different administrations and by varied groups to the "meaning" of May 4. In 1971, the editor of the *Akron Beacon Journal* remarked: "Kent State's story has not 'two sides' but thousands." Those "sides" emerged as the years unfolded, as justice was slowly reached in a civil suit, and as the institution sought to remove the "dampened Kent spirits" and to engage in "the building of a greater University," as Professor Kaplan put it in his August 1977 commencement speech, "The Kent Heritage." The building of a greater University was the constant challenge facing the three presidents, and they had to operate under the constant scrutiny of a local and national public that wanted always to know *their* (the presidents') side of the truth.

Neglect—Benign or Malignant?

The Faculty and Administrative Response

by ROBERT A. DYAL

ROBERT A. DYAL *is a former associate professor of philosophy at Kent State University. An eyewitness to the 1970 shootings, he was active in subsequent litigation related to the incident. During the gym controversy, Dyal was co-coordinator for the faculty observers. Upon leaving the University in 1980, Dyal wrote, in a letter to the* Daily Kent Stater, *that the institution was no longer "habitable" for him and cited three primary reasons: (1) administrative insensitivity to the events of May 1970; (2) a "managerial consciousness" among University officials which had created a "gulf" between faculty and administration; and (3) "a failure of nerve and imagination on the part of the faculty in general, resulting in deepening alienation and further withdrawal into individual isolation, rather than collective action." Dyal currently resides in Austin, Texas.*

On May 4, 1961—exactly nine years before gunfire struck down thirteen students on the Kent State campus—the French philosopher Maurice Merleau-Ponty died unexpectedly in Paris. He had held the prestigious Chair of Philosophy at the College de France; and, on the occasion of his inauguration to that lofty seat in 1953, he reflected candidly upon his most distinguished predecessor, René Descartes, the father of modern Western philosophy:

> Descartes has recently been honored for not having taken sides between Galileo and the Holy Office. The philosopher, it is said, should not prefer one rival dogmatism to another. . . . But this is to forget that, by refusing to speak, Descartes also refuses to vindicate and to bring into action the philosophical order in its proper place. By remaining silent, . . . he leaves them at grips with one another; he encourages them, particularly the victor of the moment. To be silent is not the same as to say why one does not wish to choose.[1]

[1] Maurice Merleau-Ponty, *In Praise of Philosophy* (Evanston, Ill.: Northwestern Univ. Press, 1963), pp. 61–62.

This essay focuses on the response of the Kent State faculty and administration to the events of May 1970 and their aftermath in the ensuing decade. As we shall see, this response has not been uniform; nonetheless, in contrast to the cacophony sounded by both the student body and the surrounding community, the response of the least transient elements of the University may be characterized as a profound silence, the net result of which has been to encourage the status quo, "the victor of the moment."

As so characterized, this is the classic stance of "benign neglect" (with a reluctant bow to Daniel Moynihan, who most recently popularized the term). It seems clear to me that "benign" is the appropriate adjective to qualify the neglect on the part of the Kent State faculty in general. It is less clear, however, that this term is sufficient to portray the less-passive culpability of the University administration. Several investigators into the Kent State shootings and the subsequent "cover-up" by the state of Ohio, the FBI, and other governmental agencies—people such as Peter Davies, I. F. Stone, and Charles Thomas—are convinced on the basis of their research that members of the University administration and the campus police force have been complicit. In this way, one might well prefer to term the administration's failure to recognize the significance of the May 4 shootings properly as "malignant" rather than benign neglect. However, it is not my purpose here to resolve this issue, but rather to catalog the elements of the neglect itself— whether benign or malignant.

To be sure, several individual members of the faculty have responded in the only way they know how—by means of research, and some of them have shared the results of their research not only with their own academic disciplines but also with the Kent State community.[2] Moreover, professors Thomas Hensley and Jerry Lewis have, since 1977, conducted or contributed to a "Great Contemporary Issues" course concerning May 4, 1970; and the Center for Peaceful Change regularly addresses May 4 issues within the context of its concern for nonviolence, as have a few instructors in other disciplines. Such faculty initiative, however, has rarely received encouragement and support from peers or the administration. I am

[2] Thomas Hensley and Jerry Lewis, eds., *Kent State and May 4th: A Social Science Perspective* (Dubuque, Iowa: Kendall/Hunt Publ., 1978); see also A. Paul Hare, ed., *Kent State: The Nonviolent Response* (Haverford: Center for Nonviolent Conflict Resolution, 1973).

aware of at least three instances where faculty colleagues were actively discouraged from May 4-related research on the grounds that such "would not be rewarded."

There have been individual and small-group cries of anguish and anger, particularly from faculty, representing both sides of the conflict so polarized that terrible Monday in May. A Kent State track coach in 1970 addressed a letter to the local newspaper applauding the employment of "real bullets" and added: "I am willing to wager that there are many more responsible citizens here in Kent who believe as I do."[3] He was correct. On the other side, several faculty members testified on behalf of the plaintiffs (families of the dead and wounded) in the civil suit litigation, and others have expressed themselves by means of poetry and the arts. Prior to 1977, however, the only "official" statement issued by the University faculty was indeed a forthright condemnation of the actions of the Ohio National Guard and Gov. James Rhodes. This statement was drafted as a resolution and narrowly passed (primarily because the graduate assistants and teaching fellows demanded and won the right to vote) at a special assembly of the faculty on May 5, 1970. In subsequent years the Faculty Senate has refused to reaffirm or even to reprint copies of the resolution; it has effectively been expunged from University records. Other than annual ritualistic cautions against violence and occasional appeals for the cancellation of classes on May 4, the Faculty Senate had fallen silent on the issue until the spring of 1978, when it supported an ad hoc and belated faculty effort to organize its own commemoration, a program which has now apparently been institutionalized. This faculty commemoration is in itself worthwhile, even if tardy, adding contemplative dignity to the day's events. It does not appear to be coincidental that it was organized only after eight years had elapsed and during the nationally publicized controversy over the construction of a gym-annex on a portion of the confrontation site and at a time when a national rally attracting hundreds of protestors from other campuses was perceived by some as an economic threat to the University and thereby to the job security of the faculty.

Three other responses by the faculty, one abortive and two successful, must be mentioned. During the remainder of the spring

---

[3] Quoted in James Michener, *Kent State: What Happened and Why* (New York: Random, 1971), p. 294.

quarter 1970, when the campus was closed by order of the county prosecutor (a period during which the faculty employed diversely innovative methods of completing the quarter's classwork without benefit of the traditional resources of classroom and library), a small ad hoc group of faculty organized themselves into the Kent Community for Nonviolent Change, the goal of which was to address, investigate, and articulate proposals regarding the conditions that had precipitated the violent confrontation or were likely to precipitate future confrontations on the campus. After an initial enthusiastic response from an otherwise rudderless faculty, the effort faded by the end of the summer of 1970, largely due to internal factional conflict over various issues as well as faculty enervation and noncooperation from the administration. What might have become an effective and articulate agent and coalition of conscience was unfortunately aborted.[4]

In 1975, Prof. John Ohles solicited funds from other faculty equally concerned that not a single memorial marker had been erected on the site of the shootings. As a result, a handsome and unpretentious granite stone was placed in an esplanade in the parking lot where the four students met death. It remains today as the only permanent memorial erected by anyone at Kent State University.

Another commendable effort was the organization and mobilization of the Faculty Observers. Though faculty members were individually present on the Commons that fateful day in 1970 (several of whom were on the target side during the shooting) and some attempted to be a responsible presence both before and after the thirteen seconds of M-1 riflefire, there was widespread regret regarding the absence of a faculty "third force." During the following summer and the next year, therefore, a small and select group of faculty were enlisted, trained, and eventually given legitimacy by the Faculty Senate for the purpose of being present at every political rally, demonstration, or march (of which there were scores in the 1970s) on the campus or in the town. Their official function was not to intervene or surveil but rather to provide and receive information, to watchdog civil liberties, and hopefully to moderate the conduct of both protestors and police. In performing their duties, often in the

---

[4] See Robert A. Dyal, "Kent Community for Nonviolent Change: An Experiment that Failed," in Hare, *The Nonviolent Response*, n. pag.

dead of night or during disagreeable weather, they knowingly subjected themselves to danger and arrest. Many were tear-gassed along with the protestors, a few were injured—though none severely—and at least two were arrested.

These faculty members expected and received no reward. Though they were sometimes verbally abused by both sides, their presence was generally appreciated by both protestors and police and sometimes privately by members of the administration. It is typical, however, of the administration's response that in his "State of the University" address in 1978, President Brage Golding lauded the efforts of the newly emerged Faculty Commemoration Committee, only a few of whom devoted more than several hours to their project, while saying nothing about the Faculty Observers, all of whom had spent scores of hours trying to keep the peace during the upheaval of the gym controversy. Moreover, on the eve of the tenth anniversary of May 4, 1970, the president of the Faculty Senate, after consultation with the administration, unceremoniously abolished the Observers. This unilateral action occurred without any prior consultation with or even notification of the group, which was then preparing for duty on an anniversary that was believed by many to be particularly portentous.

There have been only four positive responses by the administration during the years following the shootings, none of which have borne much fruit.[5] President White appointed two commissions in the immediate aftermath of May 4, 1970, both described briefly in the introduction to this book. The Mayer Commission, the Commission on Kent State University Violence, failed to consummate its task and never issued a consensus report before it disbanded or, if it did, refused to say that it did and refused to make it public. The Kegley Commission emerged as an apparent ploy to defuse the aforementioned ad hoc faculty organization, the Kent Community for Nonviolent Change. Its very structure, unsurprisingly, mirrored

---

[5] I do not include in this list the establishment of the May 4 room at the University library—not because it was not a positive contribution, which it certainly was, but because the credit should accrue not to the administration but rather to a graduate student, Paul Keane, who lobbied for it, and to the then-director of the Center for Peaceful Change, Raj Basi, who, along with Prof. Fay Biles, persuaded an alumnus to fund the project. Moreover, what might have been the centerpiece of the University Archives' May 4th Collection was lost when Peter Davies, unable to receive reasonable assurances from the administration that his materials would be protected, donated his papers to the Yale University Archives.

that of the KCNC. Its official title was "The University Commission to Implement a Commitment to Nonviolence"; and it involved a sizable number of faculty, staff, and students in exploring various issues and in compiling a thick Report of Recommendations, twenty-seven in all, covering the full span of University affairs. The mountain, alas, produced a mouse. Precious few of the recommendations were ever implemented. As Professor Kegley concluded, "Try as we might, we were unable to move the upper-level administration to act upon these concerns, or even to become aware of what we felt to be their critical nature."[6]

As a result of suggestions and pressure from a handful of faculty, the administration had in place by the fall of 1971 the semblance of a new academic unit with an appointed director—the Center for Peaceful Change, whose purpose was to design a curriculum with a major and to develop courses designed to study nonviolent alternatives to the problem of social change. Over the years, the Center has justifiably attained a very reputable status among scholars in Irenology. And while the CPC has earned praise from its own graduates, numerous public figures, and academics, it has endured largely "without honor in its own country." While the CPC has produced important research, consultative services to communities, and a number of well-trained graduates, it has locally served principally as a safety-valve for student expression of frustrated idealism and as a "soup-kitchen" for fatigued protestors. These are not ignoble services, and one shudders to imagine how the University might have survived, particularly over the long gym struggle of 1977–78, in their absence. Nonetheless, the CPC has never approximated the hopes and dreams of its supporters, much less the ringing rhetoric accompanying its inception, due to the miniscule budget, inadequate facilities, and low priority assigned it. In fact, its very existence has been threatened virtually every year of its history.

Not until the gym controversy was perceived as a genuine threat to the University's image was the administration moved to create a May 4 Commemoration Committee—eight years after the fact. This committee, made up of faculty, administrators, staff, students, and

---

[6] Charles F. Kegley, "The University Commission to Implement a Commitment to Nonviolence," in Hare, *The Nonviolent Response*, n. page. See also Eugene P. Wenninger, "Response to Crisis: The University Commission to Implement a Commitment to Nonviolence," in ibid.

townspeople, was riddled with internal dissension. Nonetheless, a consensus developed around several key issues about which recommendations were made to President Brage Golding, some of which were the following: the publication of a brief brochure for distribution to visitors at the shootings site; the installation of appropriate permanent markers at the places where students were killed or wounded; the cessation of classes on the afternoon of every May 4; and the establishment of May 4 memorial scholarships to meritorious students. Though the president accepted all but one of the committee's twenty recommendations, few of them had been implemented by the time Kent State observed the tenth anniversary of the killings.

Thus, we have the sum total of the "positive" response of the Kent State administration to May 4 during the decade following the shootings.[7] These constitute, tragically, the exception rather than the rule. Much more truly indicative of the "official" response of the administration to this event of historical importance—not only to Kent State, but also to American life in general, to the antiwar movement, and to higher education—have been the reactions of denial, defensiveness, hostility, cowardice, indifference, incompetence, and an excessive regard for the University's "public relations" image. The first reaction, after the initial shock that four students had been killed and nine wounded by a military force imposed upon the campus, was one of denial. In its neglect to display compassion and care for the dead and wounded and their families; in its reluctance openly to criticize Governor Rhodes, the adjutant general of the Ohio National Guard, and the excessive use of killing force; and, in its overriding concern to resume "business as usual," the administration seemed to want to deny what had transpired on its own campus and proceeded to pretend that it had not.

This exercise in self-deception (Sartre would call it "bad faith") was succeeded by defensiveness, by rationalizations that what happened here could have happened "anywhere," that the fact that it had happened here was purely "accidental," that the Kent State

[7] While the Experimental Programs division of the Honors College and similar educational and organizational innovations were launched and possibly found acceptance, in part, due to elevated sensitivity on the campus in the aftermath of the shootings, these ventures would doubtless have occurred anyway, given the national and local character of student unrest. In any case, no causal connection with the shootings can be attributed.

administration was in no way complicit in events precipitating the lethal confrontation, and that those demanding "truth and justice" should quietly disappear. When the protests escalated rather than diminished during the next several years, they were met not with understanding, much less support, but with hostility articulated in terms of a beefed-up and more aggressive campus police force, public condemnation of the protestors, reluctance to support a federal investigation, refusal to commission a fitting memorial on behalf of the dead and wounded, and eventually the ultimate insult: the physical obstruction of a critical portion of the site where the shootings occurred.

The administration has also reacted with equal parts of cowardice and indifference. On that awful weekend of May 2–3, 1970, it allowed its campus to be occupied by armed troops and acquiesced to the will of a governor campaigning for the Senate; and on May 4, the entire upper echelon of the administration, despite its clear knowledge that a potentially dangerous confrontation would occur at noon, chose to quarter itself not on the Commons but in the cocktail lounge of a local restaurant. No high-ranking member of the administration even bothered to visit the wounded as they lay in a hospital five miles away, nor even inquired of their parents as to their recovery. Three successive Kent State presidents have managed for a decade to avoid any personal encounter with the wounded and the families of the four slain students. And the University's rejection in 1978 of a memorial sculpture designed by George Segal, with its contemplative Kierkegaardian theme of "Abraham and Isaac," only added insult to injury—once again, Kent State made national news as President Golding's insensitivity was derided in numerous editorials throughout the country.

Yet, a distant university, Princeton, on the fall 1979 occasion of its dedication of the Segal sculpture—which it had been pleased to accept—invited the wounded and the families to share the platform with its president and trustees and honored them with a standing ovation. These victims of May 4, 1970, reported that this was the first occasion in a decade of anguished suffering and frustrated hopes for justice that *any* university administration had treated them with dignity and respect.

The most charitable appraisal of the University administration's behavior is that of incompetence. The most turbulent period in the decade since May 1970 was the series of protests involving the decision to build a huge gym-annex in a congested area of the campus, most of which covers a critical portion of the historic site of the shootings.[8] The decision itself, the excavation and construction that followed, and the massive and prolonged protests thus provoked, brought Kent State once again to the attention of the national and international news media. The sights of limp bodies being dragged away to police buses; of "Tent City" being dismantled; of persons being arrested on the steps of the Student Center while reading the First Amendment; of protestors, student peace marshals, and Faculty Observers being tear-gassed and overrun by mounted sheriff's deputies, were telecast around the world.

The results of these administrative actions, which began with their insolent indifference to pleas by concerned faculty and students to build the gym elsewhere on the campus, might have been predicted by any competent businessman: a radical decline in applications by freshmen-to-be, a diminution in total student enrollment, and a huge bill for an escalated police presence—in sum, an economic crisis from which the University has not yet recovered, and for which the administration blames the protestors rather than themselves.

Less than two months prior to the tenth anniversary commemoration of May 4, when the national news media's annual descent on the campus was multiplied, President Golding unilaterally announced his plan to construct a free-standing brick arch at the entrance to the parking lot where so many of the victims had fallen. The thirty-thousand-dollar structure, he explained, was "intended to be of sufficient size and consequence to attract the eye, and . . . acknowledge the event without interpretation." That the Roman-arch motif is *not* "without interpretation," however, was brought to public attention not by the militant student Left but by faculty members and students in the KSU School of Architecture, who gathered from among their own circle a hundred signatures to a petition opposing the arch. They reminded President Golding that, historically, the Roman arch symbolized imperial victory, ritualized

---

[8] For a thoroughgoing account of these events, see *Kent State FACT Newsletter*, co-edited by Robert A. Dyal and Herbert Goldsmith, nos. 1 and 2, 1977–78. Copies of the newsletter are available in the May 4th Collection, Kent State University Archives.

by marching through it the victorious troops, and thus conflicted with the meaning of May 4 held by those whom the president ostensibly hoped to placate by the proposed memorial. If the usually apolitical architects reacted with disdain, it is not difficult to comprehend the reaction of the more politically conscious students and faculty, one of whom observed that the arch could only symbolize "that the state had and still has the power to use military force against its citizens who oppose government policy. . . ."[9]

Hence, on March 14, 1980, President Golding issued a public statement scuttling the project: "The marker as perceived seems to have generated almost exclusively negative public comment. . . . Apparently still more time must pass before some people will be able to separate cause and effect and thus permit an appropriate and dignified recognition of the tragic consequences of May 4, 1970, to be effected." His executive assistant, Robert McCoy, was more to the point, commenting: "People aren't ready to let May 4 die as a political issue."[10] One of the tragic ironies is that, while the University administration has, throughout the years after May 4, been primarily concerned with protecting its public image as opposed to seeking justice and displaying the truth, it has by so many of its actions presented the worst possible image of Kent State to the public.

While the official response of the Kent State faculty to the terrible event of May 4, 1970, has generally been undistinguished, the official response of the University administration has been shameful. This is particularly evident when compared to the considerable efforts expended throughout the decade by various student movements and several "outsider" persons and groups. Foremost among the latter have been the parents of the four slain students as well as the parents of several of the wounded. These heroic parents became increasingly involved in the quest for justice and truth with respect to their children as it became increasingly clear, to their chagrin, that Kent State University was concerned mainly with resumption of

---

[9] The Golding statement is from the *Daily Kent Stater*, March 18, 1980, p. 2; and comments by School of Architecture faculty and students appeared in the following issues of the school newspaper: March 11, 1980, p. 1; March 12, 1980, p. 4; and March 13, 1980, p. 1. The final quote is from a letter to the editor, written by Craig Blazinski, *Daily Kent Stater*, March 13, 1980, p. 4.

[10] *Daily Kent Stater*, March 18, 1980, p. 1.

"business as usual." They were joined and supported by the American Civil Liberties Union and the United Methodist Church, the latter in the person of Rev. John Adams, director of the Board of Church and Society's Department of Law, Justice and Community Relations. Mr. Adams joined two sets of parents in being the first among 193 persons arrested on the occasion of a massive civil disobedience "sit-in" on Blanket Hill during the gym controversy. Long before that, he had offered both moral and legal support to the victims' families, particularly during the trials for the civil damages suit.

Another notable "outsider" who has given much of himself during the past decade is Peter Davies, an English-born private citizen who lives on Staten Island. He was drawn into the case, as he says, "by conscience," as a result of correspondence he initiated with Mr. and Mrs. Arthur Krause. Davies's book, *The Truth About Kent State*, remains the single most valuable book on the issue. The great majority at Kent State, however, have apparently never bothered to read it. Others could also be mentioned: Prof. David E. Engdahl of the University of Colorado Law School, Sanford Rosen and Benson Wolman of the ACLU, and Charles Thomas, formerly an employee of the National Archives, each of whom has done prodigious legal and historical research and, on critical occasions, been a responsible presence on the Kent State campus. Mention should also be made of Paul Keane, a former student at Kent State, a witness to the events of 1970, and recently a graduate of Yale Divinity School. During the gym controversy, Keane initiated, from New Haven, an organization called Kent State FACT (First Amendment Conservation Task-force), sporting a distinguished Board of Advisers, including I. F. Stone, James Wechsler, Rabbi Eugene Borowitz, Ramsey Clark, and Joseph Rhodes, Jr. Enlisting Prof. Herbert Goldsmith and myself from the University faculty as co-editors, and using money from his savings, Keane published two lengthy newsletters, describing and analyzing the state of the First Amendment at Kent State during the hectic years, 1976–78. Despite the revelation of multiple civil liberties violations by the administration, courts, and law enforcement agencies, the two publications created barely a ripple among the faculty and, as expected, were either scorned or deliberately ignored by the administration. After two issues, the newsletter and the organization died of indifference.

Student actions, whether spontaneous or organized, during the decade after May 4, 1970, have ranged from the judicious and responsible to the foolish and irresponsible. As a catalog of these activities would require a multivolume effort, I will restrict my comments to two commendable student initiatives. The May 4th Task Force was organized under student government authorization, in 1975, for the purpose of planning and conducting the annual commemorative programs. This group provides year-round "consciousness-raising" educational and other activities, bringing to the campus an assortment of notable speakers. Despite the administration's efforts to characterize them as "extremists," members of the May 4th Task Force have actually served as a moderating influence on what would otherwise be an anarchic process.

The occasion of the tenth anniversary of May 4, 1970, was obviously an appropriate milestone at which to engage in reflective analysis; hence, it should not be surprising that the idea would emerge of a commemorative volume of essays to mark the moment. The first person to propose such a project, however, was neither an administrator nor a faculty member, but Paul Keane. The idea was independently implemented, again, by students—in this case the graduate students who comprised the Kent Left Studies Forum and who published a scholarly journal, *Left Review*, largely by and for graduate students. This enterprising group of young scholars solicited a wide range of essays from faculty, students, and public figures, including Eugene McCarthy, for a handsome tenth anniversary special issue of *Left Review*, which contained in addition, a comprehensive bibliography of books and articles addressing the event commemorated.[11] It was a splendid instance of student initiative which stands in bold relief to the general neglect—whether benign or malignant—on the part of the administration and faculty at Kent State.

How might the faculty and administration have responded? They might have refused to "refuse to speak" and thereby not encouraged "the victor of the moment." Administrative representatives might have joined, instead of opposing, those forces seeking legal and moral justice for the victims; in fact, they might have taken *primary* responsibility in the effort. They might have exercised

[11] See "Kent State: Ten Years After," special issue, *Left Review* 4 (Spring 1980): passim.

academic responsibility, mobilized scholarly energy, and converted this horrible event into an unparalleled educational opportunity for successive generations of Kent State students. They might have encouraged, rather than discouraged, scholarly research into the event and its causes, particularly in the social sciences. They might have supported such research by University funding, by seeking extramural grant money, and by means of the reward system operative in the University. They might have given economic and academic priority, rather than "crumbs from the table," to the Center for Peaceful Change, making Kent State the foremost locus in the world for the study of nonviolent means of change. They might have utilized their artistic and economic resources to develop and produce at least one and preferably many memorial works of art. They might have displayed human compassion and decency toward the victims and their families and made every effort to protect the civil liberties of those students, faculty, and others who dared to exercise their constitutional rights in response to the events of 1970. As Max Weber observed, "The ethics of heart and the ethics of responsibility are not absolutely opposed but complementary, and only the man in whom they are joined has the political calling."[12] It is a calling which the University administration, sadly, has failed to grasp.

Why? Perhaps several observations are suggestive. The least damaging assertion is that the faculty and administration have lacked the requisite distance to place this event, which occurred in their very lap, in historical and sociopolitical perspective. Members of the faculty whose professional responsibilities carry them elsewhere in the nation and world are often amazed to discover that their more distant colleagues are more knowledgeable about the Kent State shootings and their significance than themselves. But why have we at Kent State lacked this perspective? Would this absence of distance prevail at any university? To an extent, perhaps. On the other hand, as a non-native Midwesterner, I cannot help but suspect that the situation reflects, in part, but another instance of the conservative parochialism so characteristic of Middle America. The academic profession, despite its educational advantage and alleged sophistication and humanism, is after all a reflection of the culture in which it is situated. Though some academics at Kent State

---

[12] Quoted in Maurice Merleau-Ponty, "The Crisis of the Understanding," in *The Primacy of Perception and Other Essays* (Evanston, Ill.: Northwestern Univ. Press, 1964), p. 210.

embody a more comprehensive, worldly attitude, the great majority apparently do not.

However an even more serious indictment must be contemplated. The University administrations during the 1970s consistently displayed insensitivity to the constitutional right of freedom of expression, opting instead to preserve "law and order" at any cost. This attitude was shown at least as early as 1968–69, prior to the killings, and has been demonstrated regularly throughout the years since. Hence, Nixon's judgment that Kent State protestors paid a necessary price for their behavior on May 4, 1970, while too harsh to fall from the lips of University administrators, has been voiced in other, more polite ways. A former provost, for example, once divulged to a small cluster of faculty that the Kent State killings were significant inasmuch as they "put an end" to campus unrest in the U.S. and this, he opined, was "good."

Even among those of a more benevolent attitude, however, we have witnessed at Kent State a failure of nerve, on the one hand, and an absence of vision, on the other. As terrible as the blow was to the University, it at least put an otherwise obscure, second-rate institution on the map. Kent State is no Harvard or Berkeley and never will be. Nevertheless, a succession of unimaginative administrations, in their headlong rush to return to normalcy (mediocrity), missed the opportunity to transform a minus into a plus. Robert White, president in 1970, proclaimed in the aftermath: "Let it be known that this is where it happened and this is where it shall never happen again." And yet, his successors—Glenn Olds and Brage Golding—nearly presided over a terrible repeat of 1970, by the decision of the former to build a gym-annex on the historic site and by the decision of the latter to see the project through. Kent State could have become the model of a *communitas humanum*. It did not.

One might ask what present value there is in reflecting on what might have been, on judging our past sins of omission and commission regarding May 4, 1970. Merleau-Ponty, who died on a May 4, answers:

> We have just as much right to judge the past as the present. Moreover, it precedes the judgments we pass upon it. It has judged itself; having been lived by men, it has introduced values into history, and we cannot describe it without confirming or weakening their historical status. . . . Knowledge and action are two poles of a single existence. Our relation-

ship to history is not merely a relation of understanding, that of spectacle and spectator. . . . History is a strange object, an object which is ourselves.[13]

The American philosopher, George Santayana, adds: "Those who cannot remember the past are condemned to repeat it."[14]

---

[13] Merleau-Ponty, "The Crisis of Understanding," pp. 202, 175.

[14] George Santayana, *Reason in Common Sense* (New York: Charles Scribner's Sons, 1905), p. 284.

The Gym Controversy

"A massive assault on this institution"

an interview with MICHAEL SCHWARTZ

MICHAEL SCHWARTZ *was born in Chicago in 1937. He attended the University of Illinois at Urbana, both as an undergraduate and graduate student, receiving his Ph.D. in sociology in 1962. He subsequently taught at Wayne State University and Indiana University; in 1970, he moved to Florida Atlantic University where he served, first, as chairman of the Department of Sociology and, later, as dean of the College of Social Sciences. Schwartz came to Kent State University in 1976 as vice president for graduate studies and research. In the summer of 1977, following the resignation of Glenn Olds as University president, Schwartz was appointed by the Board of Trustees as interim president of the institution. His appointment came in the midst of the most intense upheaval on the Kent State campus since the spring of 1970. Schwartz served as interim president from July through early September, which he says were, for him, "the longest two months in man's history." At the time of the interview, on October 10, 1980, Schwartz was provost and vice president for academic and student affairs; in September 1982 he succeeded Brage Golding as University president.*

Didn't *you suspect that there would be problems with a gym-annex located so close to the site of the May 4 shootings?*
My answer is no. When I first came to Kent State—and I started on April 1, 1976—and for several months thereafter, I didn't know anything about a plan for a gymnasium annex. I didn't know what the capital program was like, what was being planned; nothing. The first I knew of the plans for the annex was much later, when the architect brought some drawings over and the University vice presidents were invited to see them. I saw the drawings and thought they were nice, but I also thought there were a few problems: one being that there was no running track, which I remember complaining about, and another being that the pool was an awful walk from

the men's locker room. I complained about that too. At that time I didn't even know where the site was. Nobody even discussed it. I was so involved in graduate studies that the first time I really knew anything at all about the site and the problems being generated around the site was a week or so prior to the whole Blanket Hill episode. So I had no anticipation of the difficulties whatsoever.

You became interim president in the midst of the gym controversy. What would be your analysis of the program and motivations of the protestors?

That, I think, is an extraordinarily complicated question, because the gym protestors were not just a homogeneous group. They were extremely diverse. There was a group closely associated with the events of May fourth themselves, right here on this campus; some of the wounded and the parents of the students who were killed here. Then there was another group who had very little association with that event, who were on the political left looking for an issue of some kind—Kent State by then having become a good target for anything that came along. This group saw the gym, the site, all of that, as more a political phenomenon than a historical one; they wanted to make a political point and not a historical point, and certainly not a moral point. Then there was another category of students—and I think these were the students—who were involved, who were more interested in the issue of what's right and what was a good site, what was a bad site, the history of it, and so on. That was a substantial number of our own students—at least of those who were interested in it. A lot of others were not even students, or had been students off and on for a course or two. So, there were at least those three groups involved in the protest, and probably some others who were much more silent and on the fringe.

I don't think that the legitimacy of the concern was in doubt. The legitimacy of some of the people involved in the protest itself, in my view, was in doubt. For example, we saw an awful lot of people on the campus in the summer of 1977 whom we had never seen before, who had never had any association with Kent State University. We don't know particularly where they came from, but they camped out here for a couple of months. And then after the police removed the people—and I'm not going to call them students—from the hill and their "Tent City," we checked the arrest records. Then later, when a number of people—a large number of people—were arrested a second time for violating the court order, going onto the site, we checked those arrest records. The proportion of people who either were students or had ever been students was very small.

So you think that nonstudents played a major role?
I think that they played a leading role, if nothing else in numbers; but certainly they played a leading role, I also think, in terms of leadership of a number of things that went on. And so the motivation . . . the initial source of the protest was a kind of moral issue with which I could not, and did not, quibble. But the use of that for other and more peripheral political ends, which started to take over the whole thing, was something I did quibble with. I thought that when you start to abuse a moral purpose so openly—and that's what I think was going on—with regard to an issue as important to the University, then I became more than a little cynical about the whole protest. And I think it was being badly abused, seriously abused.

A major point in the interpretation of May 4 has been the appropriate form of commemoration; that is, what was the historical context in which May 4 took place? The protestors would and did say that May 4 was a political issue and must be remembered as such. You disagree with that?
No. No I don't. I really believe that the issue of the Vietnam War, but more specifically the Cambodian invasion, was clearly a political issue. No question about it. There was a rise of protest against the whole thing. That there was rioting and that students were killed and wounded here, however, is a different story. What happened was that in an ugly political event, the lives of some young people were lost and others changed, not for the better, for the rest of their lives. That strikes me as perhaps being the outcome of a political event, but I think the majority of people on this campus and elsewhere are much more concerned with the way we handled it. They are more concerned with the outcome itself than the original source of the protests. People were outraged all over this country at the consequences of those political events, which is to say the invasion of Cambodia. Vietnam was bad enough. And I suspect that there was a protest in one form or another on every university campus in America. I was in teaching and administration at Indiana University

in Bloomington on May 4, 1970, and there were the same kinds of activity there that took place here in Kent. There was the same kind of activity at my alma mater, the University of Illinois. What happened here, however, was literally a response by government—which I don't think the government planned—that had the ugliest possible consequences. That outcome was the concern of people. People were killed here, people who hadn't really done anything. They were killed by the authorities of their own government. That's an ugly phenomenon. That issue, that the students died here, is connected to the political context; but the deaths and woundings themselves, in my view, were not directly political.

As interim president, you dealt directly with the long-range impact of May 4, 1970. You were involved, among other things, in negotiations with the May 4th Coalition. In late July of 1977, you commented in a press release: "The University as well as the law has been assaulted." How did you view that assault on the institution?
In a couple of ways. I thought that there was an assault on a couple of levels. In one area, we were reasonably helpless, although in retrospect I'm not sure we should have been. We were tied up in a big federal lawsuit over the entire business. We knew that we were going to win the suit, but we were in it. And our advice from counsel was just to say as little as possible, almost nothing. Therefore, while we had dozens, literally dozens, of opportunities to use the media to our advantage, we did not. We didn't make a case. The protestors, on the other hand, used the media extremely well. I must say, I sat back from time to time and thought to myself, "This is a good job. They're doing a fine job, and they're doing it on the University." And the mail demonstrated that. We got mail from all over the country. We got mail from children, we got mail from old people, we got mail from everybody that you can imagine. I got more letters in crayon from little kids than you can believe. All the letters from children I answered personally. And some of these kids, by the way, even called. But we never made any statements to the press, except a few here and there.

Do you regret not having made your case?
Yes, I think as I look back on it, I do. I don't think that anything I would have said could possibly have injured us in court. But our

counsel was very, very cautious; and in that situation, with a federal lawsuit of that size and with that much publicity attached to it, I thought that following the advice of counsel was wise. It may really have been, but I regret not speaking out: not taking the opportunity we had, for example, on the "Today Show" or some other things which the protestors did take advantage of. On the other hand, how do you win that? We are, after all, the people with the power. And as long as you have the power and you're bulling ahead to do what you think is right, you just look like the bad guy. So maybe wisdom was "don't do it"; it's a mixed bag. But in retrospect, I'd have liked to have taken them on at least once or twice. We did in a way. In one case, we did have an aerial photograph of the site where the shootings took place. Superimposed on that photograph we put an outline of the gymnasium annex and then markings where the students were shot, to show that there was no overlap. We sent it out to newspapers all over the place. To my knowledge, the only paper that published it was the *Toledo Blade*.

One of the assaults, then, was the media campaign by the May 4th Coalition?
I think that the media campaign was a massive assault on this institution and the people associated with it. There's no question about it. In fact, a Florida newspaper characterized the administration as Nazis. I wouldn't have known that except I still have some friends there. So that was one assault. It was a publicity assault, and it did hurt us. The other assault, from which the University is only now beginning to recover, was the matter of how parents would feel about sending students to this University. It was not only an assault on the good name of the institution, not only an assault on the academic repute of the institution, it was also an assault on the potential livelihood of every employee here, because as enrollment goes down, so does the income. I would point out that in the fall quarter, 1977, our freshmen class dropped by one thousand students, and the following September it dropped by another thousand.

And you see a direct link?
I don't think there is any doubt about that. That was not a case of having lost students because there was a general enrollment decline going on around the country. Just the opposite was true. We lost

them. People did not have confidence in this place. In the public mind, the view had been established that this was an institution under siege with tanks on every corner. That was probably the most vicious part of the assault on the University. It literally did jeopardize the faculty. It jeopardized the worth of the degree at this institution for the students who are enrolled here. It was a serious matter. You could see it coming. You had to be a blind man not to see it happening. By the media's influence on prospective students and their parents, the protestors threw this place into a state of fiscal jeopardy the likes of which you can't believe. There was a question in my mind as to whether or not we were going to stay open.

Looking back at the gym controversy, then, the financial aspect would be the one item you would stress?
Yes, I would. Whether you like to talk about it in these terms or not, you don't have any choice. You do have to finish in the black every year, you do have to pay the bills; you do have a substantial faculty that has to be paid, and they can only be paid if the students come. And I think that the worst of it, from the point of view of students who were enrolled and had nothing to do with any of this, was the question in my mind: what are we doing to the value of their degree in the public view? That is, by the way, something that most people hadn't thought about. When a student walks out with a degree from a university, it's got to be marketable, it's got to speak to some worth. If all it speaks to is a university that seems to draw from all over the country, or whatever, a bunch of people who are intent on ripping it apart, what could you possibly learn in that environment? That does damage, not to an institution, which is a kind of gray and impersonal thing that nobody thinks about except the guys that have to run it and the people who have to teach in it. But now we are starting to talk about personal damage to individual degree holders: past, future, and present. That is an ugly situation, and that, I believe, did occur. That's the kind of assault I was talking about.

Did you ever seriously think about moving the gym?
Yes, we did. As a matter of fact, we talked about a number of things as options. One of the Trustees favored moving the whole thing over to what is now the University School. There was some talk about rotating the gym on its site. We talked about a number of options,

none of which really was any good. All the drawings would've had to be redone; we would've incurred enormous architectural costs and construction costs, all those kinds of things. But more important was this, and nobody ever seemed to understand it: the construction agreement was not between Kent State University and the private contractor. It was between the contractor and the state of Ohio, Division of Administrative Services. The University was a third-party beneficiary: we get the building. But for any change of the site requiring new drawings, different construction, anything like that, we had no control over whether or not the state would accept it. We were middlemen, to put it bluntly, absolute middlemen. And in fact, the state was very reluctant even to talk to us about it, thinking it was a very expensive deal. We had conversations in Columbus; we even had conversations in Washington. Nobody was going to pay the freight.

How do you think that the events of May 4, 1970, have changed or affected Kent State, in a broader way than just the gym controversy?
That's very difficult to say. This University has a history now that can be claimed by no other institution in America, except perhaps Jackson State, and even that was slightly different. And this University has that history on its sleeve, which it will wear, I think, for a long time, although the feeling about it will be tempered. In that sense, it really is a historical site, and you can't wash that away. And I think once that's in perspective, it will make very little difference to this University, except to point to a certain uniqueness. In the shorter term, I think it has had some serious and deleterious effects on the institution in terms of "well, you know who goes to school there" and "they do have tanks on every corner" and "to get to class in the morning you have to go through checkpoints and barbed wire" and all that type of thing. There is this insanity in the public view, or was through the last decade, about Kent State. And the facts were all otherwise: this is a quiet, placid, if anything remarkably conservative institution, both in terms of its student body and its faculty. More conservative than any school that I've been at, and this is my fourth. It has been a strenuous decade for everybody concerned, but it's slowly starting to fade. More and more people under-

stand this place. They know it, they've been here. And the more people come here and get to know the place a little bit, they understand that it is not what that public image is all about. We've changed this place dramatically, I think, in the last three years or so. The long-term effects for this institution, I suspect, won't be any different from what's going on anywhere else. In the short run, the fact that it survived the short run is a miracle. And the other fact about the short run is that it would not have survived the decade without the kind of faculty it's had. When this campus was closed in 1970, there were students who had to be taught; there were students who expected to graduate. Professors took the students into their homes; they housed them, fed them, taught them. Nobody talks about that. Nobody understands that it happened. The University went on literally underground; this University in fact was never closed. If it hadn't been for that, I believe that the University would not have survived the decade. So if anybody asks you, how do you account for the survival of Kent State, tell them it's the faculty.

Because of their commitment to education?
Their commitment to education, their commitment to their students. They were not going to permit any of that to stop. We knew about it even in Bloomington; we knew what was going on. There was a sense that the level of commitment to the enterprise was as strong if not stronger at Kent State University than it was anywhere in the United States, Harvard included. That's never said, but that's what Kent State really was.

When you were coming to Kent State, did you look forward to it?
Yes. I looked forward to it for many reasons. I was coming to do some things in an area which had interested me for a long time: graduate studies and research. Previously, I was at Florida Atlantic University in Boca Raton, where I was a department chairman and started a brand new master's program. We were looking forward to a little more money, more faculty, and getting a doctoral program started. I'd been there for eighteen months or so, and the state initiated a prohibition: no new Ph.D. programs; and I was stuck. So when this opportunity came along, to work in graduate studies and research at Kent State University, I grabbed it. So yes, I looked for-

ward to coming. However, I must tell you, my oldest child was in the eighth grade, and she announced to her classmates that she was moving, that her dad had taken a job at Kent State up in Ohio. And those kids, kids down in Florida, said, "Why would anybody want to go to a place like that?" And those were eighth graders, in 1976.

Tent City

"A real community"

an interview with NANCY GRIM

NANCY GRIM *was born in 1955 in Toledo, Ohio. She first attended Kent State University in 1973 and received her bachelor's degree in 1977. She recalls: "I was one of the people who was not a student when they were arrested during the gym protest, because we had just quit being students a month earlier." As an undergraduate, she was involved in student government and with the founding of the May 4th Task Force. She remembers her ambivalent feelings toward radical politics on first coming to Kent State: "I was in junior high and high school when all these 'radical things' were going on at campuses, and I saw them with contradictory feelings. On the one hand, people seemed to have some pretty good ideas, but I also read the* Reader's Digest *view that SDS was really a seditious organization." Grim played a leading role in the establishment of the May 4th Coalition in 1977, and she is currently enrolled in the University of Akron School of Law. The interview was conducted on November 5, 1980.*

You *were involved in the founding of the May 4th Task Force in 1975–76?*

Yes. When I was still in student government, when I was still in my "there must be something we can do" days, I said, "Gee, there must be something we can do about May fourth." I spearheaded the formation of the May 4th Task Force, though I didn't have much part in it as a member. I was more involved a few months later with the May 4th Strike Committee, which was basically an ad hoc group organized in the spring of 1976—and still basically the same core of people in the spring of 1977—around the issue of no classes on May 4. In contrast, the main focus of the Task Force became commemoration. As May 4, 1977, approached, there was increasing discussion about the proposed gym-annex in the *Daily Kent Stater*, but it was unclear how people felt about it. During the May 4 commemorative program, the gym was stressed by some of the speakers, and there was a great upsurge of feeling against it. I think it's fair to say that the sit-in at Rockwell Hall—which is the administration building—that same day was spontaneous. A lot of people who were saying, "I never thought I'd ever do something like this," went and occupied the building, the initial demand being to "move the gym."

What happened at the Rockwell sit-in that led to the formation of the May 4th Coalition?
I do have notes that were taken by people there: a series of people took the notebook and scribbled down the sequence of discussion. At first, as I recall, it was quite confusing. We went upstairs, then downstairs and found a place to sit. We began to coalesce and start talking. I think I ended up chairing the meeting; I'm not sure how that happened. The discussion was very broad; it took a long time because everyone had things to say and a lot got said. There was a lot of sorting out, some people were saying, "We're going to sit here until they move the gym." The eight demands were formulated. And finally a decision was reached on staying or leaving. The feeling was if we stayed we could get isolated, then arrested, and lose support. Instead, we said: "Let's break up with a show of force and go out and organize the campus." Before that happened, there was a group chosen by nomination—in fact, all the people nominated became the steering committee. I don't recall anyone being voted off the committee. It was this group which got together and wrote the demands into a list of eight. I was on that steering committee.

Were you already calling yourselves the "May 4th Coalition"; was there a sense that you were a unified group?
If we didn't have the name immediately, it developed fairly quickly. One of the decisions that was made that night, before we left, was that we would carry on: that was the reason for leaving Rockwell. That was the beginning of the organizational form of the Coalition. The steering committee would meet to formulate suggested policies, then call mass meetings. That form lasted until May 12, when Tent City was established. After that, the form of the Coalition changed, because most work was done at mass meetings in Tent City.

How important was Tent City to the work of the May 4th Coalition?
I think Tent City really kept the organization together, for a long

time. It was especially critical to people who didn't come into the Coalition with a strong ideological perspective. Tent City was a real community and provided a sense of community. It gave people a way to deal with endless meetings and discussion.

After the establishment of the Coalition's base on Blanket Hill, what were the central issues in the group's opposition to the construction of the gym-annex?
I have notes from a meeting when we discussed that, on May thirteenth, the day after Tent City was founded. We were asking ourselves what was next. Some of the demands had been met, or at least had been conceded. The administration had said, for instance, that there would be no retaliation against people who participated in the sit-in. There was something said about the Center for Peaceful Change. But it was clear to people that the gym was the issue everyone was most excited about. Realistically, it was the central issue. The discussion of May 13 came about in response to an idea of circulating a petition to get a list of supporters. What were we going to put on the petition? The decision was made to emphasize the gym. As I have it in my notes, the chief reasons for this were, first, May

Tent City, near proposed gym-annex site, 1977.

fourth, then the aesthetics and environmental issues: people saying that the hill was one of the most beautiful places on campus, saying "you're going to obliterate that?" The other issue was the politics of the Vietnam War and the protest against it.

How so?
The argument was that the students of May 4, 1970, were protesting the invasion of Cambodia and United States involvement in Vietnam, and that the shooting of the students was part of the U.S. foreign policy in Vietnam which was extended homeward. I think for most people that May fourth was the critical point, in different ways. Some were more sentimental about it than others. Certainly the rhetoric stressed "this is our land" in the sense that it was peoples' land: this is where our ancestors, so to speak, an earlier generation of students were shot down.

What about the idea, after the establishment of Tent City, that "this is our land because we have been living on it"?
That certainly became stronger and stronger. It was connected with something else that happened. As time went on, members of the Coalition would talk more and more about how many days the struggle had gone on. At first, it was to say, "Look, we've been in Tent City for twenty days, we've been together, we've been through it, let's stick together and we can keep going." And that became partly, "We've been here twenty days, this is our place." It also became something of a basis for seniority rights: "I've been on this hill for forty days, and it seems to *me.* . . ."

Many people talked and still talk about the May fourth site as "sacred ground": how important was that idea?
I personally was not too comfortable with it, but I think it was very important to the Coalition. The phrase was taken up by a number of people and became a real unifying force. It was even taken up by people who I'm sure didn't believe it, including members of the RSB —who would probably want to say that the reasons for Coalition policy were "purely political" rather than "religious." But the concept was important in keeping together people who didn't have a sense of ideology, who would reject the idea of ideology. I didn't feel that way, though I did have a certain sentimentality about the

area because I used to study on that hill and I did think it was a
beautiful place.

*How difficult was it for the Coalition to put together a political
program involving people with very different political perspectives?
How was the Coalition able to operate effectively with that kind of
mix?*
At first, quite well, and for a variety of reasons. People who came
into the Coalition from and with tightly organized leftist organizations were quite ready at the beginning at least to appear to put the
Coalition ahead of that smaller organization. They were careful to
encourage political newcomers to speak up. They were fairly careful not to put someone down for saying something that sounded
"liberal." Of course, there were others, including myself, who were
socialists and had a pretty firm sense of the ideology with which they
were involved but were not part of a tight group and had no problems "dealing with liberals" and such things. The students who came
into the Coalition from the opposite perspective—the "liberals," the
"sentimentalists," the "environmentalists"—were willing to forego
for awhile their fear of "communists." They were so excited about
what they were getting into that they were willing to try new things:
"Gee, I did a sit-in; I never did that before."

What about decision-making within the Coalition?
There was always a tension there. The beginning was, I think, the
best time in terms of dealing with tensions between the various backgrounds of Coalition members. Part of the problem was in terms of
having an equal voice. People more experienced in working with
political groups are more capable of manipulating a group. The inexperienced people might be afraid to speak up, because they might
not "say it right." The latter group was more willing to defer to experience. From the beginning, there was a certain amount of defer-
ring to the "authority" of experience. But also at the early stages of
the Coalition's development, discussion happened in a way that
most people felt was open; they would speak out. However, I notice
in looking back over my notes that even at early meetings, there was
some talk of "oh, we don't want to be liberal," which alienates
people who always thought that liberal was better than conservative. For some reason I've never really quite understood, from the

beginning, people—strangers—would come up to me and say, "I know you're friends with those radicals, but I feel like I can talk to you." And they would proceed to tell me about ideas they thought the Coalition should be listening to. So I was acutely aware that there were people who wanted to be part of the Coalition but felt that they couldn't really be part of the decision-making.

The University administration maintained that the gymnasium annex was not designed to cover up the site where students were killed in 1970. Clearly, the building would not intrude into the parking lot itself. What was the Coalition's response?
Let me go at that from two perspectives. I did some research on the history of the University's decision-making on the gym. And I think it's true that it was not deliberately designed to cover up the site. I think it's also true that the building was designed with total disregard for the history of the place. The point is not what you meant to do, the point is what's happening. The University's argument was that the gym was not going to cover any of the actual places where anybody fell down, nor the place where the guardsmen stood to fire. But the importance of the site as a historical place included the entire area. People were in fact shot about two feet from where the building was constructed. The Guard marched right across that area. One of the historical arguments to say, "Look, it wasn't the Guard's fault," was the idea that they were hemmed in. And when you put that building there, it sure looks like the Guard was hemmed in. It really changes the whole area.

So your definition of the May fourth site was much broader than simply the place where the four students were killed?
Yes, in fact one of the things we did in some of our publicity stuff was hand out a map of the site as we saw it.

When it became clear that the University was going to remove the Tent City encampment from the hill, what was the point of staying on to force the mass arrest which took place on July 12?
The initial point was, "We're going to sit here until the construction machinery comes, and they won't dig with us here." It became a symbolic point as well, though I think it was fairly clear from the beginning that what they would do was come and move us off. But the

idea was, "Okay, they're going to move us off, but we're going to show them how important this is to us." It was an important symbolic protest. It was going to hurt the resources of the state as well as Portage County. There was also the feeling, certainly by July 12, that "this is our place, we're not going to be taken out of our home." We cooked our meals there, we had our tents there, we went through some of the worst rainstorms I've ever seen in Kent that summer. And we weren't going to walk away.

Would you say that was the high point of the Coalition effort?
Yes, definitely.

What problems were created then by the loss of Tent City?
We didn't have any community to focus around. There were a number of other difficulties. People who were not dedicated, lifelong politicos had other aspects of their life to deal with. The Coalition after that continued to have meetings every night, and a lot of people just couldn't carry on with that. So it became, on that basis alone, more and more difficult for the Coalition to be a broad-based organization. People who didn't come every night were seen as being less enthusiastic members of the Coalition. "Well, if you can't be there, that's too bad." Before that, people who weren't living at Tent City knew that they could stop by any time and talk to folks and see what was going on. But it became harder to find everybody.

Did you anticipate this problem?
No, I don't really think it was dealt with ahead of time. In general, the Coalition didn't anticipate the length of the struggle. We didn't expect to be in Tent City as long as we were. Initially, we didn't even know if we would be there until the end of the school term. Even after we were moved off the hill, things continued. There was court litigation to prevent construction, defense work for the July 12 arrests and later arrests, even lobbying with the White House as well as local leafleting and rallies. And the internal divisions became more obvious.

It's been said that the May 4th Coalition was an experiment in participatory democracy. Was it a successful one?
I think it wasn't, but I don't think that's because participatory

democracy can't work. I think that the Coalition was, to me and maybe to every participant, a learning experience. I don't want to say that in a trivial way like a game that you play in school. It was a learning experience about what makes participatory democracy work and what can make it fail.

Why do you think it didn't work?
A number of things, most of which I think are going to be present in some form in every group. It's a matter of being aware of and dealing with them, though not everyone would share that opinion. One major factor was that some people came into the Coalition seeing themselves as individuals: "I am me, I have ideas, I say them, my ideas should have the same weight or impact as your ideas; we're all individuals here and together we're a group, the Coalition." There were also people from tight-knit political groups, the RSB for one. Although the Spartacus Youth League was never really a part of the Coalition, it was part of the politics of the Coalition for a short time. There was also the Young Socialist Alliance. And then there were a number of people from student government backgrounds. Members of the Revolutionary Student Brigade in particular formed a tight group within the Coalition, but that was not initially apparent to most people. They were experienced in dealing with groups, and I'm sure they saw the Coalition as an opportunity to spread their politics. The YSA also saw it that way, but they had very different ways of organizing. I was very suspicious of the Brigade—I knew they were usually opposed to broad-based coalitions. But people who came in with very little political experience were willing to take things at face value. When RSB members seemed friendly, then they were friends. We all seemed to be friends at first. This factor was important for a long time, because as it became apparent to some members of the Coalition that meetings were being manipulated, it was hard for people to think that their "friends" were doing this. You know: "We've been through fifty days together." The manipulation became more obvious after Tent City, when long nightly gatherings continued and crucial votes wouldn't happen until the end of the meeting. People who had to go to work the next day or whatever had left by then. So the hard-core folks were the ones who stayed, and they tended to be the self-styled militants. The rhetoric was important. A theme that became used more

and more was the dichotomy of "militancy" versus "liberalism." It offended those who thought of themselves as liberals, and it made it very hard for someone to take a stand that was anything other than that which the people who used the dichotomy styled as militancy.

Because people would not want to be "liberals"?
Well, it was made clear that militants were people who acted and that liberals were people who just talked fuzzily about things.

When did factionalization become critical?
It began really in August. As I mentioned, I was aware of tensions before that point, ones which many Coalition members weren't willing to say were there. There was manipulation, hesitancy on the part of some people to express themselves; and there were people dropping out, not for political reasons, but because they felt that they weren't wanted. They were offended to see their ideas brushed off. I felt increasingly that decisions ostensibly made by the group were not true Coalition decisions. I remember at the beginning of August, I left town for a few days, and I recall my own feelings when I did that. Part of it was not related to the Coalition: I was trying to decide whether or not I was indeed going to go to law school in the fall. I was having difficulty thinking about that because of the Coalition. The tensions of the Coalition were becoming very difficult for me. I was trying to convince people to do things differently, to make the organization democratic, which I felt it wasn't. But it was frustrating to me because there was so much unity among those whom I saw as manipulative. They had separate meetings, somewhere or other, and came into Coalition activities with a unified strategy; they knew what they wanted to do. And they were pretty good at getting their way. Everybody else was not unified. That is, the only point of unity was, "We're everybody else; we want to be able to be diverse." Well, it's hard to unify around diversity.

What was the Blanket Hill Council?
About the end of August, a group of people got together, and I don't remember what role I played actually in getting them together. It was a caucus concerned with the manipulation taking place within the Coalition. Initially, we tried to do what we thought the "militants" were doing: we tried to meet and talk about strategy

before the full Coalition meetings. We found it very difficult because we generally disagreed on what alternatives we wanted. What we really wanted was to be able to have open discussion. We did write up a set of principles which we felt were the original principles of the May 4th Coalition: open discussion, democratic organization, non-violence as the operative tactic. The role of nonviolence was a difficult one because there were some people in our caucus who felt that it should be a principle of life, and there were others who saw it simply as a tactic. The statement of principles was read at the next Coalition meeting, and some were even eventually adopted, or re-adopted; but the feeling continued among the caucus that all was not well and good, that the Coalition was increasingly run by a small group of people. Finally, we said: "Okay, it just isn't the Coalition anymore." And we formed the Blanket Hill Council. Unfortunately, what happened was that the Blanket Hill Council did only very non-militant things and just sort of fizzled out. By that time, it was very close to construction; it was no time to be organizing something new.

How would you evaluate the successes of the Coalition?
Let me talk first about successes in terms of external things. The gym became a national issue. When I went to New York that summer, people were concerned about the gym. Also, there was greater awareness of May fourth, of what had happened. There was, I think, a better understanding in general of the type of power structure in the University, and in the society that the University is part of. To the extent that people across the nation were aware of the gym struggle, they asked questions about the decision-making process: "How could they forget about May fourth? How could they decide to put a gym there?" And also: how could the University continue its proposal when so many people were upset about it?

Among people who were part of the Coalition, there was more understanding of the local power structure, of the role of economics. I think the main success was making May fourth again a major aspect of life at Kent State. The gym struggle brought it back into focus after several years of decreasing interest in the shootings. I think that's important. It's important to Kent State to be aware of its role in history.

The Legal Battle

Finishing Unfinished Business

by SANFORD JAY ROSEN

SANFORD JAY ROSEN *is a partner in the San Francisco law firm of Rosen &
Remcho. He is a 1962 graduate of the Yale Law School, a former law professor, a
former assistant legal director of the national American Civil Liberties Union, and
a former legal director of the Mexican-American Legal Defense and Educational
Fund, Inc. As discussed in the following essay, Rosen was chief attorney for the
Kent State families (the plaintiffs) in the 1978 retrial of the civil damages suit and
was instrumental in the achievement of the out-of-court settlement of January 4,
1979.*

For over ten years, we have lived with the echo of the barrage of
bullets that tore through the crowd of unarmed students at Kent
State University on May 4, 1970. Ohio National Guard gunfire
ended a student protest against the American invasion of Cambodia
and the war in Indochina. The deaths far away had been bad
enough, but now, the government was killing our children at home,
too.

I had been on temporary assignment as special counsel to the
national American Civil Liberties Union for only a few days when I
was assigned to investigate the May 4 shootings at Kent State. There
was very little anyone could do to ease the pain of the victims and
their families, but we could at least try to mitigate the tragedy by
asking the courts to protect the students against further abuse and to
place the blame and responsibility for the outrage where it belonged:
with Ohio's governor and adjutant general, the officers of the troops
who fired, and the troops themselves. The ACLU and other civil
liberties organizations and lawyers did what they do best: they took
pieces of the tragedy into court in a systematic attempt to make
government accountable. The list of legal actions is both long and
instructive:

—We successfully defended faculty members and students against spurious state criminal prosecutions designed to make it appear that the student victims or at least outside "agitators" were responsible for the shootings.

—A special Ohio grand jury issued a legally unauthorized report pinning all blame for the shootings on the Kent State students and faculty and outside agitators. The report exonerated all government and peace-keeping personnel. We persuaded the federal courts to expunge that report.

—The day after the shootings the Kent State campus was evacuated, and the campus police and state police conducted a sweeping search of all dormitory rooms. We successfully challenged this illegal search and seizure.

—We also succeeded in having the courts prevent the local government in Portage County from retaliating against students by denying them the vote and eligibility for food stamps. More recently, through an advantageous settlement, we imposed some control on improper police undercover surveillance of student political activity.

—Eventually we persuaded the federal government to prosecute some of the National Guardsmen most clearly responsible for the shootings. The government, however, did not put on a strong enough case to convict them under the federal criminal statute that makes it a crime for a state officer intentionally to violate a person's civil rights.

—We also attempted to persuade the federal courts to supervise the Ohio National Guard's weaponry, training, and orders. But the Supreme Court of the United States concluded that such supervision was the province of the president, Congress, and the Department of Defense, not the federal courts.

—In 1977, we attempted to persuade the courts to stop the University's actions in constructing a new gymnasium that covers and obscures a significant portion of the campus area where the May 4 demonstrations and shootings took place. Initially we had some success, and construction of the gymnasium was temporarily halted by court orders. Eventually, however, the court orders were dissolved and construction proceeded.

But perhaps the single most important legal event to come out of the May 4 tragedy was the civil damages lawsuits that were brought on behalf of all thirteen of the victims. Immediately following the shootings, twelve of the victims (or their next of kin) retained private personal injury lawyers to seek money damages on their behalf. At the same time, the parents of Sandra Scheuer, who was killed on May 4, retained the ACLU and its Ohio affiliate to seek damages for her estate. There were a number of barriers to financial recovery. For example, at that time, under both Ohio and federal law, the state of Ohio itself could not be sued. Largely because of the perceived injustice of this technical barrier to recovery by the Kent State victims, the Ohio legislature has since changed Ohio law to permit damage suits against the state.

All of the victims brought federal civil rights lawsuits against the governor, the adjutant general, the National Guardsmen who did the firing, and the officers who were in charge of those guardsmen. These suits initially were dismissed on the ground that they were tantamount to suits against the state of Ohio, and many or all of the defendants were absolutely immune from liability because they had acted within their official capacities as government officers. The United States Supreme Court reversed this ruling, holding that the suits were not suits against the state of Ohio and that the defendants enjoyed only a qualified "good faith" immunity, not absolute official immunity from liability. This decision was a landmark in the development of federal civil rights damages law.

After the Supreme Court's decision, all of the Kent State federal civil damages cases were consolidated for trial in Cleveland before federal judge Don J. Young in the spring and summer of 1975. The plaintiffs (the victims) had no unified trial team at this first trial, and there was some dissension among both the plaintiffs and their attorneys. As the trial wore on for some fifteen weeks, Judge Young became increasingly hostile toward the plaintiffs, or at least toward their lawyers.

In August of 1975, the jury brought in a verdict in favor of the defendants in the civil damages cases by a vote of nine to three. (The parties had stipulated that a concurrence of nine jurors was sufficient for a binding verdict.) After this loss, the plaintiffs joined together and retained the ACLU to handle the appeal. Perhaps because of my previous involvement with the Kent State litigation (while I had not participated in the first trial, I had moved in and out of these cases as I moved in and out of the ACLU's employ), the ACLU asked me to take on the appeal. I could not say no; it felt too much like unfinished personal business. Before I accepted the assignment, however, I made it clear that I would be answerable to no one—not the ACLU, not the previous lawyers—except my clients, the victims. The only interests I would pursue would be those of the victims. I refused to represent in any direct way the interests of any other individuals or of any organizations, or even of history.

With this understanding, I recruited a nationwide team of lawyers and legal workers to prepare the appeals brief. Included were some of the victims' previous lawyers. The lawyers on the appellate team included Nelson Karl, David Engdahl, and Michael Geltner, each of whom had been involved in the first trial. Also working with me were Nicholas Waranoff, Amitai Schwartz, Robert Baker, Ann Sayvetz, and Andrea Biren, who were recruited to work on the appeal. Perhaps the most important member of our team, throughout my involvement in the civil damages cases, was Steven Keller, our litigation consultant and documents custodian in Ohio. Many other law clerks and legal workers, too numerous to list here, also assisted the effort throughout.

Most of the financial needs for the appellate and subsequent legal efforts were met out of funds raised for that purpose on behalf of the Board of Church and Society of the United Methodist Church. Rev. John Adams, then director of the Board's Division of Law, Justice and Community Relations, ministered in every conceivable way to the Kent State victims. To this day, he continues to do so.

In preparing the appeal, we set out first to demonstrate the plain injustice of the jury verdict in favor of the defendants. Once having captured the court's attention, we hoped to persuade it of some legally sufficient reason to reverse the trial court and remand for a new trial. Even with this plan, we did not have much hope of winning the appeal; so we were ecstatic when we won. I remember screaming my joy and disbelief at the court's clerk when she telephoned with the news. Our strategy had worked. The appellate court had reversed the trial court on the technical ground that the trial judge had mishandled an outside intrusion into the trial in the form of a threat to and assault on one of the jurors.

The defendants attempted unsuccessfully to get the Court of Appeals to reconsider the decision and were equally unsuccessful in seeking a review by the Supreme Court. The damage cases were then remanded for retrial in the federal district court in Cleveland. Our work immediately escalated.

The victims retained me as lead counsel for purposes of retrial. Subject only to their ultimate review, they authorized me to recruit pretrial and trial teams and make other necessary preparations. Having studied the record of the first trial and identified what I considered numerous legal errors detrimental to the plaintiffs, our pretrial strategy was to cure these errors before the second trial started. So we drowned the defendants in a sea of pretrial motions, most of which we eventually won.

A by-product of this strategy appears to have been the sudden decision of Judge Young, who had presided at the first trial, to withdraw from the case. My clients were very pleased with this turn of events, for they had long believed that Judge Young was prejudiced against them. They and some of the previous attorneys, in fact, had pressed me hard to move to disqualify Judge Young on grounds of prejudice. I had at first resisted these efforts because I did not believe a case of bias or prejudice could be made out under prevailing legal standards. Later, I became persuaded that bias as a legal matter might be shown, and we prepared the necessary documentation to make a motion to disqualify Judge Young. He withdrew, however, before a new occasion occurred to trigger the motion.

As all the victims agreed, Judge Young's replacement, Judge William K. Thomas, was fair and just. Not only was he fair, in fact, but he also gave the appearance of being fair in his every action. After the trial, I commented to Judge Thomas about his strikingly favorable impression on the victims. He replied: "Fairness satisfies the appearance of fairness."

With the trial date approaching, I completed recruitment of the plaintiffs' trial team: principal trial co-counsel, Rees Davis, an experienced Mansfield, Ohio, trial lawyer; senior trial co-counsel, David Engdahl, who had participated at the first trial and knew everything there was to know about the photographic evidence; Steven Keller, our litigation consultant, who had also participated at the first trial and who held and organized the entire record and files of the case in his mind; Ellen Goldblatt and Robert S. Baker, recent law school graduates, familiar with the case through their work with me in my offices in San Francisco.

The trial team gathered to work on the case full-time in Cleveland in early November of 1978—nearly a month before the trial was to begin. By then we were receiving the invaluable assistance of the National Jury Project, which assisted us generally in the jury selection process. And it soon became unmistakably clear to the trial court, to the defendants, and to Ohio officialdom that we were treating the litigation singlemindedly and with utmost seriousness, expending every conceivable resource on the effort. We were gearing up to win—if winning were possible.

Yet, as we prepared the cases for trial, and even as we tried them, we also prepared to reach a settlement—on terms favorable to the victims. The new trial judge, William Thomas, did everything he could to settle the lawsuits.

And settle we did—on January 4, 1979.

Some people, including the Kent State victims' previous lead counsel, Joseph Kelner, who lost the first of the civil damages trials, have said that the settlement was inadequate. Yet, for the first time in the history of our nation, college student victims of excessive force used to disperse an assembly were given money compensation for their injuries—$675,000. More than that, for the first time the victims of such excessive force secured a signed and written statement of regret—almost universally understood as an apology— from those responsible for their injuries, the twenty-eight defendants. The victims, of course, would have preferred more money and a stronger statement of apology and responsibility. We tried, but could get no more. Under all the circumstances, the victims accepted the settlement because, through it, essentially they got everything they sought in the lawsuit. As they said on the day of the settlement: "We accepted the settlement out-of-court, but negotiated by the court, because we determined that it accomplished to the greatest extent possible under present law, the objectives toward which we as families have struggled during the past eight years."

These objectives were listed as follows:

1. Insofar as possible, to hold the State of Ohio accountable for the actions of its officials and agents in the event of May 4, 1970.
2. To demonstrate that the excessive use of force by the agents of government would be met by a formidable citizen challenge.
3. To exhaustively utilize the judicial system in the United States and demonstrate to an understandably skeptical generation that the system can work when extraordinary pressure is applied to it, as in this case.

4. To assert that the human rights of American citizens, particularly those citizens in dissent of governmental policies, must be effected and protected.

5. To obtain sufficient financial support for Mr. Dean Kahler, one of the victims of the shooting, that he may have a modicum of security as he spends the rest of his life in a wheelchair.

Point 5 was especially important. If the victims gambled on a new trial and lost again, as they had lost before an Ohio jury in 1975, Kahler, a paraplegic as a result of the shootings, would have been denied funds he needed urgently.

The settlement achieved the victims' goals in several ways. They received $675,000 to compensate them for their actual physical injuries. By paying this money as well as additional sums for part of the victims' court costs, and by underwriting the defendants' enormous legal fees and expenses, the state of Ohio acknowledged its responsibility for the shootings. So did the individual defendants (including the governor and adjutant general), by signing the unprecedented statement of regret. President Carter's refusal to issue a comparable statement to secure the release of the American hostages in Iran made clear how difficult it is to extract such statements from public officials.

The tenacity of the victims will help to deter such conduct by public officials in the future. They maintained the legal struggle for eight years, continuing it even after suffering a disastrous jury verdict against them, until they made certain that they obtained compensation. To do this, they had to tie up their own lives in litigation, but they also tied up the lives of the Ohio officials who used excessive force. They demonstrated that those who abuse public power cannot quickly escape their responsibility.

What if the victims had not settled? Having lost the first trial, what if they had insisted upon finishing the second trial? They might well have suffered the intolerable insult of losing a second time. I certainly could not predict how the second jury would have decided. If they had completed the second trial, the victims could not have proven that the defendants were guilty of murder. In fact, this was not an issue before the court in the civil damages case.

The victims could not prove that the shootings occurred in the course of a conspiracy to kill or wound students. There may well have been such a conspiracy; but there was insufficient admissible trial evidence to support such a conclusion. Further, no important new revelations would have come out of the second trial. Virtually everything we knew was already on the public record.

At the second trial all we could have done was to arrange the evidence more trimly and provide better focus to the events, pointing toward a single, simple goal of demonstrating that excessive force was used against the students on May 4, 1970. That was the issue we were trying in the Kent State civil damages cases, nothing broader or more profound. The Scranton Commission more than nine years ago had decided that issue for history. It rightly concluded that "the indiscriminate firing of rifles into a crowd of students and the deaths that followed were unnecessary, unwarranted, and inexcusable."

And even if the second trial had ended in a jury verdict for the victims, there was no assurance that the jury would have awarded them more than nominal damages. The victims of the Kent State shootings remain politically unpopular in northeastern Ohio. Unlike automobile accident cases, there were no standards that could be used to predict how much the jury would award the victims. The individual defendants may have been unable to pay substantial damages, and the state of Ohio might not have volunteered to pay if the jury award were substantial. Any award for the victims probably would have been tied up for years in further appeals that could have resulted in yet a third trial. In the meantime, there would have been no money for Dean Kahler—or for the others who suffered serious physical injuries.

By their actions, including the prosecution and settlement of the damages cases, the Kent State victims, who were made exceptional by circumstances beyond their control, have helped us all to deal both with unresolved issues of excessive government force and with the unresolved residue of the war in Indochina. History will also record that the state of Ohio and its officials were held accountable by the courts for the shootings at Kent State. It would have been better had the penalties been heavier. But the victims of the shootings deserve only admiration for persisting until they prevailed.

December Dialogues

The Settlement Reconsidered

by CHARLES A. THOMAS

CHARLES A. THOMAS *has a master's degree in military history from Duke University (1966). He was employed from 1968 to 1980 in the National Archives, Washington, D.C., where he began his research on the Kent State shootings. Thomas has written a book-length manuscript on the events of May 4, 1970, and it is available to researchers in the Kent State University Archives. Thomas is currently a resident of Philadelphia.*

I was at my desk in the Audiovisual Archives Division of the National Archives on the evening of December 29, 1975, one of the few staff members left in the building that holiday week. At the time, I was working in the Sound Recordings Unit, which I loved; I was able to spend hours discovering the unknown (to a child of the television age) world of the Golden Age of Radio. Just as I was about to leave for the day, the phone rang. The caller identified himself as Arthur Krause, a name which meant nothing to me. His call, as it turned out, resulted from the only assignment I had been given in 1975 that had not dealt with sound recordings. Between May 1 and 4, I had been detailed to the Motion Pictures Unit to write descriptions of films of the Kent State shootings, collected by the President's Commission on Campus Unrest, which had been subpoenaed for the civil trial then in progress in Cleveland. It was a strange assignment, in that I knew nothing about films and there were plenty of experienced cataloguers on the Motion Pictures staff.

In the course of writing descriptions of the films, I realized that none of the available footage showing dead and wounded students following the lethal volley had been used in assembling the compilation film shown at the public hearings which the commission had held in Kent in August 1970. Suspicious, I pulled the sound tapes that had been played at the hearings and found that the sections on the recording where the students had been shouting loudest had been "lifted," spliced together, and then juxtaposed to the sound of the fatal shots, eliminating the curious lull before the shootings that can be heard on the original tape. It looked very much as if someone had doctored the evidence to minimize any impression of the Guard's brutality and to plant the spurious notion that the soldiers had been confronted with a raging student mob.

I didn't know what to do about my discovery until a friend suggested that I contact the lawyers in the ongoing Kent State civil suit who were representing the plaintiffs, the families of the slain and wounded students. I postponed even this minimal step for weeks. When I finally did call, the attorneys thanked me for my "concern," but told me the trial was going very well and that they would not need to raise the point of such a possible cover-up. With this, I decided to drop the matter, until I received a routine solicitation for funds from the Reverend John Adams, of the Kent State Due Process in Law Fund. Still bitter about the failure of so many similar "causes," I told Adams that I no longer believed in traditional liberal expedients like writing checks for causes; but if he wanted me to give something of myself, I would "go public" with what I knew about a possible cover-up in the case of Kent State.

Now, on this December evening in 1975, Arthur Krause—whose daughter Allison had been killed on that bright noon so soon after her nineteenth birthday—was taking me up on my offer. He wanted me to discuss my suspicions with Kristine Jindra, a reporter for the *Cleveland Plain Dealer*. It was a strange conversation, because even as he urged me to do this, Krause kept saying that maybe I had better not. I couldn't completely understand his concern. On the other side of the building from my office, in an ornate rotunda on the ground floor, the Archives had on display a document called the Constitution, which had certain amendments, one of which dealt with freedom of speech. Krause of course knew what I could not as yet—that I was about to get a very thorough education in the operative state of the First Amendment in Bicentennial-era America. I was still innocent enough, on January 8, 1976, to give Kris Jindra the story. The story was a minor sensation in Ohio, attracted little attention elsewhere, and then was virtually forgotten.

Three years later, on another December evening, my phone rang again, and again the caller was Arthur Krause. My desk was no longer in the Archives building, but on the sixth floor of an abandoned department store where the Archives had leased some storage space—a creaking building, windows papered over, freezing in the winter, a steam bath in the summer. My work no longer consisted of revelling in the art form of Golden Age radio, but of taking boxes of obsolete government publications off skids and slinging them up onto shelves. I had researched my own book on Kent State and felt that I had documented proof of my initial suspicions that a cover-up had been perpetrated, beginning immediately after the murders. There was a new trial for the civil suit, and it was going well, or so it seemed. Then Art Krause asked me: "Charlie, I just want to run this by you for a reaction. What would you say to an out-of-court settlement?"

I tried not to react on the basis of the shock, even panic, I felt at even having the question raised. I tried to respond as the professional scholar that I still, despite my present circumstances, felt myself to be. I kept no record of that conversation, but I will not forget the arguments I put forth against the settlement. First, perhaps conditioned by my professional training, was my concern for the historical record. The transcript of the 1975 trial was a rich source document which, I felt, utterly devastated the Guard's defense of its actions that May. To take just the most vivid example, the guardsmen had been forced to admit under oath, one after another, that the noon rally on May 4, 1970, had been peaceful, even casual—and thus had admitted by implication and extension that there was no reason for that lethal violence that had occurred at 12:25 P.M. And that was just the beginning of the awesome weight of evidence in those pages concerning the unfolding of those twenty-five minutes: the irrationality of the Guard sally onto the practice field; the lack of any threat to their safety during the return march; even the minute analysis of a student film by a CIA-trained photogrammetrist which provided final, irrevocable physical evidence that the soldiers had been in no danger when they fired. I had cited that transcript repeatedly while researching my own book. It would be there, forever, for other historians to consult. While the jury verdict had gone against the plaintiffs in 1975, I felt that a dispassionate review of the trial's written record by future generations could only lead to their ultimate vindication. And a complete transcript of the 1978–79 trial could only reaffirm that verdict. Nothing must be allowed to halt the writing of that record.

Second, it *did* look as if, this time, the plaintiffs would win. True, there had been tremendous difficulties. The plaintiffs' attorneys had been separated by great geographical distances while preparing the trial. Individualists, like all those who take on the Establishment, they had found it difficult to work together. The plaintiffs were so emotionally drained and exhausted at this point that even a remarkable man like Rev. John Adams was having difficulty holding them together. And public apathy concerning an event that had received saturation coverage during a few weeks in the spring of 1970, and which was now eight years old, was creating enormous difficulties for the Reverend Mr. Adams in raising funds to finance the new trial.

And yet I was optimistic. I had always felt that the plaintiffs would have prevailed in 1975 but for the obvious bias of the judge. The judge in the new trial, I was convinced after sitting through part of the pretrial hearings in Cleveland in October, was scrupulously fair and careful. The evidence spoke for itself and damned the Guard, as it always had. Howard Ruffner, perhaps the most perceptive and articulate of the May 4 witnesses, had told me after his turn on the witness stand that the defendants' attorneys were acting as if they sensed defeat; even the most formidable of them, I was told, seemed listless and unenthusiastic. The scent of victory was in the air, and that made the question about a settlement all the more incomprehensible.

Third, an out-of-court settlement for cash would feed a particularly vicious Middle American rationalization of the whole eight-year struggle, one that I had heard repeatedly: "Well, you know that most of those people are Jews, and all they're interested in is the money." It was the classic example of a lie being more readily believed because it was so blatantly a lie. (When Art Krause filed his initial suit in 1970 and his attorney asked him for a figure for damages, he said, "One dollar." Told he must name a substantial figure, he chose the symbolic figure of six million, the number of lives destroyed in the death camps of the Third Reich.) All the plaintiffs had always emphasized their disinterest in the money, as opposed to vindicating their murdered children. Would they now lose the credibility for which they had fought so long by accepting money instead of justice?

Last, I cautioned Art Krause against yielding to compassion for Dean Kahler, the youth who had been paralyzed for life by a National Guard bullet. I realized how difficult this kind of emotional discipline would be. Dean, an eminently decent and gentle man, had undergone horrendous suffering, and a cash settlement would mean that he would finally be able to pay his huge medical bills. In fact, the attorneys for the defendants had played on the concern for Dean with typical cynicism, intimating that if the trial proceeded, the plaintiffs would lose and he would get nothing—a tactic so heartless that it was perhaps the best proof of how desperate they were.

But, I reminded Art, what had been maimed and crippled for life on that hillside that day had not been just a young man, but a nation. It would not be made whole again until the people of that nation, embodied in twelve jurors, stood up and publicly admitted to the monstrous wrong their government had done. The criminal justice system, controlled by the same men who had planned and ordered the murders, had covered itself with disgrace in the case of Kent State. Only now, in the civil process, could the concept of equal justice under the law be salvaged. The trial had to go on.

It did not. The families and the surviving wounded finally yielded to their own exhaustion and their anxiety for one of their own. After eight years of continuous struggle against the awesome power of state and federal governments, this small, brave band of mere citizens was ground down to defeat. As if still too brave to accept it, they have continued to rationalize the defeat as victory. They received a cash award, a tenth of the amount Arthur Krause had asked for to memorialize the victims of another episode of officially sanctioned murder. They received an apology so cool it was actually an insult. And so our society succeeded in its final attempt to evade coming to terms with May 4, 1970.

And yet, in evading the issues of Kent State, America insured that it would never escape the horror of it. In that sense, it is possible to rejoice in the settlement, for it left everything unresolved. Now the echoes of that volley of riflefire will not die. Kent State will continue to touch and transform people, as it transformed me from a typically well-meaning but ineffectual liberal into a political radical. Perhaps

as May 4, 1919, is generally regarded as the beginning of the transformation of modern China, so someday historians will cite May 4,
1970, as the beginning of the transformation of modern
America.

Some Remarks after a Decade

An Address Delivered May 3, 1980

by MARTIN K. NURMI

MARTIN K. NURMI *is professor of English at Kent State University. The address which follows was delivered as part of the faculty convocation of May 1980. The text of his remarks appeared in the Kent State University* Weekly, *No. 29 (1980), and has been edited for inclusion in this book.*

This evening we solemnly commemorate a tragic event that occurred on this peaceful campus ten years ago tomorrow. Four young people . . . lost their lives to the gunfire of troops who were here to keep the peace, and nine more were wounded. The lives of all of us here at the time were deeply altered by that event, as was in some measure the life of the nation. The words "Kent State" now refer to a signal historical event. This event became, without anyone's intending it to be, "prophetic," not in the sense that it contained a prediction of things to come but in the sense that it revealed in tragic form the result of the kind of confrontation that occurred here and at Jackson State.

The passing of a decade since the shooting here on May 4, 1970, makes it formally a historical event. Perhaps professional historians can sort out finally and exhaustively all the factors in the confusing complex of events that resulted in the killings. But I doubt it. The analysis of events here—whether it can be considered a "chain" of events or not, I'm not sure—can be succinctly stated, and has been. Political dogmatism, whether of the right or the left, has always been able to account for everything that happened as simple chains of causes and effects and to lay the "blame" for what happened clearly and obviously on one side or the other. The more rigid the dogmatism, the clearer the analysis and the simpler the laying of blame. And there has been plenty of dogmatism on both sides, resulting in a good deal of cynical exploitation of the tragedy of the young people who died here, of the grief of their parents and loved ones, and that of those who live and work here.

The event here of May 4, 1970, was indeed a tragedy in the common sense of the word: a dreadful, calamitous, and fatal event. But it was also a tragedy in another and I think deeper sense of the word, which we see exemplified in the great tragedies of literature, those symbolic structures that give form to fundamental and troubling aspects of human life, social as well as individual. The killing of the four lovely young people here, preparing themselves for a future with hope and commitment, was not only a dreadful, calamitous, and fatal event of the kind we read about in the newspapers. May 4, 1970, has a deeper meaning, however it may be interpreted, and it is that deeper meaning as well as the grief at our loss that we commemorate together here. . . .

The tragedy we share in and commemorate is, especially now, a historical event with a special significance in the chronicle of this nation. The meaning it has for all of us, especially for us here, is a symbolic one, like that of the tragedies of Sophocles' *Oedipus*, Euripides' *The Bacchae*, and Shakespeare's *Romeo and Juliet*, *Hamlet*, and *Lear*, whose personages, if they are historical at all, have no direct connection with us. And for some Christians, the great tragedy is the passion and death of Jesus, commemorated in Maundy Thursday and Good Friday before Easter.

A common feature of all these and many other tragedies is that the catastrophe occurs in a setting of some sort of social and moral disorder within which conflicting forces must move toward a climax that culminates in a catastrophe to the central figures. The tragic hero does not suffer the catastrophe because he or she has a "tragic flaw" and deserves suffering because of it. The tragic victim is almost always morally innocent, a victim to the fate that moves with a logic of its own and is overwhelmed and destroyed by it. Oedipus does not suffer his catastrophe because he had a flaw that made him morally responsible for the crimes of patricide and incest, but because he had to suffer it to affirm the will of the gods and also to rid the city of Thebes of the pollution and plague which ravaged it. In *Hamlet*, the rottenness in the state of Denmark is no way the result of a flaw in the hero, but he must die to set it right and restore order under a new king.

But literary tragedy also has another aspect, and that is, in the process of its arriving at the fateful climax, it reveals the nature of disruption out of which it developed and the character and meaning of the forces that brought about the catastrophe. It shows them in a new light and by doing so brings about a restoration, if only a temporary one, of the order that had been disrupted. After the deaths of Romeo and Juliet, the City of Verona is restored to peace; and after the deaths of King Lear and his daughter, the kingdom is restored to unity.

This restoration in tragedy is not in any sense a "happy ending," for the final vision of partial or temporary restoration is filled with grief. Tragedies reflect a sense of history and process, and there are no enduring happy endings in history. Thebes is restored to health under a new king after the exile of the blinded Oedipus, but other disruptions will arise.

In making symbolic models of phenomena, we often compress time, whether it be in literary tragedies reflecting events in human life, or in history, or even in accounts of scientific phenomena. The social disruptions in a literary tragedy, their development, the tragic catastrophe to which they bring the hero, and the final partly redeeming vision occur swiftly, in a few hours. A complex series of events in life, though it may display a pattern with symbolic meaning like that of a literary tragedy, moves much more slowly.

The conflict that resulted in the fatal catastrophe on our campus a decade ago did not develop that morning, the night before, or even the ugly nights before that. And although the fatal consequences of the conflict became clear as soon as many of us here and across the nation managed to face the gruesome shock of it, there was no real restoration of order. In another event also displaying the real-life elements of tragedy, the assassination of John F. Kennedy in November of 1963, we watched a complex drama unfold before millions of spectators on television—but we were able also to watch the nation coming together with the swearing in of a new president, Lyndon Johnson. Despite the symbolic restoration of order almost immediately after Kennedy's death, history gave us no enduring happy ending. For, though not solely responsible, President Johnson was at least instrumental in enlarging the war in Vietnam. Our tragedy occurred here in the immediate context of the apparent—and secret—further enlargement of that senseless and futile war. The invasion of Cambodia intensified the deep divisions in the nation as a whole, and these came to a tragic climax in the shooting near Taylor Hall.

The tragedy here did not promptly bring about a restoration of the orderly social fabric even in the sense that the tragedy in Dallas did. We did not have a government that functioned by the stable discourse of reason in the firm framework of law. We had instead, all too often, a governing concept backed by force that was a perversion of the separate but related concepts of law and order into a dangerous slogan of a single compound term—law-and-order—something quite different from that envisaged for the nation by the Founding Fathers. And under the constant appeal to a slippery standard called "national security," we had an executive branch of government, as Watergate later revealed, that felt free to function above the law. In fact, we had an executive branch that felt obliged to function above the law of the land.

Eventually, with some—and I stress the word "some"—restoration of confidence in the procedures of government and the termination of the divisive war in Asia, the slogan of "law-and-order" fell into disuse. And the horrifying revelations in the tragedy here at Kent State contributed to that change. At the least, peace-keeping forces came increasingly to control active dissent rather than try to suppress it. And they no longer appeared to go to assemblies of dissent armed for battle, as they did here that fateful day.

In suggesting that the tragedy here had, through what was revealed in it, some positive impact on society, I am not for a moment suggesting we take comfort in the hackneyed thought that our young people after all did not die completely in vain, hence diminishing our sense of grief. Those of us here then and others who came later cannot help but live with a continued sense of residual mourning. And the sense of rebirth in the spring season of buds and early blossoms is mingled for us with a remembrance of their deaths. For us, as the poet Shelley wrote, "Winter is come and gone, But Grief returns with the revolving year." . . . A commemoration means giving form in a ceremonial observance to a collective memory, and we are, on this occasion especially, a community sharing a common experience and, as a community, extending our sympathy to the parents of the young people who lost their innocent lives on our campus. . . .

Annotated Bibliography

The historiography of the Kent State shootings and their aftermath well reflects the ideological differences that have defined the nature of the debate over cause, culpability, and appropriate commemoration and remembrance. There have been articles and monographs, retrospectives, memoirs, political travelogues, and updates published regularly over the years. The purpose and content of such essays and articles can be glimpsed by referring to the annotated bibliography that follows.

Equally or more important, however, are the archival sources which do not easily lend themselves to bibliographical listings. There are several major collections of May 4 materials, the first of which was initiated at Kent State University. As Dean Keller, head of the Kent State Library's Department of Special Collections, wrote to the Soviet poet Yevgeny Yevtushenko on May 22, 1970: "In order to better understand ourselves and what happened here on May 4, we are assembling an archive of documents which will reflect the various views and opinions of the conflict. We hope that this archive will be the source of history, but more importantly, a guide to aid us in preventing such a thing from happening again." Since that time, the "May 4th Collection" has grown to approximately fifty cubic feet of diverse materials, including the political ephemera generated by over a decade of student activist groups at Kent State, the working papers and meeting minutes of intrauniversity commissions and commemorative committees, correspondence between faculty and students in the spring of 1970 after the closing of the University, letters received by Kent State in the wake of the shootings, and the research materials of Kent State faculty who have studied May 4 and post-May 4 events and issues. The fifty-three-volume transcript of the 1975 civil trial is available on microfilm. Other archival records not specifically related to May 4, 1970, such as administrative office files, nonetheless complement any study of the institution's response to the shootings.

But while Kent State may have seemed to many people a natural repository for May 4-related materials, an "alternate" collection has been assembled in the Yale University Archives for those whose mistrust of the Kent State University administration extends to the operation of its archives. And certainly Yale is distant from Ohio politics. Peter Davies and Paul Keane have taken the lead in encouraging the donation of May 4 papers and documents to Yale, and Davies's papers, covering seven years of his research into May 1970 events and advocacy on behalf of the Kent State families, comprise the major portion of the Yale University Archives' Kent State collection. Yale is also scheduled to receive the papers of Sanford Rosen, chief attorney for the plaintiffs in the 1978 retrial of the civil damages suit.

The other important Kent State collections are in Washington, D.C. The records of the Scranton Commission are housed in the National Archives, and James Michener's papers relating to his book *Kent State: What Happened and Why* are with the Manuscripts Division of the Library of Congress.

The final large bloc of unreleased May 4 documents consists of materials, especially investigatory files from Ohio law enforcement agencies, gathered for but not introduced into evidence during the 1975 civil trial. A February 1982 decision by the Sixth District Court of Appeals upheld an earlier ruling by Cleveland Judge William Thomas (February 1979) that much of the material should be made public following the standard practice of deleting names of interviewees, interviewing officers, and third parties, for information given in confidence. The appeals court decided that Thomas's original ruling, by excepting grand jury files and providing for redaction, adequately protected secrecy provisions concerning the documents and that the remaining items should become part of the public domain "because of First Amendment interests and the historic nature of the events portrayed in the materials concerned." However, several state agencies whose files are scheduled to be released have appealed the decision to the U.S. Supreme Court, and final disposition of the records awaits a decision at that level.

The following bibliography does not include book reviews or, with few exceptions, routine news accounts of May 4-related events. A few brief items such as newspaper opinion columns are included for historiographical purposes. All articles, scholarly and nonscholarly, have been grouped together, and a select listing of unpublished sources has been included.

Articles

Adamek, Raymond J., and Lewis, Jerry M. "Social Control Violence and Radicalization: The Kent State Case." *Social Forces* 51 (March 1973): 342–47. Reprinted in Hensley and Lewis, eds., *Kent State and May 4th: A Social Science Perspective* (1978). The authors conclude that "radicalization is positively associated with the experience of social control violence."

———. "Social Control Violence and Radicalization: Behavioral Data." *Social Problems* 22 (June 1975): 663–74. Reprinted in Hensley and Lewis, eds., *Kent State and May 4th: A Social Science Perspective* (1978). Examining the events of May 4, 1970, the authors contend that radicalization—and not pacification—is the result of "exposure to extreme social control violence."

Adams, John P. "Kent State: Why the Church?" In a special supplement to *American Report*, 12 November 1971. Characterizes the Kent State shootings as "perhaps the clearest and most classic illustration . . . of the irresponsible and unlawful use of firearms by a Government against its citizens." Concludes: "When it becomes almost impossible to distinguish between those who break the law and those who have the responsibility for enforcing the law, the church—and all other parts of the society—must be concerned and must be involved in finding the corrections."

———. "Kent State—Justice and Morality." *Cleveland State Law Review* 22 (Winter 1973): 26–47. Discussion of Adams's "pastoral role" on behalf of the families of the slain and wounded students in the aftermath of May 4, 1970.

———. "The Struggle 1970–1980." *Left Review* 4 (Spring 1980): 7–8. In the aftermath of May 4, 1970, American society "was forced to look upon itself as rarely before." Notes the gradual reconciliation that has characterized the ten-year period since the shootings: comfort, healing, and new directions for those involved in the May 4 events as well as new limitations "in the use of militia in confronting genuine citizen grievances."

Aptheker, Bettina. "In Memoriam." *Left Review* 4 (Spring 1980): 3–4. Examining the impact of the Kent State shootings, Aptheker notes a "connection between the deaths of Allison Krause and Sandra Scheuer and the rebirth of a feminist movement in the Seventies." Portrays the May 4 shootings as the end of an era: "What had begun as an effervescent decade of energetic and cheerful protest, ended."

Arthrell, Bill. "The Ones They Missed with Bullets." In *Kent State/May 4: Echoes Through a Decade*, edited by Scott L. Bills. Kent, Ohio: Kent State University Press, 1982. Description of the political atmosphere on the Kent State campus in the fall of 1970 by a former student activist and member of the "Kent 25."

Austin, C. Grey. "Editorial: Riot Notes." *Journal of Higher Education* 41 (May 1970): 337–40. Commentary on post-Kent State lessons: students must dissent nonviolently, faculty must help prevent the "paralysis of polarization," and administrators must initiate "new patterns of participatory governance."

Barnes, Sherman. "Autumn Aftermath of Kent State." *Northfield and Mount Hermon Schools* 10 (Winter 1971): 10–13. Written in the fall of 1971 by a member of the history faculty at Kent State, the article emphasizes the nonradical character of the majority of Kent State students. Barnes observes: "The strength of the reaction to the Kent tragedy is a sign of the depth of belief in higher education."

Beck, Henry. "The Ocean-Hill Brownsville and Cambodian-Kent State Crises: A Biobehavioral Approach to Human Sociobiology." *Behavioral Science* 24 (January 1979): 25–36. "Reality disjuncture" and violent upheaval.

Begala, John A. "The May 4 Disease." In *Kent State/May 4: Echoes Through a Decade*, edited by Scott L. Bills. Kent, Ohio: Kent State University Press, 1982. A life-long Kent resident and Kent State alumnus discusses his involvement with May 4 issues after 1970, including his efforts, while serving in the state legislature, to help mediate the gym controversy of 1977.

Best, James J. "Kent State: Answers and Questions." In *Kent State and May 4th: A Social Science Perspective*, edited by Thomas R. Hensley and Jerry M. Lewis. Dubuque, Iowa: Kendall/Hunt, 1978. A narrative and analysis of May 1–4 events, 1970, which concludes that a "large number" of people must share responsibility for the shootings. "Perhaps most sadly," the author writes, "the shootings on Monday morning were the result of different perceptions regarding what was at stake." Both guardsmen and demonstrators "felt they had a legitimate right to be there and to act as they did, and people who had no desire for a direct and fatal confrontation, moved inexorably toward one."

————; Hensley, Thomas R.; and Kotschwar, James L. "Causes and Consequences of Student Perceptions of Responsibility for the 1970 Kent State Shootings." *Heuristics* 8 (Spring 1978): 30–52. Examination of the impact of the federal grand jury investigation of the Kent State shootings on student perceptions of responsibility for the May 1970 events and on student attitudes toward the judicial process in general. Noting that "a person's ideology is a good predictor of perceptions of responsibility, particularly perceptions of Guardsmen and radicals," the article concludes that the grand jury had little impact on student attitudes.

Bierman, William. "Tent City: A Diary of Love and Anger." *Beacon* (Sunday magazine of the *Akron Beacon Journal*), 26 June 1977, pp. 6–9 ff. A look at the May 4th Coalition's "Tent City" on Blanket Hill in early June 1977. Noting a "spirit of human caring and an affirmation of life," Bierman observes: "The news from Tent City is the rebirth of the 'radical' protest movement among students and non-students. It appears to be national in scope. It does not seem likely to go away."

————, ed. "Kent State: Making Peace With the Past." *Beacon* (Sunday magazine of the *Akron Beacon Journal*), 4 May 1980. Special issue of the magazine to commemorate the tenth anniversary of the Kent State shootings, featuring short interviews with each of the nine people wounded on the campus on May 4, 1970.

Bigelow, Gordon S., and Kennedy, W. Robert. "Attitudes of Kent State Students Before and After the Events of May 4, 1970." *Journal of College Student Personnel* 15 (January 1974): 17–21. Commentary on student perceptions of themselves and the institution pre- and post-May 4. Notes: "The magnitude, suddenness, and inexplicable qualities of the Kent State tragedy have never been equalled in the history of higher education."

Bills, Scott L. "The May 4th Collection, Kent State University Archives: A Case Study in the Use of Contemporary Historical Source Materials." *Left Review* 4 (Spring 1980): 66–74. Description of the structure and contents of the May 4th Collection; includes a bibliography of articles, books, and poems concerning May 1970 events and their aftermath.

Brown, Steven R. "Experimental Design and the Structuring of Theory." *Experimental Study of Politics* 1 (February 1971): 1–41. Use of Kent State data to illustrate "the utility of experimental design procedures for the theoretical structuring of Q samples."

————. "The Resistance to Reason: Kent State University, 1969–1970."

Political Science Discussion Papers 3 (Spring 1971): 17–53. Examination of the events at Kent State in the spring of 1969 and May 1970: the genesis of intolerance and violent behavior. The author posits three main student points of view: "Radicalized," "Intolerant," and "Reasonable."

―――. "The Politics of Self and Other: Public Response to the Kent State Event." In *Public Opinion and Political Attitudes*, edited by Allen R. Wilcox. New York: John Wiley and Sons, 1974. Reprinted in Hensley and Lewis, eds., *Kent State and May 4th: A Social Science Perspective* (1978). Analysis of the public response to the Kent State shootings in terms of the segmentation of that response into three groups, see supra, the Radicalized, the Intolerant, and the Reasonable. Notes that the Radicalized and Intolerant groups seized upon "symbols of identification" and that "the symbols of identification for one were the symbols of rejection for the other." Characteristics of the Reasonable group were "a certain manifest tolerance, an abhorrence of violence from any quarter, and a belief that mistakes were made on both sides." Brown concludes: "Through an analysis of a brief slice of history from a single case, one can begin to become aware of the functional complexities that culminate in the visible attitudinal structure."

―――, and Ungs, T. D. "Representativeness and the Study of Political Behavior: An Application of Q Technique to Reactions to the Kent State Incident." *Social Science Quarterly* 51 (December 1970): 514–26. A discussion of representative sample designs in political research with minimal reference to the Kent State shootings.

Bryant, David. "Sowing the Wind: A Special Report from Kent State University." *Christianity Today*, 5 June 1970, pp. 13–15. American society has "sown the wind" of "permissiveness in the home" and "egoistic humanism" and reaped the whirlwind at Kent State. The church must re-dedicate itself to the Spirit. The author was pastor of Grace Baptist Church in Kent, Ohio.

Calkins, Kenneth R. "The Frustrations of a Former Activist." In *Kent State/May 4: Echoes Through a Decade*, edited by Scott L. Bills. Kent, Ohio: Kent State University Press, 1982. Discusses the "confusion and perplexity" with which Kent State faculty members faced student unrest in 1969–70, to the point that faculty were unable to play, as a group, any significant role in the events of May 1970. This article first appeared, in only slightly different form, in *Left Review* 4 (Spring 1980): 29–31.

Canfora, Alan. "A Decade of Determination." *Left Review* 4 (Spring 1980): 22–25. The experience of the Canfora family and others who have "joined together these past ten years in an effort to bring justice for our fallen martyrs." For an interview with the family, see John Spetz, "Soured dreams . . . May 4 brings Canfora's nightmares," *Kent-Ravenna Record-Courier*, 2 November 1977, p. 3.

Carey, Dennis. "The Center for Peaceful Change: An Organizational Response to the Events of May 4, 1970." *Left Review* 4 (Spring 1980): 40–41. A very brief narrative concerning the birth and growth of the Center for Peaceful Change.

————. "A Phoenix Reaction: Peace Studies at Kent State University." In *Kent State/May 4: Echoes Through a Decade*, edited by Scott L. Bills. Kent, Ohio: Kent State University Press, 1982. Narrative of the growth of the Center for Peaceful Change and its problems and successes as a "living memorial" to the students killed on May 4, 1970.

Carter, L. J. "After Cambodia and Kent: Academe Enters Congressional Politics." *Science*, 22 May 1970, pp. 955–56. In the aftermath of May 4, antiwar activism among students, faculty, and administrators is focused on the "nitty-gritty of congressional politics." A survey of that activity, its scope, and its aims and supporters.

Carter, Malcolm N. "[Interview with] George Segal." *Saturday Review*, May 1981, pp. 26–30. Includes a brief commentary by Segal on his work with the "Abraham and Isaac" sculpture.

Cizmar, Paula L. "Segal's World." *Books & Arts*, 23 November 1979, pp. 20–22. Includes a discussion of the "Abraham and Isaac" sculpture. Segal comments that the work "is my attempt to introduce difficult moral and ethical questions as to how older people should behave to their children."

Clark, Ramsey. "Violence: The American Way of Having Its Way." In a special supplement to *American Report*, 12 November 1971. "More than most, the deaths of four young lives at Kent State show how we justify, perhaps desire, violence." Asserting a connection between foreign and domestic violence, Clark concludes: "Only a renunciation of violence will avoid future Viet Nams, Atticas, Jackson and Kent States."

————. "Symposium Introduction." *Cleveland State Law Review* 22 (Winter 1973):1–2. Expressing many of the same points as his *American Report* article, supra, Clark notes: "We can never allow ourselves to be content with the present account of the Kent State killings. We must have the courage to seek the truth. We must continue the search and thoroughly understand the legal and moral issues arising out of this national tragedy."

Dante, Harris. "Kent State Tragedy: Lessons for Teachers." *Social Education* 35 (April 1975): 356–61. The author, who was chairman of the Kent State Faculty Senate from April 1, 1969, to September 1, 1970, discusses the problems of operating an educational institution in the midst of intense political polarization. Kent State, in the aftermath of May 1970, provides an example of a university under pressure from all sides. "It is because a university is basically decent and dedicated to reason that it is particularly vulnerable."

Davidson, Carl. "Lessons for 1980." *Left Review* 4 (Spring 1980): 49–50. The former national secretary for SDS urges a new generation of youthful revolutionaries to renew the struggle against American capitalism, using Kent State, May 1970, as a reference point.

Davies, Peter. "Citizens Battle for Justice: Kent State Shootings by Ohio National Guard." *The Nation*, 29 November 1971, pp. 557 ff. Davies outlines his efforts to secure a federal investigation of the Kent State shootings, discussing among other points his belief that at least several guardsmen may have conspired to fire on students.

————. "Another White House Horror Story?" *The Village Voice*, 8 November 1973, pp. 1 ff. Examines the possibility that the Nixon administration, in a desire to suppress campus activism, "obscurely filtered down" to Ohio Governor Rhodes "in the form of a hint that whatever steps the governor takes to crush the dissent at both Kent State and Ohio State University will be secure from federal intervention." Noting that there are "enough loose ends and unexplained incidents to arouse valid suspicions," Davies asks: "Will future historians some day discover that Kent State was the worst can of worms in the era of Watergate . . . ?"

————. "Caught in the Nixon-Mitchell Trap." *The Village Voice*, 6 June 1974, pp. 99–100. Davies uses his critique of the WNET-TV program "The 51st State," aired May 14, 1974, to assert: "The blacks at Jackson, and the whites at Kent, are as one: victims."

———. "The Burning Question: A Government Cover-up?" In *Kent State/ May 4: Echoes Through a Decade*, edited by Scott L. Bills. Kent, Ohio: Kent State University Press, 1982. "The shootings at Kent State, like the break-in at Watergate, were a political operation with specific political goals." Traces the genesis of the author's views relating to a government cover-up of the causes of the Kent State shootings.

DeMarco, Margaret. "Training in Nonviolence at Kent State University, August 16–23, 1970." In *Kent State: The Nonviolent Response*, edited by A. Paul Hare. Haverford, Pa.: Center for Nonviolent Conflict Resolution, 1973. Brief account of the author's experience at Kent State in August 1970 as part of team from the Haverford College Nonviolent Action Research Project to teach peace marshaling techniques.

Dunphy, John. "Guardsman Ends 10-Year Silence on KSU." *Akron Beacon Journal*, 4 May 1980, pp. A1, A10. Interview with former guardsman Lawrence Shafer.

Dyal, Robert A. "Kent Community for Nonviolent Change: An Experiment That Failed." In *Kent State: The Nonviolent Response*, edited by A. Paul Hare. Haverford, Pa.: Center for Nonviolent Conflict Resolution, 1973. Dyal recalls the informal beginnings of the Kent Community for Nonviolent Change in mid-May 1970 and the "sense of enthusiasm, purposiveness, and kinship of spirit" that characterized the group's founding. Discussing the organization's subsequent dissolution, the author asserts that the group nevertheless "contributed to a climate of institutional self-analysis and innovation" and "played a role . . . in the rebuilding of a post-May 4 Kent State."

———. "Neglect—Benign or Malignant? The Faculty and Administrative Response." In *Kent State/May 4: Echoes Through a Decade*, edited by Scott L. Bills. Kent, Ohio: Kent State University Press, 1982. A former member of the Kent State faculty critiques both the faculty and administrative response to the political issues and symbolism inherent in the events of May 1970. While the faculty response has been "undistinguished," the administrative response has been "shameful." This article first appeared, in different form, in *Left Review* 4 (Spring 1980): 33–37.

———, and Goldsmith, Herbert, eds. Kent State FACT *Newsletter*. There were two issues of this newsletter, published in October 1977 and March 1978, both dealing with the politics of the gym controversy. The short-lived organization, First Amendment Conservation Task-force, was founded by Paul Keane, who wrote in his dedication of the first newsletter issue: "No bulldozer's blade, no architectural distraction, no landscape alteration can alter the fact indelible in history: May 4th, 1970, Ohio soaked its soil with the blood of American children." The newsletters are available in the Kent State University Archives.

Engdahl, David E. "Soldiers, Riots, and Revolution: The Law and History of Military Troops in Civil Disorders." *Iowa Law Review* 57 (October 1971): 1–73. "Due process is so much a part of Anglo-American tradition as to seem almost a part of our character, and what was ravaged at Kent State was the most fundamental of all the principles of due process—the abiding conviction that military force should not be used in suppressing civil disorder." The author traces, in detail, the history of this tradition, as he sees it, as a background to the events of May 4, 1970. For a related article, but one which does not discuss Kent State, see Engdahl's "Immunity and Accountability for Positive Governmental Wrongs," *University of Colorado Law Review* 44 (1972): 1–79.

———. "Due Process Forbids Soldiers in Civil Disorders." In a special supplement to *American Report*, 12 November 1971. "No effort can undo the tragedy of Kent State; and to seek only retribution for the wrong that was done would be vain. But what a memorial to the victims of that tragedy would be our steady resolve to accomplish the redemption of that fundamental safeguard of liberty, the uncompromising subordination of military power to ordinary civilian authority and law!"

———. "Kent State Update." *American Report*, 26 February 1973, p. 6. Discusses the progress of litigation stemming from the Kent State shootings, noting that "lengthy and costly litigation remains."

———. "The Legal Background and Aftermath of the Kent State Tragedy." *Cleveland State Law Review* 22 (Winter 1973): 3–25. Following a brief legal history of the use of military force by a government against its citizens, the author concludes that the "official lawlessness" of the guardsmen at Kent State was "primarily attributable" to the "utter disregard of the rules of due process for the use of military troops in civil disorders." The guardsmen, contends Engdahl, "presented and comported themselves as a superseding military force."

Eszterhas, Joe. "Ohio Honors Its Dead." *Rolling Stone*, 10 June 1971, pp.

14–18. An observation of the first May 4 commemoration and a discussion of the points in the political debate created by the May 1970 events.

———, and Roberts, Michael. "James Michener's Kent State: A Study in Distortion." The authors, staff writers for the *Cleveland Plain Dealer*, characterize Michener's study of the Kent State shootings as an "expert application of whitewash." They also contend that the two-part, condensed version of Michener's book which appeared in the April and May 1971 issues of *Reader's Digest* excerpted material that was unnecessarily inflammatory and recast Michener's text to create a new and sinister innuendo.

"FBI: No Reason for Guard to Shoot at Kent State." *Akron Beacon Journal*, 23 July 1970, pp. A1, A8. Article relating the contents of a fourteen-page Justice Department summary of a special FBI report on the Kent State shootings. The summary noted that the shootings were unnecessary, that no guardsmen were injured by rocks or other projectiles thrown by students, and that the guardsmen were not in danger at the moment of the shootings. Excerpts from the Justice Department summary appeared in the *New York Times*, 31 October 1970, p. 30; the report is reprinted in I. F. Stone, *The Killings at Kent State: How Murder Went Unpunished* (New York: New York Review Books, 1971), chap. 4.

Fitt, Alfred. "The National Guard and Civil Disturbances." *City*, August-September 1970, pp. 41–43. The confrontation at Kent State "calls into question the ability of the National Guard to perform acceptably all the tasks our society has assigned it."

Foner, Philip S. " 'Bloody Friday'—May 8, 1970." *Left Review* 4 (Spring 1980): 19–21. The post-Kent State attack by construction workers on an antiwar demonstration in New York City.

Fricke, Edwin P. "KSU: Crisis in Communication." *College Press Review* 10 (Spring 1971): 3–6. The author, director of publications at Kent State at the time of writing, notes that the aftermath of May represented a "crisis in communication." Briefly describing the role of the University News Service, Fricke asserts that the University "reopened without any more trouble, thanks mostly to a determined, well-defined program of communication."

Furlong, William Barry. "The Guardsmen's View of the Tragedy at Kent

State." *New York Times Magazine*, 21 June 1970, pp. 12 ff. Interview with members of the 145th Infantry, First Battalion, Ohio National Guard, who had been at Kent State on May 4. "Clearly," Furlong writes, "the men of this unit are not gung-ho military types."

Gelman, David. "Even At Kent State, The Fervor Has Faded." *Newsday*, 15 October 1973, pp. 4A ff. Kent state at the beginning of the fall quarter, 1973. Despite the "symbolic aura" of May 4, 1970, the author sees the school as "typical of its time" and observes: "The campus consciousness has become vague, fragmented—unfocused really."

Gerth, Jeff. "Kent State Massacre." *Fifth Estate*, 14–27 May 1970, p. 24. Report on the Kent State shootings, noting that guardsmen "gunned down over 20 sisters and brothers." Gerth writes: "The war abroad and repression at home are inextricably linked—Kent State has shown that once again."

Ginsberg, Allen. "War and Peace: Vietnam and Kent State." In *Allen Verbatim*, edited by Gordon Ball. New York: McGraw-Hill, 1974. Ginsberg spoke at Kent State in April 1971; this selection is a transcription of his remarks before a class on war and peace, where he makes reference to antiwar ritual and the symbolism of Kent State and May 4.

Gorden, Robert I., and Kelley, Robert. "A Look at the Fire Symbol Before and After May 4, 1970." In *Free Speech Yearbook 1974*, edited by Alton Barbour. New York: Speech Communication Association, 1975. The authors argue that one reason for the violence of May 1970 was that "radical political protest came to be identified with fire by the people of northeastern Ohio. Destruction by fire and the recurrent threat of arson by a few dissenters blinded many people to the societal concerns of many students." Further: "It is our conclusion that the escalation of events moved, in large part, from fire symbol to fire-power to death, because the rhetorical symbol and the destructive element could not be separated."

[Gordon, Bill]. "Kent State University's Petition to the White House: Ten Months of Deceit." In U.S., Congress, House, *Congressional Record*, 92d Cong., 2d sess., 1972, 118, pt. 22:29210–12. This report, prepared in August 1972 for the KSU student government office, traces the efforts by students Paul Keane, Greg Rambo, and others to secure a federal grand jury investigation of the May 4 shootings. Petitions calling for such an investigation, containing over ten thousand signatures of Kent State students and faculty, were presented to a White House official on October 20, 1971; no formal response was received until July 10, 1973, when it was announced that no grand jury would be convened. The report contends that the Nixon administration never intended a serious consideration of the petitions. The report was inserted in the *Congressional Record* by Congressman William Moorhead, who commented: "It is the account of bureaucratic runaround and blatant lying carried on by the administration. . . ." The original typescript is available in Box 21 of the May 4th Collection, Kent State University Archives.

————. "Kent State Indictments Leave Crucial Questions Unanswered." *American Report*, 15 April 1974, p. 16. Identifies "one of the more curious aspects of the Kent State tragedy": "For years, government investigators and newsmen have been unable to produce conclusive answers as to why the triggers were pulled." Gordon wrote a number of news articles in the early 1970s concerning the shootings, and has written a book-length manuscript on the topic.

Grace, Don. "Campus Unrest." *Ohio Bell/Perspective*, 24 July 1970, pp. 10–12. Three articles focusing on the opinion of Ohio Bell officials on campus dissent—two of them directly connected to Kent State: Don Wrentmore, whose son was among the wounded, and Bill Clossey, who as a second lieutenant in the Ohio National Guard was present at Kent State on May 3–4. Both men advise moderation and an effort to separate the "honest" peace movement from the "militants" or "radicals" in its leadership.

Grace, Tom. "Kent State . . . ten years on." *The Spectrum*, 30 April 1980, pp. 1, 14. Brief retrospective by a former Kent State student, wounded on May 4, 1970. He writes: "A decade of investigations and legal proceedings have reinforced the lessons that the state can kill with impunity and not be held accountable."

Greene, Daniel St. Albin. "When a World Collapsed: Kent State's Wounded Tell Their Grim Story." *The National Observer*, 3 May 1975. The "wounds of war . . . aren't all physical": "Some linger as traumas in the minds of combatants and victims. And some remain as scars on a national conscience still haunted by the ghosts of an internecine era that exploded a 'generation gap' into generational warfare." Greene examines the post-1970 lives of the nine people wounded at Kent State on May 4.

Grigg, Susan. "The Kent State Collection, Yale University Archives." *Left Review* 4 (Spring 1980): 75. A very brief survey of the contents of the Kent State Collection at Yale University.

Grim, Nancy. "The Politics of History." *Left Review* 2 (Fall 1977): 7–9. Mythologization of May 4, 1970, as a "tragedy" obscures the political reality of the shootings: "The Tragedy is frozen into a past in which we do not participate, to be remembered with religious piety at annual services, or cited by officials with feigned concern when students again show anger." The author asserts: "The debate over 'the truth about Kent State' is partly a debate about facts, but it is also a struggle over meaning."

Halliday, Kirk W. "Why Home Rule?" *Political Science Discussion Papers* 3 (Spring 1971): 79–103. Author advocates student-faculty selection of the University's Board of Trustees as part of the process of generating a better post-May 4 institution.

Hamburger, Philip. "Aftermath." *The New Yorker*, 5 June 1971, pp. 106 ff. Visiting Kent nearly a year after the shootings, the author describes the town and its people, reporting an "air of friendliness and openness at Kent State." He notes: "As I wander about Kent State—in and out of the open doors—I have the feeling that I am wandering through a dream."

Hare, A. Paul. "Instituting Peaceful Change at Kent State: Moving Toward Life's Center by Grasping Truth and Realizing Love." In *Kent State: The Nonviolent Response*, edited by A. Paul Hare. Haverford, Pa.: Center for Nonviolent Conflict Resolution, 1973. The process, at Kent State after May 4, 1970, whereby University and community representatives "have begun to seek nonviolent solutions to the problems of social change."

————. "Kent State, May 4, 1971: Nonviolence This Time." In *Kent State: The Nonviolent Response*, edited by A. Paul Hare. Haverford, Pa.: Center for Nonviolent Conflict Resolution, 1973. Account of the first-anniversary commemorative activities, written in June 1972: "Unlike the previous year, many students and faculty had been trained in methods of nonviolent action and third party intervention. They were constantly and unobtrusively on hand and at work."

————. "Noon Rally at Kent: A Dramatic Statement of a University's

Problems." In *Kent State: The Nonviolent Response*, edited by A. Paul Hare. Haverford, Pa.: Center for Nonviolent Conflict Resolution, 1973. The author recounts a noon rally of February 4, 1971, at Kent State, where "several thousand students assembled, marched, listened to speeches, and chanted slogans." Hare observes: "The problem for the university and for the nonviolent movement is to discover how this rally and other rallies can become a functional part of the university life . . . by acknowledging the problems they dramatize and using the commitment they generate in the participants to work toward solving the problems."

———. "The Tale of Peter Rabbit (And Paul Hare) at Kent State: Or the Role of the Inside and Outside Agitator." In *Kent State: The Nonviolent Response*, edited by A. Paul Hare. Haverford, Pa.: Center for Nonviolent Conflict Resolution, 1973. Essay on conformity and nonconformity in attitude and presentation as exemplified by speakers at a student rally at Kent State on October 23, 1970; discussion of restraints imposed upon members of an institution and not shared by nonmembers. The title is drawn from a Peter Rabbit costume worn by a Yippie speaker at the rally, a device which allowed him, according to Hare, to step outside certain bounds placed on student behavior and speech.

———. "Who Needs a Revolution to be a Human Being? Some Observations at Kent State University." In *Kent State: The Nonviolent Response*, edited by A. Paul Hare. Haverford, Pa.: Center for Nonviolent Conflict Resolution, 1973. Written during an October 1970 "Think Week" at Kent State. The author notes: "This year the subject of discussion was nonviolence and its application to Kent State in the form of life style, avoiding further violence, and creative dissent."

Harkness, Bruce. "The Educational Consequences of the Tragedy: An Address Delivered May 4, 1979." *Left Review* 4 (Spring 1980): 44–46. The consequences of May 1970 must not be allowed to overwhelm the institution; the University must renew its commitment to education: "There can be no better memorial to our students than that."

Hassler, Donald M. "The Poet and the Republic After May 4." *Left Review* 4 (Spring 1980): 42–43. The ambiguity of art in the expression of political themes. The author supports the University administration's decision not to accept the George Segal sculpture, "Abraham and Isaac," for placement on the campus.

Hayes, John. "An Exclusive Interview with James Michener (part 1)." *Writer's Digest*, April 1972, pp. 20 ff. Michener discusses the writing of his book *Kent State: What Happened and Why*, the reaction to it, and his views on the case of the "Kent 25." The second part of the interview, which appeared in the May 1972 issue of *Writer's Digest*, contained no reference to Kent State.

Heisey, D. Ray. "Sensitivity to an Image." In *Kent State/May 4: Echoes Through a Decade*, edited by Scott L. Bills. Kent, Ohio: Kent State University Press, 1982. A Kent State professor contends that the University administration, during the years after May 1970, was sensitive to the issues raised by the shootings and, within the various public and private constraints imposed upon it, tried to deal effectively with May 4 matters.

Henderson, Ron. "18 Months Later: Families of Kent Dead Speak Out." In a special supplement to *American Report*, 12 November 1971. Interview transcript includes remarks by Florence Schroeder, Arthur Krause, Martin and Sarah Scheuer, and Steven Sindell.

Hensley, Thomas R. "Kent State 1977: The Struggle to Move the Gym." In *Kent State and May 4th: A Social Science Perspective*, edited by Thomas R. Hensley and Jerry M. Lewis. Dubuque, Iowa: Kendall/Hunt, 1978. Background to and discussion of the May 4th Coalition and the gym controversy. The author notes: "I believe university officials were insensitive to the depth of feelings of some people concerning the events of May 4th, but it also seems to me that the trustees' decisions on November 11, 1976 and May 12, 1977 were reasonable given the circumstances which they faced at the time."

———. "The Kent State Trials." In *Kent State and May 4th: A Social Science Perspective*, edited by Thomas R. Hensley and Jerry M. Lewis. Dubuque, Iowa: Kendall/Hunt, 1978. Good summary of Kent State litigation, focusing on six judicial investigations and/or trials: (1) the 1970 state grand jury probe; (2) the 1971 criminal trials resulting from the "Kent 25" indictments; (3) the 1973–74 federal grand jury investigation; (4) the 1974 federal criminal trial in which the guardsmen were acquitted; (5) the 1975 trial of the civil damages suit; and (6) the 1977 ruling by the Sixth U.S. Circuit of Appeals which overturned the 1975 civil trial decision.

———. "The 1979 May 4th Federal Civil Trial." *Left Review* 4 (Spring 1980): 55–58. Discussion and evaluation of the 1979 out-of-court settlement. Hensley contends that "the decisions by both the plaintiffs and the defendants were reasonable and defensible in light of the existing realities. Further, the type of case represented by the May 4th shootings does not lend itself to easy resolution by the courts."

———. "The Impact of Judicial Decisions on Attitudes of an Attentive Public: The Kent State Trials." *Sociological Focus* 13 (August 1980): 273–92. "Kent State students' attitudes about responsibility for the shootings did not change to conform with the decisions of authoritative judicial structures."

Howard, Bob. "The Manipulation of May 4 for Political Ends." *Left Review* 2 (Spring 1978): 14–15. The use of "official language . . . to define May 4 as a day isolated from the past and present, and without any bearing of the future." He notes: "The purpose is clear enough, and the benefits are obvious. If May 4 can be sanitized, questions of the legitimacy of the authorities are neatly sidestepped."

———. "The Fourth of May: An Overview." *Left Review* 4 (Spring 1980): 13–14. "Official murder" at Kent State was "mythologized and mystified." Howard asserts: "It is time to say that this country is ruled by a small minority, and that when that rule is challenged, the weapons are loaded and fired."

Howarth, Robert F., Jr. "Sovereign Immunity—An Argument Pro." *Cleveland State Law Review* 22 (Winter 1973): 48–54. Against the background of the efforts by the Kent State families to file a civil damages suit against officials of the state of Ohio, the author argues for a traditional view of sovereign immunity.

Hubbell, John. "A Point of Clarification." *Left Review* 4 (Spring 1980): 32. A brief comment on the May 3, 1970, statement by "23 Concerned Faculty" by one of its authors.

Huber, James, and Rosen, Carl. "What Should Be, What Could Be: While Educating the Children, Who Will Guard the Guards?" *Left Review* 4 (Spring 1980): 9–12. The events of May 1970 within the broad context of what the authors see as the prior process of growing alienation of universities from society at large, culminating in the opening of the "abyss of reality" on May 4.

Jackson, Miriam R. "The Kent State Legacy and the 'Business at Hand.' " In *Kent State/May 4: Echoes Through a Decade*, edited by Scott L.

Bills. Kent, Ohio: Kent State University Press, 1982. Leftist perspective on the events of May 1970 and their aftermath. The author writes: "We must link 1970 to the great questions of the past two decades— none of which have diminished in urgency—and honor its memory by pledging ourselves to expose and alter the general conditions that produced the specific tragedy of Kent State." This article first appeared, in different form, in *Left Review* 4 (Spring 1980): 26–28.

Johnson, Haynes. "1970 to 1980: Where Have We Gone?" *Washington Post*, 16 December 1979. End-of-the-decade survey, focusing on Kent State 1970 and the changes within the institution during the interim years.

Joy, Ted. "Quite Legal, Quite Ethical: Espionage at Kent State." *The Nation*, 29 January 1973, pp. 144–48. The use of undercover agents by the Kent State campus police department.

———. "Cost of Freedom." *Rolling Stone*, 25 August 1977, pp. 28–31. Background to and narrative of the gym controversy.

Kaplan, Lawrence S. "The Kent Heritage: A Commencement Address Delivered August 27, 1977." In *Kent State/May 4: Echoes Through a Decade*, edited by Scott L. Bills. Kent, Ohio: Kent State University Press, 1982. Kaplan observes: "May 4 is part of our heritage, as it is part of America's heritage. We should remember the past, not to re-open old wounds or to seek new villains, but to learn from it and to use it for the building of a greater University." Reprinted in edited form from the alumni magazine *Kent*, July 1977. For the text of a speech evoking similar themes, see Kaplan's remarks at a faculty convocation of May 4, 1978, as reprinted in the *Daily Kent Stater*, 9 May 1978, pp. 5, 8.

———. "A View From Europe." In *Kent State/May 4: Echoes Through a Decade*, edited by Scott L. Bills, Kent, Ohio: Kent State University Press, 1982. Lecturing in Europe in the spring of 1970, the author recounts student reactions to the Kent State shootings. May 4 became the "flashpoint of all discontents with American leadership" in international affairs. This article first appeared, in only slightly different form, in *Left Review* 4 (Spring 1980): 15–18.

Kasparek, Timothy G. "American Grand Jury—Investigatory and Indictment Powers." *Cleveland State Law Review* 22 (Winter 1973): 136–56.

Using the state grand jury report, issued October 16, 1970, as his point of departure, the author notes that it raises "a recurring issue which has been debated within the legal and political communities for years: whether or not the grand jury system in the United States is a viable institution within the framework of modern justice." Kasparek argues for changes in the current system.

Kegley, Charles F. "University Commission to Implement a Commitment to Nonviolence." In *Kent State: The Nonviolent Response*, edited by A. Paul Hare. Haverford, Pa.: Center for Nonviolent Conflict Resolution, 1973. Discussion of the origins and development of the commission, which Kegley chaired. Initially concerned primarily "with recommendations seen as critical to the survival of the University," the commission later felt confident "to move to more controversial concerns." Kegley sees the commission's work, "despite some glaring failures, [as] an exciting and on balance successful experiment."

Keller, Gordon W. "Kent State a Year Later." *Dissent* 18 (April 1971): 171–74. The author argues that the "underlying causal factors" of the Kent State shootings "are more diffuse and apolitical than is generally realized." Kent State is a "symbol for institutions and systems that have gotten out of human and humane control."

———. "Middle America Against the University: The Kent State Grand Jury." *The Humanist*, March/April 1971, pp. 28–29. The state grand jury report of October 1970 as a "microcosm of the tensions in American society today."

Kelner, Joseph. "The Kent State Killings: Among the Victims Was Justice." *Los Angeles Times*, 4 May 1980, pt. 4, p. 3. "The gunsmoke at the Kent State University shooting had hardly cleared when the cover-up began." Kelner recounts the Kent State litigation, dismissing the 1979 out-of-court settlement as a "pittance" and concluding that justice failed.

Keniston, Kenneth, and Lerner, Michael. "Unholy Alliance Against the Campus." *New York Times Magazine*, 8 November 1970, pp. 28 ff. The authors argue that campus dissent has been overwhelmingly peaceful and moderate and that there is a recognizable pattern of police restraint in response to student unrest, although the shootings at Kent State and Jackson State "provided the tragic and inexcusable exceptions." The authors conclude: "Higher education must be reformed to serve society better, not destroyed as a scapegoat for national problems."

"Kent State Revisited: An Appeal for Justice." Special supplement to *American Report*, 12 November 1971. The introduction to the supplement was written by Ron Henderson, who asserts that the May 1970 events at Kent State were closely connected with the Vietnam War and with racism in American society: "The events surrounding Kent accentuate a national emergency that has been with us for so long as to be virtually chronic. Kent, in many ways, is the essence of the American problem." The supplement includes the following articles: "Violence: The American Way of Having Its Way," by Ramsey Clark; "The Kent Story: An Eyewitness Account," by Jerry M. Lewis; "Kent State: A Legal Overview," by Steven A. Sindell; "With Liberty and Justice for All," by Barry Levine; "18 Months Later: Families of Kent Dead Speak Out," by Ron Henderson; "The Church Responds to Kent," by Carolyn Wilhelm; and "Kent State: Why the Church?" by John P. Adams. See the individual article listings for annotations.

Kilpatrick, James J. "Many Share KSU Blame." *Cleveland Plain Dealer*, 10 May 1970, p. 4AA. Asking who is to blame for the Kent State shootings, Kilpatrick answers: "I suggest that a terrible responsibility lies upon the heads of student revolutionaries who have kindled the wild torches of unreason." Noting that there is "plenty of blame to go around," the columnist also points to administrators who refused to listen to students' "valid complaints," to faculty members who failed to provide "examples of maturity and restraint," and to apathetic students who were "too timid to stand up for their rights."

Knight Newspapers, Inc. "Tragedy In Our Midst—A Special Report." *Akron Beacon Journal*, 24 May 1970, pp. A17–A24. The 30,000-word report, which appeared in all Knight newspapers, on the Kent State shootings. The introductory section to the report notes: "The incident at Kent State has divided the generations of our country; the price of our misunderstanding has grown to become intolerable. . . . It is our hope that this report will prove common ground and a shared version of the facts from which dialog and understanding may grow. There must be a lesson in this tragedy and it can be learned if only we try." The report offered the following conclusions: (1) the slain students "did nothing that justified their deaths"; (2) there was no sniper; (3) the guardsmen "fired without orders to do so"; (4) the killing and wounding of students was unnecessary; guardsmen had "several other options"; (5) there was no SDS involvement; (6) there was "no reasonable excuse" for three violent and illegal acts by the students: the destruction in downtown Kent, the burning of the ROTC building, and rock-throwing on May 4; (7) the "prime and immediate cause of the trouble was President Nixon's decision to invade Cambodia."

Krause, Arthur S. "May 4, 1970." *New York Times*, 4 May 1972, p. 43. In this brief note, Krause writes: "Within twenty-four hours of my daughter's murder, I knew justice would not only be delayed, it would be denied as long as this Administration remained in office."

———. "A Memo to Mr. Nixon." *New York Times*, 7 May 1978, sec. 4, p. 23. Sparked by comments in Nixon's memoirs, Krause—disbelieving the former president's claim of sympathy for the families of the students killed at Kent State—focuses on Nixon's decision, while president, not to convene a federal grand jury to investigate the shootings: "To learn of your personal veto of a Federal grand jury months before Justice Department officials were assuring me that the killings were still under 'intensive investigation' is to prove, in my opinion, all the charges leveled against you in the Watergate scandal."

Lander, Byron G. "Kent State University's Organized Response to the May 1–4 Crisis: A Study in Administrative Confusion." *Political Science Discussion Papers* 3 (Spring 1971): 104–38. "A better organizational structure that also included unity of command, authority for delegation, and communication extending upward and downward throughout the chain of command may have prevented the National Guard from coming on campus, avoiding the confusion as to whether peaceful rallies were prohibited and, at the same time, provided for accurate downward communication to faculty and students."

———. "Functions of Letters to the Editor: A Re-Examination." *Journalism Quarterly* 49 (Spring 1972): 142–43. Study of letters to the editor of the *Kent-Ravenna Record-Courier* in the aftermath of the May 4 shootings to determine the validity of the assumption that such a letters column functioned as a "social safety valve." Noting that the "overall reaction was one of hatred and contempt," the author concludes that the letters had a double negative impact: (1) the "encouragement of future violence and killing," and (2) the "effect that these letters could have in shaping the political environment in the community."

———. "James Michener's Kent State Personalities." *Left Review* 4 (Spring 1980): 59–62. Criticizing Michener's *Kent State: What Hap-*

pened and Why, the author cites areas where the former's research and exposition should have been more substantial: "Some material unfavorable to people in authority is not included or only briefly mentioned. . . . On the other hand, people in non-authority roles are criticized on the basis of limited facts."

Lerner, Max. "Agony at Kent State." *New York Post*, 8 May 1970. Columnist writes of the Kent State shootings: "Not since the Martin Luther King and Robert Kennedy slayings has anything so traumatic happened in the world of the young. . . . Clearly this has united again the badly fragmented extreme left in America, and given it martyr symbols and a devil figure [Richard Nixon] it is overjoyed to use."

Levine, Barry. "With Liberty and Justice for All." In a special supplement to *American Report*, 12 November 1971. Levine was Allison Krause's boyfriend at the time of her death on May 4, 1970. Asking himself about the character of American justice, Levine answers: "If there is justice it is administered so selectively that it goes unnoticed. Justice must be a tool that is used by the rich and the power hungry."

Lewin, Nathan. "Kent State Revisited: Another Skeleton in the Closet?" *The New Republic*, 18 and 25 August 1973, pp. 16–19. Examines the decision by Attorney General John Mitchell in 1971 not to convene a federal grand jury in the Kent State case.

Lewis, Jerry M. "The Kent Story." *New Politics* 8 (Fall 1970): 44–50. Brief narrative of May 1–4, 1970, and subsequent investigations into the shootings. Lewis concludes his article with the following: "The story at Kent is a continuing one and consequently this article really has no ending. One of my students communicated the depth of the tragedy when he wrote, 'Their bullets left four large holes in the beauty of the world that some thought could have been.' "

———. "The Moods of May 4, 1970: The Students' View." *Political Science Discussion Papers* 3 (Spring 1971): 1–15. Brief description of the University, the town, and the events of May 4, 1970. Asking why students were on the Commons that day, Lewis concludes (based on essays written by his students in a course on collective behavior) that they "were on the campus because they were motivated by a real opposition to the war and its extension on to the campus. They felt the National Guard had invaded their sacred turf. The Commons, for many Kent students, was seen as a sacrosanct place of assembly where students could hear speeches or demonstrate."

———. "The Kent Story: An Eyewitness Account." In a special supplement to *American Report*, 12 November 1971. Essentially the same article that appeared in *New Politics*, supra.

———. "Review Essay: The Telling of Kent State." *Social Problems* 19 (Fall 1971): 267–79. Reprinted in Hensley and Lewis, eds., *Kent State and May 4th: A Social Science Perspective* (1978). Kent State historiography: a comparative review of the following studies: (1) the Knight Newspapers investigation published on May 24, 1970 (see esp. *Akron Beacon Journal*); (2) Bill Warren, ed., *The Middle of the Country*; (3) the Scranton Commission report; (4) Joe Eszterhas and Michael D. Roberts, *Thirteen Seconds*; (5) I. F. Stone, *The Killings at Kent State*; (6) Ottavio M. Casale and Louis Paskoff, eds., *The Kent Affair*; (7) James Michener, *Kent State: What Happened and Why*; (8) Phillip K. Tompkins and Elaine Vanden Bout Anderson, *Communication Crisis at Kent State*; (9) Stuart Taylor et al., *Violence at Kent State*; and (10) Peter Davies's at that time unpublished manuscript, "An Appeal for Justice" (which appeared in 1973 as *The Truth About Kent State*).

———. "A Study of the Kent State Incident Using Smelser's Theory of Collective Behavior." *Sociological Inquiry* 42 (1972): 87–96. Reprinted in Hensley and Lewis, eds., *Kent State and May 4th: A Social Science Perspective* (1978). Application of Neil Smelser's theoretical model "to data derived from diverse sources dealing with the events at Kent State University" on May 4, 1970.

———. "Faculty Marshals and Student Dissent: A Sociological Analysis." In *Kent State: The Nonviolent Response*, edited by A. Paul Hare. Haverford, Pa.: Center for Nonviolent Conflict Resolution, 1973. Review of student protests at Kent State, 1968–71; discussion of faculty peace marshaling. The author notes a "fundamental problem": "In becoming a marshal the faculty member is forced to assume a social role whose content is unclear and changing. . . . Further it is often devoid of any clear structural support from significant others with whom a faculty member deals."

———. "Making Sense of Kent State." *Intellect*, March 1976, pp. 448–50. "In making sense of Kent State, there is a tendency to take one of two approaches. The narrower political approach stresses the approval or disapproval of the killings and related events in the context of the use of force to deal with mass protest. The broader historical approach views the events of Kent State in a context of social change in America or as one part of the impact of the Vietnam war on this society."

―――. "The Quest for a Federal Grand Jury." In *Kent State and May 4th: A Social Science Perspective*, edited by Thomas R. Hensley and Jerry M. Lewis. Dubuque, Iowa: Kendall/Hunt, 1978. Asserts that efforts to secure a federal grand jury investigation of the May 4 shootings were guided by a feeling "that the U.S. government, and particularly its justice system, could work. The movement was never a radical movement guided by views on the failings of the basic system. Rather, it was a movement governed by the more conservative belief that the system could work if only 'good' men would act properly to make it work."

―――. "The May 4th Coalition and Tent City: A Norm Oriented Movement." In *Kent State and May 4th: A Social Science Perspective*, edited by Thomas R. Hensley and Jerry M. Lewis. Dubuque, Iowa: Kendall/Hunt, 1978. Examining the period from May through July 1977, the author seeks to provide a narrative of events dealing with the gym controversy and "to demonstrate the utility of Neil Smelser's (1962) model of collective behavior for looking at a variety of collective behavior events." Lewis notes that "readers should know that I supported the idea of building the gym on an alternative site because destruction of the original site would interfere with sociological research on social control violence."

―――. "*Kent State*—The Movie." *Journal of Popular Film and Television* 9 (Spring 1981): 13–18. Commentary on the television movie "Kent State," shown on February 8, 1981. Lewis finds that the movie had numerous "factual errors"; as a result, there is a "public conception of fact about what happened at Kent State which is based on error and a distortion of reality."

―――, and Adamek, Raymond J. "Anti-R.O.T.C. Sit-in: A Sociological Analysis." *Sociological Quarterly* 15 (Autumn 1974): 542–47. Reprinted in Hensley and Lewis, eds., *Kent State and May 4th: A Social-Science Perspective* (1978). "This study compares social characteristics, political and protest activities, and the impact of social control violence on participants and nonparticipants in a sit-in ending in arrest at Kent State University." The sit-in took place on April 26, 1972.

——, and Hensley, Thomas R. "Teaching a Course on May 4th." *Left Review* 4 (Spring 1980): 63–65. Structuring an undergraduate course.

——, and Weaver, Teresa J. "Student Interest in May 4th, 1970." In *Kent State and May 4th: A Social Science Perspective*, edited by Thomas R. Hensley and Jerry M. Lewis. Dubuque, Iowa: Kendall/Hunt, 1978. Study designed to "examine the impact of the May 4th shootings on students attending Kent State several years after the event." Based on a 1976 sample of undergraduate attitudes, the authors note a "high expressed interest" in the shootings coupled with a "low use of resources" beyond the student newspaper.

Logue, John. "Official Violence: An American Tradition." In *Kent State/May 4: Echoes Through a Decade*, edited by Scott L. Bills. Kent, Ohio: Kent State University Press, 1982. The author sees a tradition in America of "official violence" against groups that depart from the political mainstream. Thus, there is a thread that connects government violence against the labor movement in the nineteenth and twentieth centuries with the actions of National Guardsmen at Kent State in May 1970. This article first appeared, in much shorter form, in *Left Review* 4 (Spring 1980): 6.

Lombardi, John. "A Lot of People Were Crying and the Guard Walked Away." *Rolling Stone*, 11 June 1970, pp. 6–8. Early account of May 1970 events which includes statements from students, faculty, townspeople, and guardsmen.

McCarthy, Eugene. "On Being Born Again." *Left Review* 4 (Spring 1980): 5. "It is time for the United States to put aside its conception of its innocence, either original, or as reborn, and face the realities of our past."

McGhee, Edward G. "A Case of Civil Disobedience." *Christian Century*, 28 December 1977, pp. 1217–23. Explanation of the author's involvement with the May 4th Coalition and his arrest along with sixty others at the construction site for a new gymnasium annex in the early morning hours of July 29, 1977.

Malone, Robert, and Eastman, George D. "Kent State Story: Part 1." *The Police Chief*, November 1978, pp. 38–40; "Kent State Story: Part 2." *The Police Chief*, December 1978, pp. 77–82. Malone was director of police and security at Kent State during the gym controversy. The authors assert: "In 1977, perhaps beginning in late 1976, a new type of activist movement seemed to take hold based on cooperative efforts of students and nonstudents, perhaps with control lying with the latter."

Marovitz, Sanford E. "Kent Ohio: The American Crisis." *Lake Forest Alumni Quarterly* 6 (Summer 1970): 10–17. Kent State faculty member notes continued polarization within the Kent community two months after the May 4 shootings. Marovitz praises President Robert White for his commitment to academic freedom and argues that controversy is an essential element of a university: "Without strong conflicting points of view, a university would stagnate; moreover, if a university is not stable enough to cope with the outspoken views of a handful of radical students, then as a viable institution it is in serious trouble."

Matijasic, Thomas D., and Bills, Scott. "The People United: A Tentative Commentary on the Kent State Struggle 1977." *Left Review* 2 (Fall 1977): 10–35. Narrative and analysis of the May 4th Coalition and the gym controversy; offers for the first time the thesis of a "May 4th Movement": "It is not merely a struggle to preserve history but rather an effort to discern truth in history: a romance with the future."

May 4th Coalition. "Kent State: Political History." *The Truth Demands Justice*, 10 April, 17 April, 24 April, and 4 May 1978. This four-part series was published unsigned in a May 4th Coalition newspaper. Although the organization was virtually defunct by the spring of 1978, the themes expressed in the articles represent viewpoints commonly articulated during the gym controversy, e.g., "Students at Kent State, with life and blood, wrote a proud and heroic chapter in the history of the American student movement in May of 1970." The articles express the following points: that the ROTC building was set afire by students and that the action was justifiable; that the May 4 shootings were "a coldly calculated maneuver"; and that in the aftermath of the deaths there was a massive cover-up.

Michener, James. "Kent State—Campus Under Fire." *Reader's Digest*, March 1971, pp. 57 ff.; April 1971, pp. 217 ff. Michener's book-length study of the Kent State shootings appeared in condensed form in two installments, under the above title, in the spring issues of *Reader's Digest*. The articles subsequently appeared together in booklet form with an introductory section, "Behind the Lines," describing the two-part series as a "relentlessly honest re-creation of the May events." The introduction continued: "It is the result of an intensive and laborious collaboration by many people: the consulting editors who sought to find clarity in chaos; the researchers who hounded down elusive facts; the Pulitzer-Prize-winning author who skillfully bound the divers elements together, utilizing the compassion of a born novelist, the hard-nosed objectivity of a master journalist."

————. "Kent State: Ten Years After." *The Directive Teacher* 2 (Spring 1980): 20. Interview with Michener conducted by Thomas M. Stephens, executive editor of the journal. Michener notes: "The shootings at Kent State hang more heavily on my conscience than any other subject about which I've written. It was a turning point in American education, for it showed us in bare ugliness what might happen if we all went down wrong paths."

Miller, Arthur. "The War Between Young and Old, or Why Willy Loman Can't Understand What's Happening." *McCall's*, July 1970, p. 32. Miller characterizes May 4 as the day "the war finally came home." Remarking that "there are millions of Americans who simply hate the young," he writes: "Can anyone doubt that if everyone over thirty vanished tomorrow, there would be racial peace in this country in a year and a way found to end the Vietnam War?"

Miller, T. David. "An Account of the Historic Incident by the Man That Was There! An Open Letter from Tom Miller of the Kent 25." *Freedom Bell*, [1974?], pp. [1, 3]. An ex-radical and eyewitness to the May 4 shootings looks at his troubled life before he found Jesus, "the heaviest revolutionary of all time." *Freedom Bell* was published by the Kent New Generation Church and is available in the Kent State University Archives. Miller wrote a similar letter, dated May 7, 1971, which appeared in *Acorn*, No. 6 (1971), p. [8].

Molyneaux, David G. "The Kent State Trials End." *Rolling Stone*, 20 January 1972, pp. 14–18. Sharp criticism of the grand jury indictments of October 1970 and the "Kent 25" trials that eventually followed.

Moran, Barbara. "For Someone Who Was There, Reasons Still Elusive." *Atlanta Journal/Constitution*, weekend edition, 3 May 1980, pp. 1A ff. Moran was a student at Kent State in 1970. Returning to the campus in 1980, she recalls her experience of May 4, 1970: "I remember that naive, scared middle-class coed who thought that the bloodied

student stumbling toward her was painted as part of a Yippie demonstration. . . . What I did was not courageous or memorable. I ran,
tears swept away by the speed of my flight. Gaping homemakers and
their children stared as I tore through their neat suburban streets."

Munves, James. "More Than People Died at Kent State." *The Nation*, 26
April 1980, pp. 492–94. Referring to the Kent State shootings as "the
most blatant violation of civil rights since the Palmer Raids of 1920,"
the author writes that "most of the grave issues raised [by the shoot-
ings] were never dealt with by the judicial process." He concludes pes-
simistically: "Nothing that grew out of the Kent State shootings will
discourage another national administration or governor from seeking,
when expedient, another bloody confrontation. Nothing that grew out
of the shootings affirms that our liberties remain intact. The real
victims of Kent State are all of us."

Nadig, Henry Davis, Jr. "Kent State, Cambodia, and the Classroom." *The
Independent School Bulletin*, February 1971, pp. 33–36. The author
recounts the post-Kent State experience of Rye Country Day School
of Rye, New York. He concludes: "Trying to look at the deep-seated
feelings of our students which rose to the surface in the aftermath of
Kent State and Cambodia has led us back to the reality of what all too
often has been going on in our classrooms. We have failed to involve
most of our students in the process of their own education and provide
the kind of climate where what we do is germane to their emotional
needs as human beings, as well as to their intellectual needs."

Nurmi, Martin K. "Some Remarks After a Decade: An Address Delivered
May 3, 1980." In *Kent State/May 4: Echoes Through a Decade*, edited
by Scott L. Bills. Kent, Ohio: Kent State University Press, 1982.
Speaking at a special faculty convocation, the author makes use of the
"great tragedies of literature" as a vehicle to explore the meaning of the
Kent State shootings. The speech is reprinted, in edited form, from the
Kent State University *Weekly*, No. 29 (1980).

Rangel, C. B. "Kent State Reopened." *The Progressive*, March 1974, p. 12.
Cong. Charles B. Rangel, a New York Democrat and member of the
House Judiciary Committee, applauds the Justice Department's deci-
sion to impanel a federal grand jury to investigate the Kent State
shootings. He writes: "How America accepts and understands Kent
State will tell us the answer to the question, does America work?"

Rosen, Sanford Jay. "The Greening of the Scranton Commission." *AAUP Bulletin* 57 (December 1971): 506–10. Compares the Scranton Commission's assumptions about the youth counterculture with Charles Reich's thesis in *The Greening of America*. Rosen notes: "Haunted by the spectre of escalating violence and a flight to repression lest anarchy prevail, the Commission quite properly called for a return to civility and for reform. It tried to be even-handed in its call. But even-handed pleas for moderation confuse the immoderate. The reception of the Commission's work showed that."

——. "The Legal Battle: Finishing Unfinished Business." In *Kent State/ May 4: Echoes Through a Decade*, edited by Scott L. Bills. Kent, Ohio: Kent State University Press, 1982. The chief counsel for the Kent State families in the 1978 retrial of their civil damages suit offers his views on the positive aspects of the 1979 out-of-court settlement. This article first appeared, in somewhat different form, in *Left Review* 4 (Spring 1980): 51–54.

Rudwick, Elliott, and Meier, August. "The Kent State Affair: Social Control of a Putative-Value Oriented Movement." *Sociological Inquiry* 42 (1972): 81–86. Using the theorctical model provided by Neil Smelser's *Theory of Collective Behavior*, the authors examine the reactions of University, local, and state officials and residents to the events of May 1–4, 1970. The authors note: "The radical rhetoric of a few individuals, and the outbursts of violence had frightened townsmen and their officials to perceive the students' protest as the opening shots of a violent revolution, and to act accordingly."

Ryan, Bruce. "They Shoot Students, Don't They?" *Australian Quarterly* 42 (September 1970): 10–23. As a teacher at the University of Cincinnati, Ryan recounts the events on his campus following the Kent State shootings; he is generally unsympathetic toward student and faculty activists.

Salem, Richard A. "The Use of Mediation and Conciliation to Resolve Racial Disputes in the USA." In *Race and Ethnicity: South African and International Perspectives*, edited by Hendrik W. van der Merwe and Robert A. Schrire. Cape Town and London: David Philip, 1980. In outlining the conflict mediation role of the federal government agency, the Community Relations Service (CRS), the author includes a brief study of the 1977 gym controversy on the Kent State campus, where the CRS "worked closely with law enforcement and the demonstrators, urging each side to plan carefully to avoid a confrontation." Though not all such planning worked smoothly, "the important point is that each side planned to the limits of its capacity and that this planning contributed to a season of demonstrations that were fraught with danger, yet ultimately were free of serious physical injury."

Salyer, Sharon J. "13 Seconds on May 4, 1970 May Never Be Explained." *Atlanta Journal/Constitution*, weekend edition, 3 May 1980, pp. 1A, 4A. Like Barbara Moran, supra, Salyer was present on the Kent State campus on May 4, 1970. Visiting the campus again in 1980 for this retrospective piece, Salyer interviews Glenn Frank, Doris Krause, and Rev. Carl Pierson, a Kent minister. "Its power," she writes, referring to the May 4 incident, "is . . . shown by the fact that no matter who is questioned and is willing to talk—former students, national guardsmen, professors—everyone seems to agree that his life has been irrevocably changed."

Sanford, David. "Kent State Gag: A Very Special Grand Jury." *The New Republic*, 7 November 1970, pp. 14–17. Concludes: "The Ohio grand jury found guilt almost everywhere. Demonstrators, arsonists, onlookers, outsiders, obscenity shouters, faculty, and, most of all, the administration was to blame—but not the Guard."

Sayre, Nora. "Kent State: Victims, Survivors, Heirs." *Ms.*, September 1975, pp. 53 ff. The author writes, after a visit to the University, that there is "no reek of history at Kent; for today's undergraduates, the shootings of May, 1970, are as remote as Gettysburg." Further: "Today, although 1970 means less within Kent than outside it, the university also seems like a paradigm of the nation at large: it appears to reflect and distill the anxieties and the dilemmas of this country more than any other institution I've encountered."

Schollenberger, Charles. "Justice Denied at Kent State." *The New Republic*, 12 May 1973, pp. 13–14. An update on efforts to secure a new investigation of the May 4 shootings.

Schrag, Peter. "After Kent State: The First Hundred Days." *Saturday Review*, 29 August 1970, pp. 12 ff. Examines the post-May 4 student movement: what emerged was "an attempt to reorganize the student peace movement in what some called a 'professional basis,' to give

political activism a 'responsible' flavor, and . . . to cleanse the image
of student involvement of the taints of freakiness and violence."

Segal, Erich. "Death Story." *Ladies Home Journal*, October 1970, pp. 100
ff. Primarily writing about the death of Allison Krause, the author
concludes: "The meaning of the deaths of Allison, Sandy, Jeffrey and
Bill is that they had no meaning. And yet even this is not the real
tragedy of Kent State. The real tragedy is that some people think they
deserved to die."

Shaw, Harry F. "Thoughts on the Movement Surrounding May 4, 1970."
Left Review 4 (Spring 1980): 47–48. Former New Left activist looks
back at the student movement: "The shootings at Kent State shattered
not only the bodies of our comrades but also our fantasies of miracu-
lous revolution."

Sinclair, Patricia. "Whither Freedom?" *Journal of Teacher Education* 21
(Summer 1970): 163–64. Brief commentary denouncing the violence
against demonstrators at Kent State on May 4 but also calling for
reasoned discussion between polarized camps: "The real issue is the
right of dissent. . . . Violence on one side leads only to the violence of
reprisal, thus establishing an ugly cycle that results in the brutal suppression of dictatorship."

Sindell, Steven A. "Kent State: A Legal Overview." In a special supplement to *American Report*, 12 November 1971. Kent State as "a call
to the conscience of America." Sindell sees the legal system as an effective means to unravel responsibility for the shootings. The "best
hope" for justice, he writes, lies in the lawsuits brought by the Kent
State families against the state of Ohio.

———. "Sovereign Immunity—An Argument Con." *Cleveland State Law
Review* 22 (Winter 1973): 55–71. The doctrine of sovereign immunity
as an anachronism: "It is the contention of this article that the reason
for the rule no longer exists and that it should, therefore, be abolished
as a controlling legal principle. Moreover, it is submitted that sovereign immunity violates the due process and equal protection clauses of
the United States Constitution."

———. "Kent State: Opening the Doors." *Trial*, July 1974, pp. 43–44.
With reference to the Supreme Court decision *Scheuer* v. *Rhodes*,

Sindell argues that it will "deter state officials from flagrant abuses of power" and concludes that "we have embarked upon a new recognition of civil rights litigation and a healthy check on executive power."

Smelser, Neil T. "Some Additional Thoughts on Collective Behavior." *Sociological Inquiry* 42 (1972): 97–101. The author comments on the use of his theoretical model to interpret May 1970 events at Kent State; reference to articles by Jerry M. Lewis and Elliott Rudwick and August Meier in the same journal issue.

Stang, Alan. "Kent State: Proof to Save the Guardsmen." *American Opinion*, June 1974, pp. 1–20. Rightwing analysis of the Kent State shootings purporting to show that revolutionary communist elements based within the SDS chose Kent State for a confrontation that would create martyrs.

Stevens, Mark, and McGuigan, Cathleen. "Kent State Memorial." *Newsweek*, 11 September 1978, p. 99. Summary of the controversy surrounding the rejection of "Abraham and Isaac," the George Segal sculpture, by the administration of Kent State University.

Stone, I. F. "Fabricated Evidence in the Kent State Killings." *New York Review of Books*, 3 December 1970, pp. 28–31. Stone posits a conspiracy among several guardsmen to fabricate an account of May 4 events favorable to their interests.

Thomas, Charles A. "The Kent State Investigation: The Dilemma of the Historian in Technocratic Society." *Left Review* 3 (Winter/Spring 1979): 26–28. Thomas's version of his problems as a National Archives staffer involved in research of the Kent State shootings.

———. "The Kent State Massacre: Blood on Whose Hands?" *Gallery*, April 1979, pp. 40 ff. The author points to a government conspiracy against student demonstrators.

———. "Kent State Documentary Collections, Washington, D.C." *Left Review* 4 (Spring 1980): 76–77. Description of pertinent archival/record sources in Washington: Scranton Commission records in the National Archives, Michener's Kent State papers with the Library of Congress, and FBI holdings.

———. "December Dialogues: The Settlement Reconsidered." In *Kent*

State/May 4: Echoes Through a Decade, edited by Scott L. Bills. Kent, Ohio: Kent State University Press, 1982. A negative view of the 1979 out-of-court settlement which ended the Kent State families' civil damages suit against Ohio officials: "And so our society succeeded in its final attempt to evade coming to terms with May 4, 1970."

Thomas, Dani B. "Radicals and Moderates: Psychological Issues in Students' Response to Kent State." *Political Science Discussion Papers* 3 (Spring 1971): 55–78. The author examines the "perceptual behavior" of six moderate students and six radicals as it relates to the "political world," specifically to the crisis at Kent State.

————. "Psychodynamics, Symbolism, and Socialization: 'Object Relations' Perspectives on Personality, Ideology, and Political Perception." *Political Behavior* 1 (Fall 1979): 243–68. "This paper proposes a theoretical perspective on—and outlines an operational means of analyzing—the attributional element involved in symbolic identification. The substantive focus is the perceptual behavior of six radical and six moderate persons." The author uses data gathered at Kent State in spring 1970.

Thomas, Judge William K. "Jury Selection in the Highly Publicized Case." *Columbus Bar Association Journal* 35 (May 1979): 3 ff. "Selecting an impartial jury in a highly publicized case gives trial by jury real tribulation." Cites retrial of the Kent State civil damages suit as one of the pertinent examples; drawn from the author's experience between June and December of 1978.

Thulin, S[teven] R. "Introduction: May 4, 1980." *Left Review* 4 (Spring 1980): 1–2. Introduction to the special issue of the journal commemorating the tenth anniversary of the Kent State shootings. Thulin notes: "The May fourth movement is the logical expression of our common struggles against imperialism, militarism, and domestic oppression. . . . For the spring of 1980, all roads lead again to Kent."

Vernon, Thomas S. "The Laius Complex." *The Humanist*, November/December 1972, pp. 27–28. The reference is to Oedipus' slaying of his father Laius. The author points to the Kent State shootings as a display of generational hatred, using the term "laius complex" to designate the hostility of older people to the younger generation, of parents to their children.

Wallace, Weldon. "After four years, Kent State wants the tragedy purged." *The Sun* (Baltimore), 29 April 1974, p. B1. "Students on campus today go about the ordinary university routine of study and play and the incident of four years ago has sunk beneath the surface, rising into view only briefly . . . in annual memorial services." Yet, contends the author, the May 1970 events have "deeply" affected life at Kent State.

Wechsler, James A. "Unsolved Murders." *New York Post Magazine*, 24 December 1972, p. 5. Columnist supports a federal grand jury investigation of the Kent State shootings.

Wicker, Tom. "In The Nation: The Dead at Kent State." *New York Times*, 7 May 1970, p. 42. Columnist examines Nixon's Vietnam policy in light of the Kent State shootings, charging that the "re-escalation" of the war with the Cambodian incursion was a "monumental blunder." Asking what the invasion can accomplish, Wicker answers: "Whatever the answer, the dead at Kent State are far too high a price for it. Like the dead in Cambodia and Vietnam, they can be buried; but somehow the nation has to go on living with itself."

Wilhelm, Carolyn. "The Church Responds to Kent." In a special supplement to *American Report*, 12 November 1971. Brief narrative of actions by national and Ohio church groups in 1970–71 with regard to the Kent State shootings.

Wenninger, Eugene P. "Response to Crisis: The University Commission to Implement a Commitment to Nonviolence: Kent State University, May–September 1970." In *Kent State: The Nonviolent Response*, edited by A. Paul Hare. Haverford, Pa.: Center for Nonviolent Conflict Resolution, 1973. Outlines commission conclusions, noting that "the lesson . . . is that there is no way to absolutely prevent violence. Our hope lies in our ability to score, to orchestrate, our community in such a way as to minimize the probability of violence occurring."

Wolman, Benson. "Kent State Five Years Later." *Civil Liberties*, April 1975, p. 1. Summary of ACLU work on Kent State litigation. Wolman, at the time, was executive director of the Ohio ACLU.

Young, Stephen M. "Murders at Kent State." *American Report*, 28 April 1972, pp. 6–7. Brief narrative of May 1970 events which concludes: "How can anyone claim guardsmen shot in self-defense?!" Young was a former Democratic senator from Ohio, retired in 1970.

Books and Booklets

Bills, Scott L., ed. *Kent State/May 4: Echoes Through a Decade*. Kent,
Ohio: Kent State University Press, 1982. Contents: "Introduction:
The Past in the Present," by Scott L. Bills; "Fact-Finding: 'To dispel
the rumors,' " interview with Mary Vincent; "Town in Crisis: 'It's life,
liberty, *and* property,' " interview with Lucius Lyman. Jr.; "Chain
Reaction: 'A series of mistakes,' " interview with Leigh Herington;
"After May 4: 'Kent State haunts you,' " interview with Ruth Gibson;
"The Ones They Missed with Bullets," by Bill Arthrell; "The Frustra-
tions of a Former Activist," by Kenneth R. Calkins; "A View From
Europe," by Lawrence S. Kaplan; "Random Bullets: 'It rains on the
just as well as the unjust,' " interview with Charles Kirkwood; "En-
forcing the Law: 'What did they expect?' " interview with Robert
Gabriel; "The May 4 Disease," by John A. Begala; "The Kent Heri-
tage: A Commencement Address Delivered August 27, 1977," by
Lawrence S. Kaplan; "Official Violence: An American Tradition," by
John Logue; "The Burning Question: Government Cover-up?" by
Peter Davies; "A Phoenix Reaction: Peace Studies at Kent State University," by Dennis Carey; "The Candlelight Vigil: 'A way of participating,' " interview with Jerry M. Lewis; "The Kent State Legacy and
the 'Business at Hand,' " by Miriam R. Jackson; "Sensitivity to an
Image," by D. Ray Heisey; "Neglect—Benign or Malignant? The
Faculty and Administrative Response," by Robert A. Dyal; "The
Gym Controversy: 'A massive assault on this institution,' " interview
with Michael Schwartz; "Tent City: 'A real community,' " interview
with Nancy Grim; "The Legal Battle: Finishing Unfinished Business,"
by Sanford Jay Rosen; "December Dialogues: The Settlement Reconsidered," by Charles A. Thomas; and "Some Remarks after a Decade:
An Address Delivered May 3, 1980," by Martin K. Nurmi. Annotated
bibliography. See the article listings for annotations for the essays.

———; Smith, Tim; and Thulin, S. R., eds. *Kent State: Ten Years After*.
Kent Ohio: Kent Popular Press, 1980. Contents: "Introduction: May
4, 1980," by S. R. Thulin; "In Memoriam," by Bettina Aptheker; "On
Being Born Again," by Eugene J. McCarthy; "An American Tradi-
tion," by John Logue; "The Struggle 1970-1980," by John P. Adams;
"What Should Be, What Could Be: While Educating the Children,
Who Will Guard the Guards?" by James Huber and Carl Rosen; "The
Fourth of May: An Overview," by Bob Howard; "May 4, 1970—A
View From Europe," by Lawrence S. Kaplan; " 'Bloody Friday'—
May 8, 1970," by Philip S. Foner; "A Decade of Determination," by
Alan Canfora; "The Legacy of 1970," by Miriam R. Jackson; "The

Frustrations of a Former Activist," by Kenneth R. Calkins; "A Point
of Clarification," by John Hubbell; "Too Little and Too Late: The
Kent State Faculty and Administrative Response in the Decade After
May 4, 1970," by Robert A. Dyal; "The Center for Peaceful Change:
An Organizational Response to the Events of May 4, 1970," by
Dennis Carey; "The Poet and the Republic After May 4," by Donald
M. Hassler; "The Educational Consequences of the Tragedy: An Ad-
dress Delivered May 4, 1979," by Bruce Harkness; "Thoughts on the
Movement Surrounding May 4, 1970," by Harry F. Shaw; "Lessons
for 1980," by Carl Davidson; "Kent State 1980: Finishing Unfinished
Business," by Sanford Jay Rosen; "The 1979 May 4th Federal Civil
Trial," by Thomas R. Hensley; "James Michener's Kent State Person-
alities," by Byron G. Lander; "Teaching a Course on May 4th," by
Jerry M. Lewis and Thomas R. Hensley; "The May 4th Collection,
Kent State University Archives: A Case Study in the Use of Contem-
porary Historical Source Materials," by Scott L. Bills; "The Kent
State Collection, Yale University Archives," by Susan Grigg; and
"Kent State Documentary Collections, Washington, D.C.," by
Charles A. Thomas. This publication was a reprint of a special issue of
Left Review 4 (Spring 1980). See the article listings for individual
annotations.

Casale, Ottavio M., and Paskoff, Louis, eds. *The Kent Affair: Documents
and Interpretations*. Boston: Houghton Mifflin, 1971. Useful volume
which reproduces local and national newspaper articles on the Kent
State shootings as well as radio and television broadcasts. Includes
excerpts from such official reports as the Justice Department summary of the FBI investigation into the shootings, the Scranton Commission, and the special state grand jury investigation. In their introduction, the authors note: "Like the killing of John Kennedy, of
Robert Kennedy, of Martin Luther King, Jr., the killing of the Kent
students was a public and personal shock, a shock which forced people
to examine their deepest definitions of themselves as citizens and as
mortals."

Center for Peaceful Change. *Voices: Speeches*. Kent, Ohio, 1980. This
booklet was part of a CPC project to commemorate the tenth anniversary of the Kent State shootings. It contained the text of three
speeches made originally as part of the Center's Lectureship in Peaceful Change: "Four Students," by Peter Davies, May 1974; "Is Peace
Possible?" by Robert Theobald, May 1976; "To Re-possess America,"
by George Wald, May 1972. The speeches have been reprinted pre-

viously by the CPC as pamphlets, and the series includes the lecture, "Perpetual Dissent or Fundamental Change?" by Gene Sharp, delivered May 1977.

Davies, Peter. *The Truth About Kent State: A Challenge to the American Conscience*. New York: Farrar, Straus & Giroux, 1973. "Now it appears that what was initially reported to be wild, indiscriminate shooting on the part of some thirty ill-trained and frightened young Ohio National Guardsmen may well have been a premeditated barrage by about ten experienced, riot-trained guardsmen, with the remaining troops firing in reaction. . . . It was an event of tragic proportion, but what happened afterward is the real tragedy of Kent State." Detailed narrative and analysis of May 1970 events and their aftermath; includes seventy-four photographs. Appendixes, bibliography.

Eszterhas, Joe, and Roberts, Michael D. *Thirteen Seconds: Confrontation at Kent State*. New York: Dodd, Mead, 1970. Two Cleveland journalists use extensive interviewing of students, faculty, and guardsmen to provide a background to and narrative of May 1970 events. Conflicting viewpoints are presented, but there is little analysis by the authors.

Grant, Edward J., and Hill, Michael H. *I Was There: What Really Went On at Kent State*. Lima, Ohio: C.S.S. Publishing Co., 1974. Two former guardsmen provide a narrative of May 1-4 events, emphasizing the hostile environment in which the guardsmen operated. The authors assert that the National Guard requested nonlethal weapons before arriving in Kent but that the army refused the request: "Had we had this equipment at Kent State, much heartache could have been avoided. The Guard would have been able to control or subdue demonstrators without the use of deadly force."

Hare, A. Paul, ed. *Kent State: The Nonviolent Response*. Haverford, Pa.: Center for Nonviolent Conflict Resolution, 1973. Contents: "Training in Nonviolence at Kent State University, August 16-23, 1970," by Margaret DeMarco; "Who Needs a Revolution to be a Human Being? Some Observations at Kent State University," by A. Paul Hare; "The Tale of Peter Rabbit (And Paul Hare) at Kent State: Or the Role of the Inside and Outside Agitator," by A. Paul Hare; "Noon Rally at Kent: A Dramatic Statement of a University's Problems," by A. Paul Hare; "Kent State, May 4, 1971: Nonviolence This Time," by A. Paul Hare; "Instituting Peaceful Change at Kent State: Moving Toward Life's

Center by Grasping Truth and Realizing Love," by A. Paul Hare; "Faculty Marshals and Student Dissent: A Sociological Analysis," by Jerry M. Lewis; "Kent Community for Nonviolent Change: An Experiment That Failed," by Robert A. Dyal; "Response to Crisis: The University Commission to Implement a Commitment to Nonviolence: Kent State University, May-September 1970," by Eugene P. Wenninger; and "University Commission to Implement a Commitment to Nonviolence," by Charles F. Kegley. See the article listings for individual annotations.

Hensley, Thomas R. *The Kent State Incident: Impact of Judicial Process on Public Attitudes*. Westport, Conn.: Greenwood Press, 1981. Examination of three cases of Kent State litigation: (1) the 1974 federal grand jury investigation; (2) the 1975 civil trial; and (3) the 1978 retrial of the civil damages suit, which led to the out-of-court settlement. "These legal activities have provided us with the opportunity to analyze the impact of authoritative legal decisions on attitudes of Kent State University students concerning responsibility for the shootings, support for specific legal structures, and general support for the American judicial system." Hensley notes: "While the May 4 trials spanned the decade of the 1970s, no clear judgments emerged from these extensive legal activities about who was responsible for the shootings." Bibliography.

————, and Lewis, Jerry M., eds. *Kent State and May 4th: A Social Science Perspective*. Dubuque, Iowa: Kendall/Hunt, 1978. Contents: "Kent State: Answers and Questions," by James J. Best; "Review Essay: The Telling of Kent State," by Jerry M. Lewis; "The Kent State Trials," by Thomas R. Hensley; "The Quest for a Federal Grand Jury," by Jerry M. Lewis; "A Study of the Kent State Incident Using Smelser's Theory of Collective Behavior," by Jerry M. Lewis; "The Politics of Self and Other: Public Response to the Kent State Event," by Steven R. Brown; "Social Control Violence and Radicalization: The Kent State Case," by Raymond J. Adamek and Jerry M. Lewis; "Anti-R.O.T.C. Sit-in: A Sociological Analysis," by Jerry M. Lewis and Raymond J. Adamek; "Social Control Violence and Radicalization: Behavioral Data," by Raymond J. Adamek and Jerry M. Lewis; "Student Interest in May 4th, 1970," by Jerry M. Lewis and Teresa J. Weaver; "Kent State 1977: The Struggle to Move the Gym," by Thomas R. Hensley; and "The May 4th Coalition and Tent City: A Norm Oriented Movement," by Jerry M. Lewis. Bibliography. The collection reprints a number of earlier articles, but articles covering

Kent State litigation and the gym controversy were written specifically for this volume. See the article listings for individual annotations.

Kelner, Joseph, and Munves, James. *The Kent State Coverup*. New York: Harper & Row, 1980. Kelner was chief counsel for the Kent State families in the 1975 civil trial. The authors provide a description of the trial, noting the contradictory portraits of the May 4 shootings presented by the opposing trial teams. Kelner is very critical of Judge Donald Young, asserting that his decisions during the course of the trial placed the plaintiffs on trial for their political beliefs: "What the judge was doing in the courtroom was as great an affront to civil liberties as what the guardsmen had done on the campus." Kelner is critical of the 1979 out-of-court settlement. Appendixes.

Knight Newspapers, Inc. *Reporting the Kent State Incident*. American Newspaper Publishers Association, 1971. Booklet containing an account of the investigation undertaken by Knight Newspapers which resulted in the 30,000-word report appearing in the May 24, 1970, editions of the Knight newspaper chain. "This is an account of what they did and how they did it, offered in the hope that it may provide some help and guidance to other journalists who may be faced with special problems of covering campus unrest."

Michener, James. *Kent State: What Happened and Why*. New York: Random House and Reader's Digest Books, 1971. The author's detailed examination of the Kent State shootings was widely read in the early 1970s. Michener concludes that there was no sniper, that there was no order to fire, that "it seems likely that some kind of rough verbal agreement had been reached among the troops when they clustered on the practice field," and that the guardsmen were "in no mortal danger at the time of firing." "No student," writes Michener, "performed any act on May 4 for which he deserved to be shot."; yet there is "one final significant conclusion": "The hard-core revolutionary leadership across the nation was so determined to force a confrontation—which would result in gunfire and the radicalization of the young—that some kind of major incident had become inevitable. . . . That it happened at Kent State was pure accident, but the confrontation itself was not." Recounting his own stay in Kent and his work with the *Reader's Digest* research team, Michener contends: "This is as true a picture of one small aspect of a great state university as we could construct."

O'Neil, Robert M.; Morris, John P.; and Mack, Raymond. *No Heroes, No*

Villains: New Perspectives on Kent State and Jackson State. San Francisco: Jossey-Bass, 1972. A report prepared by a special committee of the American Association of University Professors, this study "concentrates upon the implications of the student deaths and subsequent events for the future of academic freedom, institutional autonomy, and democratic governance." The authors contend that "similarities between Kent State and Jackson State—largely unappreciated on other analyses—are far more revealing than the obvious differences." The authors note: "There are no heroes and few villains in this unhappy chronicle. There are people who made mistakes, some grave."

Payne, J. Gregory. *Mayday: Kent State.* Dubuque, Iowa: Kendall/Hunt, 1981. The author writes: "The passage of ten years provides an historical perspective needed to permit less passionate assessment of the event and the people it touched." The book is divided into three parts: (1) a sketchy chronicle of May 4 issues from 1970 to 1980; (2) excerpts from letters and interviews with members of the Kent State families and other observers of Kent State affairs; (3) discussion and narrative of the making of the TV-movie "Kent State," for which Payne was the historical consultant. Appendixes and bibliography.

Peterson, Richard E., and Bilorusky, John A. *May 1970: The Campus Aftermath of Cambodia and Kent State.* Berkeley: Carnegie Commission on Higher Education, 1971. Foreword by Clark Kerr. Part 1 discusses the reaction to the Kent State (and Jackson State) shootings on the nation's campuses: "Cambodia, Kent, and Jackson triggered a period of perhaps unparalleled strife between the academic community and the national government." Peterson conducted a survey, via a questionnaire sent July 1970 to all college and university presidents in the nation, and the response is the basis for his overview. Part 2, by Bilorusky, focuses on Berkeley, titled "Reconstituting University and Society: Implications from the Berkeley Situation."

Rosenblatt, Stanley. *Justice Denied.* Los Angeles: Nash Publishing, 1971. Chapter 7, "The National Guard Is a National Menace," deals with Kent State.

Stone, I. F. *The Killings at Kent State: How Murder Went Unpunished.* New York: New York Review Book, 1971. Introduction by former Ohio senator Stephen Young. Stone writes: "At Kent State as at Jackson State, it looks as if the killers will go unpunished and only demonstrators will be prosecuted." Review of investigative commissions connected with the Kent State shootings and an appeal for a federal grand jury. The first three chapters were written between October and December 1970 and appeared originally in *I.F. Stone's Bi-Weekly*; chapter 4 reprints the Justice Department summary of the FBI investigation of May 4 events; appendixes follow. The book is skimpy but was often cited when it first appeared because of its strong denunciation of the shootings.

Taylor, Stuart; Shuntlich, Richard; McGovern, Patrick; and Genther, Robert. *Violence at Kent State, May 1 to 4, 1970: The Students' Perspective*. New York: College Notes & Texts, 1971. The authors undertook "to evaluate the perceptions, feelings, attitudes and reactions of as many students as possible" concerning May 1970 events. A questionnaire was sent out on May 28, 1970, to all students then enrolled at Kent State; by June 24, seven thousand had been returned. The analysis, based on this response, includes all major events of May 1-4. Fifty-seven percent of the respondents, for instance, felt that the major purpose of the noon May 4 rally was to protest the presence of the National Guard on the campus; only 14 percent felt that protesting the Cambodian incursion was the major purpose. Sixty-one percent of all students responding felt that the guardsmen were not justified in shooting.

Tompkins, Phillip K., and Anderson, Elaine Vanden Bout. *Communication Crisis at Kent State: A Case Study*. New York: Gordon and Breach, 1971. Tompkins was chair of a task force on communication, a subcommittee of the University Commission to Implement a Commitment to Nonviolence. This book is based on interviews conducted by the task force and examines the breakdown in communication at the University in the days previous to the May 4 shootings. The authors write: "It seems conclusive to us that the disintegration of Kent State University during the crises of May, 1970, can be traced to certain organization-communication *imperatives* which were present in the routine functioning of the university: a highly centralized and indecisive administration which operated 'blind' because of inadequate upward-directed communication; a President with little appreciation for his communication responsibilities; the absence of a two-way system of communication designed to integrate all segments of the rapidly expanded university; academic officers who were shut out of administrative decision-making; a fragmented, print-oriented faculty whose loyalty was to the department and discipline rather than to the university; large numbers of students who had been alienated from the university because of communication denial; and non-academic divisions which were found to be isolated from the academic sector."

Urban Research Corporation. *On Strike . . . Shut It Down! A Report on the First National Student Strike in U.S. History.* Chicago, Ill., 1970. Reports that at least 760 campuses "participated in some way in the strike that started almost immediately after the President's announcement on April 30 that U.S. troops were being sent into Cambodia." The Kent State shootings "escalated years of student unrest to historic heights that shocked the nation." A superficial summary of student activism in May 1970 is followed by a state-by-state listing and brief description of actions on campuses that experienced significant disruption. Since the book was printed in May 1970, the accounts no doubt contain inaccuracies; but it does provide a good overview.

Viorst, Milton. *Fire in the Streets.* New York: Simon & Schuster, 1979. Chapter 14, "Days of Death, 1970," focuses on Alan Canfora and the Kent State shootings. Viorst notes: "The 1960s ended in a small town in Ohio called Kent."

Warren, Bill, ed. *The Middle of the Country: The Events of May 4th as Seen by Students & Faculty at Kent State University.* New York: Avon, 1970. This book, reproduced from typescript pages, was, according to the blurb, "hastily conceived and hastily executed" and shows it. The editor was a Kent State sophomore in the spring of 1970; in his introduction, he writes: "What happened at Kent on May 4 was only a part of a worldwide, day-to-day drama. When such tragic events occur, many individuals suddenly realize that they are no longer in the audience but are in reality part of the play." The faculty and students whose brief essays appear in the book are as follows: Lew Fried, Chris Plant, Bill Rubenstein, Saul Daniels, Allan and Linda Dooley, Claudia Van Tyne, Rita Rubin, Kathy Lyons, and Douglas Vaughan. There are no annotations for the individual essays.

Young Socialist Alliance. *May 1970: Birth of the Antiwar University.* New York: Pathfinder Press, 1971. The introduction was written by Frank Boehm, then national chairman of the YSA, who noted: "To millions throughout the country, the Kent massacre showed the link between the endless slaughter of Indochinese people and American troops in a hated war and the willingness of the government to turn its guns on those in this country who fight to end that war." Most of the articles are reprinted from *The Militant* and deal with a variety of "May events" across the nation. "Eyewitness Report of Kent Massacre," by Mike York and Fred Kirsch, is a very brief narrative of the shootings in Kent.

Documents

Kent State University. *Commission on KSU Violence.* 4 vols. Kent, Ohio, 1972. Typescript. An introductory note from Glenn Olds, dated January 25, 1972, observes that the volumes are "not a commission report but rather a collection of papers which express the opinions and findings of the authors noted on each respective document." Volume 1 contains several essays by Harold Mayer, chairman of the commission, including a background to and narrative of the commission's operations. In "The Image and Reality of Kent State University," Mayer notes: "The apparent conflicts of interest between the university community on the one hand and a significant proportion of the non-university population of Kent on the other hand . . . constituted a major factor in setting the stage for the violence of May 1–4." Further: "The university is now well-known—regardless of the reasons—and its image must be modified. It can be, and the reality— the university's potential—fulfilled, if the desire is present and serious efforts are made to benefit from the painful experience of 1970." Volume 2 contains various surveys of the constituent elements of the University community. Volume 3 contains subcommittee reports on administrative attitudes, community relations, and the impact upon the University of federal, state, county, and local government agencies during the May 1970 events. Volume 4 contains the minority report, titled "The Events of May 1–4, 1970 at Kent State University," written by Doris Franklin, Kathy Stafford, Kathleen Whitmer, and Jeffrey Zink. The minority report draws heavily upon statements submitted to the commission by faculty and students who witnessed the shootings as well as the events previous to May 4. According to Franklin, the report "deals neither in making nor in unmaking legends."

U.S. Congress. House. Ad Hoc Committee. *Student Views Toward United States Policy in Southeast Asia, Hearings before an Ad Hoc Committee of the House of Representatives,* 91st Cong., 2d sess., 1970. Includes the testimony of Kent State student Greg Rambo; the hearings were held on May 21 and 22, 1970. Rambo, later a May 4 activist and especially prominent in the leadership of the May 4th Coalition during the 1977 gym controversy, asserted during these hearings that President Nixon had made a "wise decision" in sending American troops into Cambodia. Rambo denounced "hard-core radicals who seek to change society and close the universities by violent demonstrations." For Rambo's views on his political transition, see Charles Buffum, "Turnabout: Rambo examines his trip from GOP to Marxism," *Akron Beacon Journal*, 2 October 1977, pp. Al, A12.

U.S. Congress. House. Committee on Internal Security. *Investigation of Students for a Democratic Society, Part 2 (Kent State University), Hearings before the Committee on Internal Security*, 91st Cong., 1st sess., 1969. Hearings on June 24 and 25, 1969. Part of a series of hearings on the activities of SDS on various campuses. In his testimony before the committee, Robert White stated: "The SDS is an enemy of democratic procedure, of academic freedom, and of the essential university characteristics of study, discussion, and resolution." There is a lengthy appendix which reproduces a number of Kent SDS leaflets and other materials as well as pertinent newspaper articles.

U.S. Department of the Interior. National Park Service. Historic Sites Survey Division. *Kent State May 4, 1970 Site*. Report prepared by James Sheire, January 1978. Typescript. Sheire was historian for the Historic Sites Survey Division and prepared this report as part of the National Park Service's response to a request by Sen. Howard Metzenbaum and Cong. John Seiberling that the Kent State campus be considered for designation as an official historical landmark, a designation that was not conferred. Sheire examines three areas of possible significance for the Kent State shootings; political, social, and symbolic. Only in the third category does he find a possible enduring impact: "The tragedy of young American soldiers killing young American college students reinforced an already present psychological and intellectual climate within which Americans questioned their role in the world and within which they became increasingly willing to recognize and accept limits to the American vision and to American power. . . . As tragic as it was, Kent State as symbol may have had the positive effect of indirectly contributing in some degree to the maturing of the United States."

U.S. President. Commission on Campus Unrest. *Report*, 1970. Reprint edition by Arno Press. The commission was established on June 13, 1970, chaired by William Scranton, and held its first meeting on June 25. Other commission members were James F. Ahern, Erwin D. Canham, James E. Cheek, Lt. Gen. Benjamin O. Davis (USAF ret.), Martha A. Derthick, Bayless Manning, Revius O. Ortique, Jr., and Joseph Rhodes, Jr. The commission's report included general commentary on student upheaval of the 1960s as well as specific commentaries and analyses of the shootings at Kent State and Jackson State Universities in May 1970. Concerning events in Kent, the commission concluded: "Those who wrought havoc on the town of Kent, those who burned the ROTC building, those who attacked and stoned National Guardsmen, and all those who urged them on and applauded their deeds share responsibility for the deaths and injuries of May 4." Yet, the decision by Guard commanders to disperse the noon rally was a "serious error." Further: "The timing and manner of the dispersal were disastrous. . . . The indiscriminate firing of rifles into a crowd of students and the deaths that followed were unnecessary, unwarranted, and inexcusable."

Selected Unpublished Sources

Manuscripts and Papers

Hammond, Ken. "History Lesson: Kent State, A Participant's Memoir." Box 21, May 4th Collection, Kent State University Archives. Hammond offers his essay, written in March 1974, as a "memoir, a recollection of a time and place that seem remote to me now, but which I will never forget, and I think will never be forgotten." Account of radical political activity among Kent State students prior to and including the events of May 1970. The author notes: "In the immediate aftermath of the shootings, no one knew just what to expect next. It seemed that the revolution, or something like it, was on, and that things were likely to get pretty rough real soon."

Heisey, D. Ray. "University and Community Reaction to the News Coverage of the Kent State Tragedy." Revision of a paper presented at the Central States Speech Association Convention, Cleveland, 16 April 1971. Revision as of November 15, 1971; Heisey attempts to answer the question: ". . . What are the expressed opinions of the community and the university on how well the news media handled the Kent crisis?" Notes that "the reaction to the news coverage of Kent

State was as varied as the truth was of what happened here," though, "in general, the reaction of the community was largely unfavorable to the news coverage . . . and that of the university, favorable."

Keane, Paul. "The Bound and the Unbound: Oedipus, Isaac, Jesus: Commentary on the Segal May 4 Sculpture." Typescript. New Haven, Conn., 1979. Not seen.

———. "Kent State: A Ten-Year Ministry." Typescript. New Haven, Conn., 1980. Not seen.

Lewis, Jerry M., and Kirschner, Betty Frankle. "Public Interpretation of Tent City Arrestees: Kent State, 1977." Paper presented at the annual meeting of the Southern Sociological Society, New Orleans, April 1978. The authors assert: "Officials took a narrow view both of legitimacy and motivation of demonstrators and of the geographic area relevant to the memory of those who died in 1970. . . . We found that public accounts about the event neglected the sense of community that was present particularly at the time of the first arrest [of Tent City residents on July 12, 1977]."

Moore, Carl M., and Heisey, D. Ray. "Not a Great Deal of Error . . . ?" Mimeographed. Kent, Ohio, 1972. Noting that Michener's *Kent State* "is a dramatic, powerful book" and is considered the "definitive account and has been advertised as, and claims for itself, the truth of what happened at Kent State in May 1970," the authors contend that Michener's work contains numerous errors of form and substance. Questionnaires were sent to approximately 200 people quoted by Michener; about one-half were returned; and the authors conclude: "A casual reading through the responses made it quite apparent that misquotation and distortion of what had been said were not isolated instances."

Thomas, Charles A. "Four Days in May: Kent State and the Nixon Scenario for Suppressing Campus Dissent in the United States, May-October, 1970." Box 63, May 4th Collection, Kent State University Archives. Completed in September 1979, this book-length manuscript provides a background to and narrative of May 1970 events and their aftermath. Thomas writes from a leftist perspective but contends that after the shootings, "everyone, whichever point on the political spectrum they occupied, realized that this day would stand for something ghastly and unprecedented in American history. . . . America had tried to wash away its own guilt in the blood of its children."

Dissertations and Theses

Crocker, James W. "A Rhetoric of Encounter: A Content Analysis and Comparative Study of Selected Sources at Kent State University During the Quarter Following the May 4th Confrontation." Ph.D. dissertation, Kent State University, 1974. There was a "real desire by the Kent State University campus community for unity, working together, and sharing following the trauma of May 4."

Jackson, Miriam Ruth. "We Shall Not Be Moved: A Study of the May 4th Coalition and the Kent State University Gymnasium Controversy of 1977." Ph.D. dissertation, Purdue University, 1982. Describes the rise of the May 4th Coalition "as a result of long-term discontent with the lack of accountability on both local and national levels for the casualties of 1970, and as a result of short-term indignation at University insensitivity for planning a construction project slated to destroy part of the most famous national symbol of student opposition to the Vietnam War." Narrative and analysis of the gym controversy from a participant in the May 4th Coalition.

Kegley, Charles F. "The Response of Groups to the Events of May 1–4, 1970 at Kent State University." Ph.D. dissertation, University of Pittsburgh, 1974. Observes that established groups within the University had problems reorienting themselves to deal with the crisis and that ad hoc groups, created in the aftermath of May 4, attracted much interest but "seemed to suffer from a failure to develop internal operating procedures which dealt effectively with the management of group work." Source: *Dissertation Abstracts International* 35, pt. 12 (1975): 7683A.

Kotschwar, James L. "Judicial Impact: A Case Study of the Impact of the 'Kent State' Federal Grand Jury on Student Attitudes Toward the May 4th Shootings." Master's thesis, Kent State University, 1975. Notes that those students most likely to change their attitudes regarding responsibility for the May 4 shootings were "those who before the [federal] grand jury probe had taken a 'middle position' in assigning blame. This would suggest that judicial decisions have more impact on people who have not yet 'taken sides' or who have no strong preferences as to the outcome of the case in question."

Owens, Alfred W., II. "A Correlation Between the News Reports by WJW-TV and the Scranton Commission Report of the Events at Kent State, May 1–5, 1970." Master's thesis, Kent State University, 1971. Study of

WJW-TV news coverage of May 1970 events to determine if accuracy varied "as a function of time such that as time passed the scripted news reports became more accurate." The author concludes: "Even though the nature of the Kent tragedy was such that objectivity was difficult to maintain, the WJW-TV news scripts evidenced little editorialization."

Payne, James Gregory. "A Rhetorical Analysis of Selected Interpretations of the May 1970 Kent State Incident." Ph.D. dissertation, University of Illinois, 1977. "The purpose of this study is to analyze rhetorically two divergent interpretations offered in explanation of the shootings incident at Kent State University in May 1970"—as typified by the state grand jury report of October 1970 and Peter Davies's book, *The Truth About Kent State*. Payne notes that the grand jury report was "characterized by inadequate and selectively used data employed to support unsubstantiated but clearly popular claims." Source: *Dissertation Abstracts International* 38, no. 11 (May 1978): 6399A–6400A.

Rodkey, James D. "The Administrative Behavior of Kent State University, May 4, 1970–May 4, 1971: A Dedication to Communicate." Honors College thesis, Kent State University, 1971. Whether or not ultimately successful, the University administration has tried to reach out to its constituent elements and develop effective programs. The author writes: "The administration . . . and especially our president, Robert White, have carried the university through the most critical period in its history. The very existence of Kent State as an institution of higher learning has been preserved, at least for the time being, and hopefully forever."

Summers, Kurt. "A Study of Decisions Made by the Board of Trustees of Kent State University from 1968 Through 1977." Ph.D. dissertation, Kent State University, 1978. Includes comparisons of decision-making in 1970 and 1977, each being a "year of controversy" when a higher percentage of policy decisions were "mandated by the Board." Summers notes that "not until the November 1976 gymnasium annex controversy, was an item which explicitly concerned the May 4, 1970 issue voted on by the Board."

Addendum

Archival holdings regarding the Kent State shootings have not increased appreciably since the first publication of this volume. The James Munves Papers at Yale University Archives contain a number of interviews which should be of interest to researchers. In addition, J. Gregory Payne, author of the play *Kent State: A Requiem* and consultant for the television movie "Kent State," has donated similar materials to the archival collections at both Yale and Kent State University. The large bloc of May 4–related documents gathered for the 1975 civil suit trial has not yet been made public; their release awaits completion of court-ordered redaction.

The following bibliographical listings include both older and newer items. I have included a few retrospective articles and columns which appeared on the fifteenth anniversary of the Kent State shootings, many of them written by former KSU students. There is one correction from the first edition bibliography, p. 261, where the citation should read: Eszterhas, Joe, and Roberts, Michael, "James Michener's Kent State: A Study in Distortion," *Progressive,* September 1971, pp. 35–40.

Published Sources

The most significant new source of published documents is the awkwardly titled collection, *FBI Files on the Fire Bomb and Shooting at Kent State* (1985), available on seven reels of microfilm from Scholarly Resources, Inc. (Wilmington, Del.) The first reel contains materials from the FBI's investigation of the burning of the ROTC building on the night of May 2, 1970, and the remaining six reels consist of materials from the FBI's investigation of the May 4 shootings. Most of the documents have been sanitized, such that names and other personal descriptive data were marked out or deleted, and numerous pages were withheld by the FBI and not available for filming. The utility of the collection would have been much enhanced, especially for use by undergradute students, if there were (1) a prefatory narrative of May 1970 events and an overview of subsequent related litigation, and (2) an index for the location of key documents. As it is, effective use of the collection requires that a researcher already be well acquainted with the Kent State shootings and be willing to look through reels of material in search of particular items. The only explanatory note from the publisher is this:

> This material has been reproduced in exactly the condition and order as provided by the Federal Bureau of Investigation. Some documents have been deleted and portions of documents have been expunged under exemptions of the Freedom of Information Act. Other material, such as that forwarded to the Office of the Legal Advisor of the National Guard Bureau, was removed prior to FOIA review.

In lieu of a comprehensive index to the collection, the following summary offers a means to locate certain groups of documents, with a few examples of specific items. Reel One contains fifteen numbered sections, and there are forty-six numbered sections stretching over the remaining six reels of microfilm. With the exception of Reel One, the microfilm image is generally clear and easy to read.

Reel One. This reel contains only material generated by the FBI's investigation of the ROTC building fire of May 2, 1970. Section One shows the FBI's initial efforts to discover evidence of the use of incendiary devices and to identify likely suspects, especially through interviews concerning the behavior of "hippie type" individuals. An internal memorandum of May 8, 1970, notes that FBI agents are conducting two separate investigations at Kent State: a "civil rights type" regarding the deaths of May 4 and a "sabotage type" regarding the ROTC fire, with deadlines for preliminary reports set for May 12 and May 14 respectively. Sections Two through Five contain an FBI report of May 21, 1970, featuring extensive interviews with ROTC personnel, students, and faculty; included are a May 11 statement from Peter C. Bliek, later charged with first degree riot and arson (sec. 2), a May 11 interview with G. Dennis Cooke (sec. 3), a May 8 interview with Glenn Frank (sec. 4), and inquiries directed toward gathering information about the occupants of 230 East Main Street, Kent, whom the FBI quickly identified as prime suspects (sec. 5).

Sections Six and Seven contain materials from an FBI report of May 13, 1970; included are interviews with ROTC personnel, local police and firemen, students, and KSU staff. There is a May 9 interview with student Craig A. Morgan (sec. 6) and a listing of people receiving medical treatment on and off campus for injuries possibly sustained during several days of disturbances (sec. 7). Section Eight consists of several pages of unreadable material.

Sections Nine through Twelve contain materials from supplementary FBI reports, largely further interviews designed to confirm the FBI's identification of those responsible for the ROTC fire. Some of the interviews in Section Nine focus on May 4 events as well as the fire, as in a four-page statement from a student who witnessed the shootings: "It seemed like there were dead and wounded all over. One boy was holding a rag over one girl's throat, only there wasn't much of her throat left. Another boy was lying face down in a pool of his own blood. . . . People were screaming for help, but there just weren't enough ambulances. . . . About this time, I just sat down and started crying. I still can't believe that it really happened." Many pages were withheld from Section Eleven.

Section Thirteen contains correspondence between FBI Director J. Edgar Hoover and presidential assistant John D. Ehrlichman, who was being furnished copies of all FBI reports on Kent State matters. Included here are the results of the laboratory examination of physical evidence gathered by the FBI and a discussion of what charges might be brought against the suspects. There are materials from a supplementary report of June 4, including interviews with Thomas G. Foglesong (June 2), Richard C. Felber (June 4), and Jerry Rupe (June 4).

Section Fourteen contains commentary related to the trials of the "Kent 25" which began in Ravenna, Ohio, in November 1971; included is a full list of the defendants and the charges brought against them. Section Fifteen includes correspondence between Hoover and J. Walter Yeagley, assistant attorney general, Internal Security Division, Justice Department, from June 1970; there are also internal memorandums discussing the actions of Portage County prosecutor, Ronald Kane, and his plans for a grand jury. According to one memo, Kane told FBI agents on June 18, 1970, "that he is extremely interested in initiating as many local prosecutions as possible, and cited his record of having convicted approximately 60 individuals as a result of disruptions on the KSU campus during April, 1969." Interviews directed toward providing further evidence of campus arson focus on the actions of Jerry Rupe and Peter Bliek. Included is the text of the grand jury report of October 15, 1970, clipped from the *Kent-Ravenna Record-Courier*.

Reel Two. The documents in Section One show the FBI setting up its investigation of the Kent State shootings at the request of Assistant Attorney General Jerris Leonard, Civil Rights Division, Justice Department. Included is correspondence between J. Edgar Hoover and Ohio Governor James Rhodes. On May 8, 1970, Hoover authorized use of the codeword KENFOUR in intra-Bureau communications concerning the shootings. There are interviews with members of the Ohio National Guard (ONG). Section Two contains a lengthy interview with Chester A. Williams, director of the KSU campus police, summarizing his view of local SDS activity. Standing near the burnt remains of the ROTC building on May 4, Williams recalled, "I saw students throwing objects, but could not tell what they were. I heard the wildman chants, screaming and yelling. I remember one chant Sunday night. The whole group as they were marching to get to downtown saying, 'KSU fuck you, KSU fuck you,' " There is a summary of an FBI interview with KSU President Robert White and a statement from Leroy Satrom, Kent's mayor, who requested the presence of National Guard troops. Both Sections One and Two include interviews with guardsmen who were on the Kent State campus.

Section Three contains interviews with ONG members and KSU students; Section Four consists largely of interviews with students and faculty. Section Five includes interviews with faculty member Seymour H. Baron and student activist Steven A. Sharoff; also included are surgical pathology reports on the slain and wounded students. There is, for example, an account of the efforts to help William Schroeder, who was still alive and conscious when he reached Robinson Memorial Hospital, Ravenna, complaining of shortness of breath and back pains. There are autopsy reports for Schroeder and Jeffrey Miller.

Section Five concludes with materials provided by the Kent Police and the Ohio State Highway Patrol; Section Six begins with materials from the Portage County Sheriff's Office. Section Seven

concerns the assembling of physical and photographic evidence regarding Kent State events. Section Eight includes Governor Rhodes's
proclamations authorizing ONG activity in Akron on April 29 and
subsequently in Kent. There are documents from the City of Kent,
the KSU administration and student government, and also a copy of
the injunction sought by Ronald Kane, Portage County prosecutor,
to close down the campus following the shootings. Also included is
background information on the slain and wounded students gathered through interviews.

Reel Three. Section Eight is continued from the previous reel, with
interviews concerning Sandra Scheuer and others. The information
gathered shows that Scheuer attended her morning class on May 4
and was en route to her 1:10 Speech 448 class at the time of the
shootings. There are autopsy reports for the four students killed and
medical reports on the wounded. Section Nine contains reports
from local law enforcement agencies; Section Ten contains interviews with guardsmen; Sections Eleven and Twelve consist of interviews with students about the events of May 1–4. Section Fourteen
contains additional interviews: with students, staff, and faculty, including workers at the site of the new library then under construction.

Reel Four. Section Fourteen is continued, with interviews designed
to gather information about campus activist groups; there is a copy
of a speech read at the noon rally of May 1 by a member of the ad hoc
group, World Historians Opposed to Racism and Exploitation
(WHORE). FBI investigators were especially interested in gathering
information about the New University Conference (NUC) in their
effort to establish links between activist faculty and student radicals.
Section Fifteen is largely composed of interviews conducted in order
to assess the accuracy of claims that a sniper fired before the
guardsmen discharged their weapons. Interviews with students, faculty, and guardsmen show widely differing opinions as to whether or
not someone did fire, whether someone fired from the roof of a
nearby building or from a parking lot, whether someone in the
crowd pulled out a weapon to fire at guardsmen, and so forth. Much
of the student commentary focuses on the role of photographer
Terry Norman, who did have a pistol with him on May 4 and sur-
rendered it to KSU police, claiming he carried it for protection

against student radicals. Section Sixteen contains a summary of the physical and photographic evidence gathered by the FBI; there is a statement by Robert Stamps, dated May 12.

Section Seventeen contains further materials regarding the analysis of such physical evidence as the clothing worn by those who were killed and wounded, bullet fragments, etc. There is a May 11 memorandum by J. Edgar Hoover, reporting a conversation with presidential assistant Egil Krogh, Jr., in which the FBI director noted that while his agents were getting both sides of the Kent State story he had already reached his own conclusions: "I said I think it is a situation of six of one and half-dozen of the other and that the students invited and got what they deserved." Section Eighteen contains internal FBI memorandums, mostly related to the preliminary findings of the Bureau's investigation. Section Nineteen contains materials from an FBI report of May 22, 1970, concerning the shootings; there is a statement by Lt. Col. Charles Fassinger of the Ohio National Guard. The FBI report continues through Sections Twenty and Twenty-one, including numerous interviews.

Reel Five. Section Twenty-two continues the FBI's May 22 report, with special focus on identifying (through student interviews) those faculty members whose classroom remarks expressed antiwar or what FBI agents considered otherwise radical views. Interviews with a wide range of KSU students, scattered around the country, often produced fairly idiosyncratic testimony, as in the follwoing account:

> [The interviewee] advised he had been eating breakfast in Perkins Pancake House in downtown Kent, Ohio [along the northwest edge of the campus] the morning of May 17, 1970, when he saw an individual, apparently meeting with a group of other individuals in the Pancake House, whom he had seen two or three weeks earlier at the KSU [Student] Union. He said when he saw this individual earlier, he was discussing revolution with a group of militant activists. In the group at that time there appeared to be Leninist-Marxists, Maoists, and Socialists. He stated that at that time this individual, who is unknown to him, had a heavy, full, long beard and shoulder-length hair. He advised that when he saw him in Perkins Pancake House, his appearance was changed in that his beard had been closely trimmed and his hair was now extremely

short, with it still being long enough to comb. . . . [He] stated that he felt certain that this individual has something to do with the organization of the hard-core militants activities at KSU.

Interviews were also directed toward securing evidence about the possible presence of a sniper on May 4 and identifying demonstrators from photographs.

Section Twenty-three contains interviews regarding the lifestyles of the slain and wounded students interspersed with materials concerning the analysis of physical evidence from the scene of the shootings. A letter from Sen. Strom Thurmond to Will R. Wilson, assistant attorney general, dated May 7, 1970, asserts that Jerry Rubin was "largely responsible" for events at Kent State because of an inflammatory speech he delivered on the campus. An internal FBI memo of May 23 reveals the continued sense of Bureau officials that the guardsmen "fired when they were in grave danger of being surrounded and overrun." Sections Twenty-four through Twenty-six contain materials from an FBI report of May 26, 1970. Interviews in Section Twenty-five show that allegations of improper conduct on the part of Prof. Thomas Lough were unfounded—that he did not use his classes as a forum to advocate the violent overthrow of the U.S. government or teach students how to make molotov cocktails. There is a copy of Lough's letter to his students after the University closed down in the wake of the shootings, which read in part: "It is tragic that only after our tragedy do the nation's campuses rise to confront the issues students have long tried peacefully to present. But now many are realizing the obvious connections between the national guard on the campuses and the national guard in the ghettos, the rule of military violence at Kent and the rule of military violence overseas. Kent's sorrow has become the nation's outrage, and you were there. Don't forget it." Section Twenty-six includes a mailing from the Committee of Kent State Massacre Witnesses, intended to recruit KSU students to speak about May 1970 events on other campuses through the summer.

Section Twenty-seven includes an interview with Mary Vecchio in latter May 1970, in Indianapolis, where she was in the custody of the Marion County Juvenile Court. A memo from Hoover to the Cleveland FBI office, dated June 4, ordered agents to discontinue efforts to locate and interview additional students, faculty, and ONG personnel except in special cases. Sections Twenty-eight and Twenty-nine contain further materials regarding the May 26 FBI report.

Reel Six. Section Twenty-nine is continued and includes an editorial from the *Canton Repository,* dated May 28, 1970, critical of the reluctance of so-called radical professors to be interviewed by FBI agents. Hoover wrote to the newpaper's editor on June 4: "It was certainly encouraging to read your favorable comments in connection with our investigative endeavors at Kent State University." Section Thirty contains miscellaneous memorandums about the Kent State case, including an exchange between John D. Ehrlichman and Hoover confirming that FBI investigative materials would be made available to the Scranton Commission. An internal memorandum of July 15, 1970, shows that at the peak of the investigation 302 agents were assigned to the KENFOUR inquiry, at a cost (at that time) of $258,125, with agents driving a total of 92,160 miles; by June 30, only four agents were still active in the investigation.

Section Thirty-one contains supplementary reports and interviews regarding May 1970 events, including a May 21 letter by Thomas Lough, to his students, protesting FBI efforts to investigate classroom discussions. Section Thirty-two contains materials which detail the FBI's angry response to the release of a Justice Department memorandum, first printed in the *Akron Beacon Journal,* which observed (based on the FBI's investigation) that guardsmen on the KSU campus had acted wrongly (see the listing for "FBI: No Reason for Guard to Shoot at Kent State," *ABJ,* 23 July 1970, supra, p. 261). A memo by Hoover, dated July 24, 1970, reported a conversation with President Nixon about the Justice Department memorandum, and thereafter the FBI issued routine denials that it had ever proffered any conclusions about the Kent State shootings: rather, the agency had simply gathered information. But as a result of the *Beacon Journal* story and similar reporting elsewhere, much of the general public believed that the Bureau itself had criticized the actions of National Guardsmen, and the FBI received many letters of complaint.

Sections Thirty-three and Thirty-four contain a supplementary FBI report of July 30, 1970, with additional interviews with campus and local officials. Section Thirty-five consists of miscellaneous correspondence and memorandums, including new cost estimates for the FBI's KENFOUR investigation, an exchange between Hoover and publisher John S. Knight, and various letters from citizens. A letter, for example, from Kent resident Isabel D. Veon, dated August 31, 1970, asserted that a number of suspicious characters were still living in the town: "I hope the F.B.I. will keep an eye on our city, if such a thing is possible. I still think it may be in danger." She was subsequently interviewed by FBI agents. Sections Thirty-six and Thirty-seven contain many newspaper clippings as well as further internal memorandums stimulated by media reporting about the KENFOUR investigation. Sections Thirty-eight and Thirty-nine contain materials regarding the actions of photographer Terry Norman on May 4 and also a listing of the physical evidence gathered by FBI agents.

Reel Seven. Section Thirty-nine is continued and includes interviews regarding the injuries of wounded students Alan Canfora and Douglas Wrentmore. Sections Forty and Forty-one contain investigative materials generated by the re-opening of the Kent State case by the Justice Department, formally announced on August 3, 1973; see C. L. McGowan to Gebhardt, November 13, 1973. Terry Norman is again a subject of interest. Sections Forty-one and Forty-two include materials concerning the re-examination of the M-1 rifles fired at Kent State, twenty-seven of which had been shipped to the Letterkenny Army Depot in Chambersburg, Pennsylvania, in April 1971. Also in Section Forty-two are materials related to the work of the federal grand jury which issued indictments of eight guardsmen in late March 1974.

Sections Forty-three, Forty-four, and Forty-five contain materials related both to the federal grand jury and to the subsequent trial. An FBI memo of November 11, 1974, notes the difficuty of assembling the pertinent evidence because the KENFOUR investigation "possesses an almost limitless number of witnesses, photographs, and other physical evidence" (sec. 45). Section Forty-six includes documents and newspaper clippings related to the 1975 civil suit litigation.

Articles

Armao, Rosemary, and Farkas, Karen. "One Day in May." *Plain Dealer Magazine,* special issue, 28 April 1985. A fifteenth-anniversary retrospective on the Kent State shootings, featuring interviews with Dean Kahler, Elaine Holstein, Doris Krause, the Canfora family, Prof. Jerry Lewis, and Charles Fassinger, a former National Guard officer who was on Blanket Hill, May 4, 1970.

Berry, R. William. "Four Dead in Ohio: 15 years after the shootings at Kent State." *Ironton Tribune,* 1, 2, 3, and 5 May 1985. This five-part retrospective summarizes the background to and the events of May 1–4, 1970; the author was a KSU junior in spring 1970 and witnessed the shootings from atop Johnson Hall. He recalls: "When the gunfire stopped, there was hardly a sound to be heard, other than the muffled groans of the injured students and the isolated screams of terror from those who first realized just what had transpired. . . . I was stunned to the extent that probably a half an hour expired before I was able to utter an intelligent word." Presently an attorney in Ironton, Ohio, Berry notes that "there is no question in my mind that the shootings constituted homicide. The shots were not fired out of any reasonable fear of physical harm on behalf of the Guardsmen."

Boerner, Dave. "Memories of gentle man committed to peace, justice." *Akron Beacon Journal,* 13 December 1983, p. A11. A brief summary of the career of the Rev. John P. Adams, best known to KSU students for his role as counselor to the Kent State families and advocate of nonviolence during the gym controversy in 1977.

Brett, Regina. "KSU graduate recounts the death of a friend." *Daily Kent Stater,* 3 May 1985, pp. 3, 4. An interview with Sharon Lee Swanson, friend of Sandra Scheuer, who was present in the Prentice Hall parking lot at the time of the shootings on May 4, 1970. Swanson recalls: "So many people had a bad impression of the students. We were just on our way back to class. We just happened to be in the wrong place at the wrong time."

_____. "Experience, innocence try to understand May 4." *Daily Kent Stater,* 25 April 1985, p. 5. A native of Ravenna, Ohio, Brett recalls her thoughts on hearing news of the Kent State shootings: "Everyone was panicking. At the tender age of 13 I didn't understand why. It seemed like a war had started."

Corelis, Jon. "Kent State Reconsidered as Nightmare." *Journal of Psychohistory* 8 (Fall 1980): 137–47. The author argues that the Kent State shootings must be placed within the context of a "universal human tendency to infanticide," such that May 4, 1970, should be treated "as an episode in the aggravated struggle between the generations which took place in the late 1960s." Thus, writes Corelis, the theme of the *Abraham and Isaac* sculpture was simply too close to the truth to be accepted by KSU officials.

Drexler, Michael. "13 Seconds at Kent." *Cleveland Edition,* 2–8 May 1985 edn. A fifteenth-anniversary retrospective on the Kent State shootings, featuring comments by Bill Arthrell.

Dyer, Joyce Coyne. "Confronting 'anguish of truth.' " *New Directions for Women,* May/June 1983, p. 11. A graduate student at KSU in May 1970, Dyer comments on her experience in offering a course on the Kent State shootings, focusing especially on the utility of James Michener's *Kent State: What Happened and Why* (1971). Dyer faults Michener for his "descriptive digressions" concerning female students: "Whether Michener intended it or not, knew it or not, through such descriptions [emphasizing the physical attractiveness of the female students interviewed] he had been able to avoid confrontation with the hard facts, the distressing reality of the crisis." This sentiment provides the basis for the author's reexamination of her own feelings about May 1970 events.

"The Filming of 'Kent State.' " *American Cinematographer,* April 1981, pp. 354 ff. No author listed. An interview with James

Goldstone, director for the television movie "Kent State," which aired in February 1981. While much of the interview focuses on filming techniques, Goldstone comments: "All the college kids today know about Kent State, even though they might not know the details. It was the climax of a polarized period between the college age generation . . . and the adult generation."

Hall, Mitchell K. " 'A Crack in Time': The Response of Students at the University of Kentucky to the Tragedy at Kent State, May 1970." *Register of the Kentucky Historical Society* 83 (Winter 1985): 36–63. An in-depth analysis of student activism on the campus in Lexington, Kentucky, where "antiwar actions occurred only sporadically until the spring of 1970, when activity seemed to increase." The author concludes that the use of National Guard units, arriving on the University of Kentucky campus on May 6, was "not only unnecessary and ineffective, but counterproductive."

Hensley, Thomas R., and Griffin, Glen W. "Victims of Groupthink: The Kent State Board of Trustees and the 1977 Gymnasium Controversy." *Journal of Conflict Resolution* 30 (September 1986): 497–531. An application of Irving Janis's theory of "groupthink," a process "by which a small group of decision makers subjected to intense stress may become more concerned with achieving concurrence among their members than in arriving at carefully considered decisions." The authors conclude that the KSU Board of Trustees did exhibit groupthink during the gym crisis, characterized by "the incomplete survey of alternatives, the poor search for information, the failure to reappraise initially rejected alternatives, and a selective bias in processing information."

Klibanoff, Hank. "Today, a far different Kent State" and "Scarred by tragedy, Kent State survivors return and remember." *Philadelphia Inquirer,* 4 and 5 May 1985, respectively. A fifteenth-anniversary retrospective on the Kent State shootings and the 1985 commemoration.

Lelyveld, Joseph; Kifner, John; and Smith, Robert M. "The View From Kent State: 11 Speak Out." *New York Times,* 11 May 1970. Partial transcript of a long interview with a "diverse" group of Kent State Students regarding the events and emotions of May 4: Ronald Arbaugh, Wayne Bragg, Tom Difloure, Ellen Glass, Yvonne Mitchell, Lucia Perry, Michael Stein, Tom Stephan, Buzz Terhune, Jeff Tetreault, and Jeffrey Zink.

Robinson, William. "Commemorating the Past." *Inland Architect* 30 (July/August 1986): 4—8. Discusses the national design competition for an appropriate memorial to the Kent State shootings following the initial announcement (on April 4, 1986) that Ian Taberner was the winner. "KSU apparently wanted something non-political, non-specific, non-committal, homogenized, and generic. What it got is a distinctive, subtly provocative testimonial to the ability of human imagination and inspiration to transcend bureaucratic timidity."

Vaughan, Doug. "Remembering Kent State." *Denver Post,* 4 May 1985. A fifteenth-anniversary retrospective from a former KSU student activist, who was with Sandra Scheuer when she was shot on May 4, 1970.

Wischmann, Lesley. "Dying on the Front Page: Kent State and the Pulitzer Prize." *Journal of Mass Media Ethics* 2 (Spring/Summer 1987): 67—74. With reference to the widely distributed photograph of Mary Vecchio kneeling beside the body of Jeffrey Miller on May 4, 1970, taken by John Filo, the author argues that photojournalists have a responsibility to take pictures that do not cause pain to innocent victims. Further, they have a responsibility to take photographs which communicate the reality of complex events. Wischmann asserts that Filo's photograph constitutes an invasion of privacy when it is shown, and also that it "explains very little. The National Guard is nowhere to be seen. Nothing in his photograph tells us that this is a college campus. The cause of the young man's death is a complete mystery."

Booklet

Whitney, R. W. *The Kent State Massacre.* Events of Our Times
series, no. 20. Charlotteville, N.Y.: SamHar Press, 1975. This
32-page booklet is a brief narrative of May 1970 events and
their aftermath. The author observes: "Who was to blame,
how it might have been avoided—these have become questions for private reflection, not judicial decision. . . . If history makes sensible use of the Kent State massacre, let it de-
cree that never again will the guardians of a free society aim
loaded weapons at any of their own countrymen."

Selected Unpublished Sources

Banks, James, and Banks, Paula. "Kent State: How the War in
Vietnam Became a War at Home." Paper presented at an
international conference on the Vietnam War, Manchester
Polytechnic, England, September 1986. In the spring of
1970, the authors were the directors of Wright Hall dormitory at Kent State. This paper is a somewhat personal recollection of the increasing politicization of the campus after
1967, into and through the "authority crisis" and shootings
of May 1–4, 1970. After the events of May 4: "I thought I was
part of a nightmare of stark unreality; everyone in authority
seemed to be literally coming apart. One got the impression
that only madness was normal. Most of our colleagues in the
University thought Kent State was finished as an institution.
Life had gone out of the University and in a sense out of each
of us."

Gregory, Stanford W., Jr., and Lewis, Jerry M. "Symbols of Collective Memory: The Social Process of Memorializing May 4,
1970 at Kent State University." Revised version of a paper
presented at the 12th Annual Conference on Social Theory,
Politics, and the Arts, University of California-San Diego,
October 1986. The authors use a "social process model of
collective memory" to analyze the support for and design of a
May 4 memorial on the KSU campus, often with reference to
the construction of the Vietnam Veterans Memorial in Wash-

ington. The May 4th Task Force and KSU President Michael Schwartz are identified as pivotal forces in the successful search for an acceptable memorial. The article contains a useful discussion of the role of professional elites (in this case, architecture and landscape design) in shaping the form of contemporary memorials to complex historical events.

Kriese, Daniel Paul. "Experience as Philosophical Method: A Study of Student Radicalization." Ph.D. dissertation, Purdue University, 1977. Examines the utility of experiential approaches to an analysis of the dynamics of social change. Kent State events are included in the discussion. Source: *Dissertation Abstracts International* 38, pt. 7 (1978): 4350A–51A. Kriese was a Kent State student in 1970.

Lough, Thomas S. [Untitled.] 25 April 1986. Written in the format of a letter to the editor of the *Daily Kent Stater,* this essay sets forth Lough's perspective on key events of May 1–4, 1970. The author was among the twenty-five people indicted by a state grand jury in October 1970, charged with inciting to riot, and recalls, "I was honored as the token radical professor." Lough believes that the burning of the ROTC building on May 2 was a work of "professional arson" carried out while the building was under police control; he asserts that the shootings of May 4 were ordered and rehearsed. The essay is available in the May 4th Collection, Kent State University Archives.

Payne, J. Gregory. "Historical Accuracy Versus Dramatic License in Television Docu-Drama: The Making of 'Kent State.' " Paper presented at the 67th Annual Conference of the Speech Communication Association, Anaheim, California, 12–15 November 1981, Folder 19, Box 67, May 4th Collection, Kent State University Archives. Asserting that television "reigns as our modern day oral poet," shaping the American view of reality, Payne discusses the filming of the movie "Kent State" with reference to the conflicting goals of those favoring a strictly accurate storyline and those favoring the use of "dramatic license." Payne was the historical consultant for the movie, and he describes it as a bittersweet experience, confronted with "the seepage of increased dramatic license into the film, especially as the director's vision became more shaped by the dramatic forces during the editing phase of the project."

Spofford, Timothy John. "Lynch Street: The Story of Mississippi's Kent State—The May 1970 Slayings at Jackson State College." Ph.D. dissertation, State University of New York at Albany, 1984. Provides a "documentary narrative" which reconstructs the events surrounding the May 15, 1970, shooting deaths of two students at Jackson State College. "This account depicts the racial unrest in Jackson and the lawmen's alleged coverup after the killings." Source: *Dissertation Abstracts International* 45, pt. 3 (1984): 672A–73A. A book drawn from this dissertation is forthcoming from the Kent State University Press.

Index

Scott L. Bills is associate professor of history at Stephen F. Austin State University. He received his Ph.D. from Kent State University in 1981 and was a resident of Kent from 1974 until 1982. He is also the author of *Empire and Cold War: The Roots of US-Third World Antagonism, 1945-47* (1990).